Children of the Series
and
How They Grew

Children of the Series
and
How They Grew

Or
A Century of Heroines and Heroes, Romantic, Comic, Moral

Faye Riter Kensinger

Bowling Green State University Popular Press
Bowling Green, Ohio 43403

Acknowledgements

Where copyright exists, the author has made every effort to obtain authorization to quote, and makes grateful acknowledgement to the following publishers and individuals for permission to use excerpts from material previously published.

Bruno Bettelheim: *The Uses of Enchantment,* Vintage Books Edition, May 1977, A Division of Random House. Copyright 1975, 1976 by Bruno Bettelheim. Originally published by Alfred A. Knopf, Inc., in 1976. "A Primer for Literacy," Part V of special section entitled "The Child's Mind," *Harper's,* April 1978.

Doubleday and Company, Inc.: *Penrod* by Booth Tarkington. Copyright 1914 by Doubleday, Page & Company. *Penrod and Sam* by Booth Tarkington. Copyright 1916 by Doubleday Page & Company.

Dover Publications, Inc.: *The Tales of Peter Parley about America* by Peter Parley (Samuel Griswold Goodrich), facsimile of the 1828 edition with a new Introduction by Barrows Mussey. Copyright 1974 by Dover Publications, Inc. *Billy Whiskers* by Frances Trego Montgomery. Unabridged and unaltered republication of the first (1902) edition.

E.P. Dutton: "From *The Riflemen of the Ohio* by Joseph Altsheler. Copyright 1910 by D. Appleton & Co., renewed 1938 by Sallie B. Altsheler. A Hawthorn book. Reprinted by permission of E.P. Dutton, a division of NAL Penguin Inc."

"From The *Eyes of the Woods* by Joseph Altsheler. Copyright 1917 by D. Appleton & Co. A Hawthorn book. Reprinted by permission of E.P. Dutton, a division of NAL Penguin Inc."

"From *The Lost Hunters* by Joseph Altsheler. Copyright 1918 by D. Appleton & Co., renewed 1946 by Sallie B. Altsheler. A Hawthorn book. Reprinted by permission of E.P. Dutton, a division of NAL Penguin Inc."

Edgar Rice Burroughs, Inc.: "Excerpts from *Tarzan of the Apes,* by *Edgar Rice Burroughs,* Copyright © 1912 by *Frank A. Munsey Company,* Used by Permission of *Edgar Rice Burroughs, Inc.*"

"Excerpts from *The Beasts of Tarzan* by *Edgar Rice Burroughs.* Copyright © 1914 by *Frank A. Munsey Company.* Used by Permission of *Edgar Rice Burroughs, Inc.*"

Paul S. Eriksson: *Small Voices* by Josef & Dorothy Berger. Copyright 1966 by Josef & Dorothy Berger.

ISBN: 0-87972-375-0 Clothbound   0-87972-376-9 Paperback

Cover design by Gary Dumm

Gratitude needs expression as well to publishers judging limited utilization of material as falling into fair usage, to individuals in permission departments, along with library personnel of the R.R. Bowker Company, for valuable help in solving the mysteries of copyrights and other-day publishing houses, and to the author's siblings, who gave willing aid where needed.

*Dedicated
to old loves—the children of the series
and their creators*

Contents

He who ne'er learns his A, B, C,
Forever will a Blockhead be;
But he who to his Book's inclin'd,
Will soon a golden Treasure find.
The New England Primer

Foreword

When the Friends of the Library of a Midwestern university expanded their "want" list in the late 1960's, we welcomed the opportunity to collect in their behalf more than elementary textbooks of historical interest. One request concerned titles missing from Dr. Frank Luther Mott's *Golden Multitudes* of best sellers which dated back as far as the 17th century; another was less restricted: that of old American juvenile fiction series many of which "...have become almost classic."

A connection not immediately perceived existed, for the complete *Golden Multitudes* roster contained, from the 1880's on, a number of books written for children as first volumes of series. At that time a few old copies of childhood series stood on our shelves, but names such as the Rover Boys I knew only through facetious references made by my husband. This became a time for widening acquaintanceships.

Frequent hunting grounds were thrift outlets, organizational and private sales, old-book stores, antique shops, and there were gifts now and then from friends who knew of our search. Particular pleasure lay in personal discovery of special "finds;" the challenge lay in stretching what we cared to spend in this manner of contributing to the university where we had met.

A good many years have followed the first packing-up of series examples for the Friends' collection. Meanwhile, re-visiting literature of childhood by means of books passing through our hands, I began a collection of my own. Once read, with attention-span depending upon author-ability, these volumes went into cardboard boxes until the time came when a handyman transformed a great shoe-closet fashioned apparently for someone with an unbelievable wardrobe of footwear—and that of a size my brothers used to refer to as "gunboats" or "violin-cases." Slanted shelves became horizontal and were spacious enough for shelving books two-deep. Therein is housed with overflow accommodated nearby, an accumulation of about three hundred volumes representing one hundred and thirty-four series and one hundred and seven authors. In addition, there has grown a lengthening list of other series mentioned in the back pages of old books and, later, on the interiors of dust-jackets.

The absorbing pastime led to more than reading dog-eared books with flyaway illustrations, injured spines, inscriptions, cryptic comments, bits of verse or other mementos of someone's lost childhood. It excited inquiry into how this lavish flowering of series came about, and one element caught fire from another as investigation continued.

Whisked back to the 19th century in its youth when a boy called Rollo made his modest appearance in the first fictional series written for children, I made my irregular way through a century to a girl named Laura, whose creator followed the pattern set by Rollo in playing out a role chronologically through a cycle of years and a series of books. Thus the use of a century for time structure seemed reasonable frame-work for exhibiting the evolution of fiction designed in the serial manner, for showing mutation and expansion and for making judgment.

The pursuit led into by-ways and forgotten places; it led to honest respect for writers long forgotten, to silent meetings with characters in fiction and outside it; it led to laughter, to sentiment, and to appreciation of individuals and the sometimes uncertain American spirit in its development. Even that was not all; intimacy with a favored subject, young children, increased.

It would be impossible to share this study properly without generous use of verbatim sampling, often delightful in itself. Furthermore, the citations suggest reasons for certain young personages entering the store of classics and reasons why others fell like duplicate paper dolls from slashes of a scissors.

To look into private lives, wholly fictional or not, and discover generations of children who were book worms even as you and I, was itself an adventure rivaling those of some children of the series.

Chapter 1
In The Beginning

"This is my decision. The knife is Rollo's. When a person gives or sells any property to any other person, it is called a conveyance. If this is done under such circumstances, and in such a manner, as to make the thing fairly and fully the property of the person who receives it, it is a *valid* conveyance. If it is made in such a way, or under such circumstances, as not to entitle the new possessor to it, it is said to be *null* and *void*, and goes for nothing...."[1]

These careful statements are not spoken in a court of law, nor by a professor lecturing to students of elementary jurisprudence. They are the words of Miss Mary, young Rollo's teacher, as she settles a dispute in the fifth of a series known as the Rollo Books, forerunners of hundreds of fictional series which American writers would put before boys and girls for all the decades to follow. The prefatory notice is here dated Oct. 18, 1838, and the author is Jacob Abbott, schoolmaster and minister as well as writer.

Unique for their time, the books carry a narrative line which extends throughout and into a second series concerning the stage-by-stage development of a little boy. That they go beyond dispensing information, education and moral maxims is another triumph. Wrote author Abbott, "...these little books are intended to exhibit some of the temptations, the trials, the difficulties, and the duties, which all children experience in circumstances similar."[2] (Note the somber quality of those four nouns.) That he wished for the young reader to be "profited as well as amused" is plain. Yet the gentle Abbott provided an equally gentle Miss Mary as guide during the sedate adventures of Rollo and Henry, Dovey and Ann, and the other small pupils through a world of pietism and serious learning with setting not only of schoolroom but also woods and country lane, meadow and orchard where, epochs later, the Bobbsey Twins might come for a frolic.

The volume *Rollo at School* finishes with Miss Mary's "keeping holiday" in her father's orchard, a pastime considered more appropriate than attendance at the "training" of Light Infantry on the village common. True, the children spend the morning helping gather apples, but at noon the entire company adjourns to the woods. There the rewards unfold: a play tent, a fire for roasting corn and apples, a basket yielding bread and butter

ROLLO AT SCHOOL.

THE ROLLO SERIES

IS COMPOSED OF FOURTEEN VOLUMES, VIZ

Rollo Learning to Talk.	Rollo's Museum.
Rollo Learning to Read.	Rollo's Travels.
Rollo at Work.	Rollo's Correspondence.
Rollo at Play.	Rollo's Philosophy—Water.
Rollo at School.	Rollo's Philosophy—Air.
Rollo's Vacation.	Rollo's Philosophy—Fire.
Rollo's Experiments.	Rollo's Philosophy—Sky.

A NEW EDITION, REVISED BY THE AUTHOR.

BOSTON:

PHILLIPS, SAMPSON, AND COMPANY.

NEW YORK: JAMES C. DERBY.

A revised edition repeats Jacob Abbott's Prefatory Notice of 1838.

They mounted up into a large wagon.

Muddy watercolors applied by some small hand brightened this frontispiece from *Rollo at School.*

and "one or two pies." What is more, there is time for storytelling and for sailing toy boats in the brook.

Rollo is rather far removed from the hordes of children and creatures of the caravan stretching to the fictional horizon: the orphaned or half-orphaned children, family groups, foursomes, twins and cousins, juvenile organizations, official and unofficial. There appeared totally unrelated sets of characters as well, grouped together for some reason or for no reason. Finally they came in swarms, Elsie, Anne, Gypsy, Rebecca, Pollyanna and Laura, Tarzan and Tattered Tom and Tom Sawyer and Tom Swift, the families March, Pepper and Parlin, the Blue Grass Seminary Girls and the Rover Boys, the Camp Fire Girls, the Boy Pioneers, Boy Allies and the Red Cross Girls, moving from mountains to lake or from sea to sea. While the first heroes and heroines began with geographical settings largely of the Northeast, backgrounds expanded rapidly and exploratively to every continent. Rollo himself, suitably chaperoned by his uncle, Mr. George, and other family members, went journeying in the second series from one European city to another, presaging the voyaging of the future. It very soon seemed that the world had opened itself to young people engaged in every activity under the sun or moon ranging from common everyday happenings through the adventurous into the fantastic.

Eventually animal friends and enemies followed suit. Uncle Wiggily and his entourage streamed through woods and field with the creatures of the West Wind, Sleepy-Time Tales or Hollow Tree, while the Oz players and Doctor Dolittle's crew were a good deal bolder in their wanderings.

When the century turned, some children were still making Rollo's acquaintance. One dare say that among these were readers with curious minds that impelled their owners to focus upon any written word, whether it be between covers of a book, on a cereal box or scrawled on a scrap of notebook paper blowing in the street. Such is the nature of one for whom reading is the foremost pleasure and occupation.

This is not to say that Rollo did not deserve attention. After all, as the counterpart of any child he followed a natural pattern of one inclined to neither intensive piety nor downright badness, although as primary character of one story after another, and possessed of frequent home counseling, he perhaps exhibited more virtues than vices. So that the feminine readers would not feel slighted, Abbott thoughtfully prepared the Lucy Books of lesser number, these *after* the Rollo Books, naturally, since Adam appeared before Eve and woman modestly followed a step behind man and, incidentally, was not always accorded so complete an education.

In the Notice appearing in one of the first Lucy Books, Abbott stated: "The simple delineations of the ordinary incidents and feelings which characterize childhood, that are contained in the Rollo Books, have been found to interest, and, as the author hopes, in some degree to benefit the young readers for whom they were designed—the plan is herein extended to children of the other sex. ...Lucy was Rollo's cousin; and the author hopes that the history of her life and adventures may be entertaining and useful to the sisters of the boys who have honored the Rollo Books with their approval."[3] And that would seem to indicate that the author's definition of "children of the other sex" might read as "sisters of boys," turning the tables on a non-fictional 20th century small girl's explanation of holy, winged messengers by announcement that boys were merely "angels' brothers."

Abbott was not alone in turning from one sex to the other. The many-storied Louisa May Alcott, writing feverishly to supply the needs of her expanding and early-impoverished family, turned from girls to write *Little Men* and *Jo's Boys*. By the time that she was producing book after book, fiction for children had advanced noticeably and it is to the credit of Abbott that he early introduced "children of the other sex" into series of their own.

The literary inheritance of the early 19th century child reputedly was meager. According to a writer who, a century ago, so immersed herself in the domestic and social history of colonial times in New England and New York that she wrote more than a dozen volumes associated with that period, it was a tightly circumscribed world for the young. "There were few American children until after the Revolution who had ever read from any book save the Bible, a primer, or catechism, and perhaps a hymn book or an almanac."[4]

Rigid rules of behavior had been printed and reprinted in book form. A "Revolutionary patriot and printer, Isaiah Thomas," published small cheap books, often English reprints, including some of John Newbery's "penny books." Other matter, from American writers as well as from across the Atlantic, treated of morals and the avoidance of sin, and could be terrifying. Strangely, among miniature publications for children were abridged adult novels such as Henry Fielding's *Tom Jones* and *Joseph Andrews*, and Samuel Richardson's *Pamela, Clarissa Harlowe*, and *Sir Charles Grandison*. There were also the fairy tales, myths and legends, rhymings and such classics as *Pilgrim's Progress, Gulliver's Travels* and *Robinson Crusoe* which, although written for adults, had been taken over by the younger generation.

Perusal of some of the early books designed for children may well conclude with the belief that advent of adventures of Rollo provided light-hearted reading indeed. Too much light-heartedness would have seemed folly in a day when the apparition of mortality hovered so close. Early death continued to stalk through youthful heritage, and terror of hell was perhaps as much in mind as salvation and the glories of heaven, for God was a stern and demanding presence. Preparation for that final physical disaster and for entry into heaven entwined itself with education in the beginning.

Consider that which awaited the young child at school and in church. The *New England Primer*, modeled after British primers and known to appear in America before the 17th century ended and to be still in use beyond 1800, sold to an estimated number of three million copies,[5] American publishers, perhaps changing the title if that suited them, augmented or subtracted from earlier contents at will and bound the tiny books in thin board covered lightly with paper, or in paper itself. To learn the alphabet by picture and rhyme is one thing, but to go into catechism while still confined to a primer and to, let us say, "A Dialogue between Christ, Youth, and the Devil" could be more than sobering. After such nourishment the Rollo Books would seem deliriously escapist.

Meanwhile Sunday School "union" and tract societies were putting out text-only hymnals for children, again borrowing from the British but making whatever revisions pleased them. Thus young Ann and Jane Taylor's *Hymns for Infant Minds*, showing quaint little figures on their knees with hands folded, appeared under American imprint with sometimes pleasant hymns, sometimes one with title such as "For A Child That Feels It Has A Wicked Heart." One entitled "About Dying" begins with a child's pondering.

Tell me, Mamma, if I must die,
    One day, as little baby died;
And look so very pale, and lie,

Down in the pit-hole, by its side?[6]

In still another a child, confessing guilt along with knowledge of imminent death, addresses a Heavenly Father in the following manner.

How soon my health and strength are fled!
  And life is nearly past!
O smile upon my dying bed,
  And love me to the last....[7]

Can one wonder at the paralyzed imagination and spiritual indigestion that must have been common? Couchant lambs atop sandstone markers were prevalent long after Rollo and Lucy appeared on the scene. While historical statistics for the United States do not show any dramatic decrease in infant mortality until the 1920's, there were phantoms created by respiratory disease, diphtheria and typhoid, by mysterious ailments, by the paucity of treatment for disastrous diseases. In the state of Massachusetts first records in 1850 show that expectation of life at birth was 38.3 years for males and 40.5 years for females.[8]

A minuscule hymnal first entered in 1854 in Cincinnati by a Sunday School union, *Hymns for Sunday Schools, Youth and Children*, testifies to the continuing need of making ready in all respects for early departure. Titles descriptive enough to make an adult shudder include: "Death of a Child," "Death of a Pious Child," "The Early Dead," "Go to Thy Rest, my Child," "At the Grave of a Child," "The Wicked Child Judged."

Nor did the religious boards stop with hymns. Out from the busy presses came not only papers for Sunday distribution but books such as *Lessons for the Little Ones*, with intent of more than teaching. A chapter on "Heavenly Arithmetic" overflows with warnings that could frighten a small boy out of his red-topped boots or a girl-child out of her pinafore.

Our days may be very few. We do not know that we shall live till we are old. Many of my old school companions are in their graves...Some of your young companions are dead also. But you think you will be sure to live a long time yet. They thought so, too; but death came, and took them away. You may never live till you are men or women. Ah, dear children, before another year closes you may be in your graves! The snow of next winter may be your covering, and the moon look down upon you where you lie cold. Yea, even before this winter has passed away you may die, and the green grass and the little flowers of spring grow over you...[9]

In this pious and anonymous literature an invisible Old Dame Care seems to phrase the underlying message in such colloquial language as: Better be good—or else! The awful spectre of death must have followed any child like a shadow in daytime and remained close, behind a chair or door, during evening. Recorded testimony to the existence of fearsome thoughts within young hearts of those early days appears in a compilation of diary and journal excerpts drawn from children's notations over several centuries.

Esther Edwards, daughter of minister Jonathan Edwards, and future mother of the political duelist Aaron Burr, was noting in 1742 the thirty-third birthday of her mother and wondering whether she herself would live to a mature thirty-three. (She did not; she died at twenty-three.) On another occasion she spoke of riding in the woods with her usually "taciturn or preoccupied" father on a spring day. "...he discoursed to me of the awful sweetness of walking with God in Nature..."[10] Remark that "awful sweetness." Even though the adjective probably indicated emotion "worthy of reverence," quite possibly Esther also felt it "terrifying."

In the century which followed, Euphemia Mason Olcott, born in 1844, expressed at age twelve unmistakable terror of death and the feeling of her own unworthiness.

Feb. 21 (1857) I can count in our family during the last two years seven deaths. Oh, what a warning it should be to me! Last night it seemed as if I heard a voice whispering warnings into my ear and telling me to prepare to die...
March 15 When I began my last birthday to keep a journal I hardly thought I would finish it. I have finished that book and commenced another. God only knows whether I will live to finish it. Oh!—I wonder if I am prepared to die. I wish I knew. I feel my sins more than I ever did in my life before...[11]

In Miss Mary's little school Bible-reading began the day, and the instructor explained verses to the pupils. "God will not listen to us when we pray to him, if he is displeased with us; and he is displeased with us just as much when we have iniquity *in our hearts,* as when we exhibit it in our actions..." Obviously education was of a no-nonsense quality, dealing as it did with morals and religion as well as formal schooling and manners. Once Miss Mary told some of her charges that a school "...is in some respects like a hospital. Children are sent here partly to be cured of their faults and improved in character..."[12]

It is rather amazing that with all else incorporated Abbott could and would devise means of weaving simple narrative through the series devoted to development of small Rollo. It was quite time for that. Over the decades he was to write the Jonas Stories, the August Stories and the Franconia Stories, considered his best, but it was Rollo whom readers seemed to remember. Lucy remained rather an afterthought.

The recognition was growing, against a fearful, arid background, that sin did not lie in reading for pleasure as well as for dutiful instruction. Even if youths ignored the teachings of piety running throughout a story they would by osmosis absorb these principles to some degree. And fiction writers would not put piety entirely aside. The verbal pointer focusing on a moral would never quite vanish. Indeed, virtue has seemed to find some sort of reward for decades while mean conduct results in contrition and/or punishment. And if the philosophy holds true that a child must like himself in order to be at all content, then likely his instinct will bid him mind his manners and morals to one extent or another. Disapproval from some directions is a strong guiding force, and it is natural to desire approval and certain admiration. It is also natural and normal to conduct oneself sometimes with grace, sometimes without it, and of this children are quite conscious. To behave only with piety is non-human, and they recognize this, too.

Like the child who asks, "And then what?" at a pause or even at the end of a tale if the teller did not sign off with "And so they lived happily ever after," the investigator seeks to discover what did follow the pious, doctrinal molding of the 19th century child.

Rising from every phase of the exploration of how the series grew, diversity distinguishes itself as prime characteristic. Even the term "series" itself needs interpretation since it defies precise and confining definition. With the gradual transition from didactic writing to that with an honest story line, the press supplied not only books but periodicals with serial fiction. The Sunday School, preceding the development of the public library, was a boon, making available reading matter and introduction to authors, for here it was that the early series appeared.

Variety in backgrounds and qualifications differentiated the authoring throng. Scribes were often private persons concealing themselves in pseudonyms, not to be coy, perhaps, but because of sometime modesty or recognition of social opinion that fiction did not contribute to strengthening Christian character. Too, the notion conveyed a certain mystique, as with the assumed name of "Aunt Florida" or "Cousin Mary."

Heroes and heroines progressed from sanctimonious nature to more realistic make-up, thus more honestly representing their eras. Even the constitution of the child alone, or almost alone, in the world and exhibiting common conditions of destitution, altered in accordance with civic handling of indigence. That lowly protagonist, frequently a child of stubborn will to survive and of determination to aid in shaping his own future, became a notable character for his quick tongue, leadership and individuality. Later he was often given a special niche among acquaintances merely because of his lack of immediate family.

Of craftsmanship there was a wide range from that of literary to competent to mediocre to gauche. These degrees of ability displayed themselves in manipulation of protagonists and plots, scope of setting, foreign and domestic, portraiture and verbal style. Authors challenged readers and visionary girls and boys with dreams and fancies, with adversity, with adventures both homely and extravagant, eventually with comedy. The thread of early instruction in moral philosophy continued for long in the weaving of narration but not forever with the original somber predications, and not always in the same pattern. Styles in writing were individual for the most, and of many colorations and ranks.

Rules of conduct did not confine themselves to contrived experiences of human beings but carried over into the kingdom of small animals in the simpler series written for the very young, the listeners on their way to becoming readers. Here writers aimed to find favor, too, with the adults of a household.

That the age of untold series made history remains evident on shelves of bookstores and libraries where one can still find new printings, usually freshly illustrated, exemplifying the best from that vast accumulation built up as basis for American children's literature. Several strictly of the classification of recreational reading, updated, have joined them. Often-handled early editions grace old-book stores and antique shops, awaiting collectors. This is not all that survives. There exist as well less visible fragments, souvenirs in phrase or word or sound, that occasionally rise like echoes out of the capricious mists of the past.

Chapter II
Sunday Schools and Libraries, Presses and Authors

What began at a disciplined pace with the Rollo Books increased gradually to a moderate trot and eventually to a gallop. An interweaving of events and individuals and institutions required time and some harmonizing before the caravan of fiction series, appearing in book form, rose like a pastel mirage on the horizon.

Germinating at the same time and resembling "papers" rather than magazines, other publications for children joined the modest contest to place reading material into young hands. Although periodicals of a general nature in the new republic had their beginnings before the revolution there had been no immediate concern for "second-class citizens," in this case the second sex and children. During the spring of 1784 *Gentlemen and Lady's Town and Country Magazine* had made its bow but withdrew after eight issues, while five years later *Children's Magazine* stepped out—for three appearances only.

Nevertheless, acknowledgement of some activity in the field of juvenile printed matter came in the form of an 1829 announcement by the *New York Mirror*. "The mania for periodicals has extended itself to children."[1]

Center of the early Sunday School movement and the primary source of church-sponsored papers was Philadelphia. Already the American Sunday School Union was putting out *Youth's Friend and Scholar's Magazine*, which sold for twenty-five cents a year. By 1827 its circulation was ten thousand, its pages sixteen, its contents religious essays and anecdotes.[2]

Good fortune came in guise of the spread, also from England, of the Sunday School library movement. While the little libraries may have been mean, their establishment in the earlier part of the 19th century was significant. Similar institutions of that era were limited to an occasional small community affair and, after 1838, to schools which might follow the New York plan. There the state granted a sum of money for school libraries with the stipulation that each school must itself produce a sum corresponding to that offered by its governing body. It was not until 1876 that the public library movement brought about organization of the American Library

Association. And first training class for children's librarians had to wait until the advent of the next century for it was only in the final decade of the 19th that recognition came of the youthful segment of the population as library patrons and of the need for specialized service.[3]

Interestingly enough, the aim of the Sunday School was that of a charity school teaching reading and morals to its one-day-a-week pupils.[4] In order to fulfill this design officials and volunteers provided a store of books as well as pamphlets. "The expanding West gave the Union great concern and in 1830 all efforts were directed to the needs of the 'heathen of the Valley of the Mississippi.' The 'Valley' embraced all territory west of the Alleghenies, with the first concentration of effort in Ohio, Kentucky, Indiana and Illinois."[5] An advertisement among the back pages of a series begun in the 1860's offered "CARTER'S CHEAP SABBATH SCHOOL LIBRARY 50 vol. In neat cloth. In a wooden case. Net $20.00."[6]

Young readers were to find in the Sabbath School library more than the virtuous religious volumes considered proper to their nourishment. There were the Rollo Books and, from time to time, additional series including those of Pansy and of Elsie Dinsmore. Some of the same caliber came into use as Sunday School prizes. Looking back, an historian reviewing the development of children's literature, while criticizing the tone of the offerings, still called these libraries "...probably the greatest source of books for children."[7]

Annie Fellows Johnston, who spun the many Little Colonel volumes, was familiar with such library shelves. One of her characters, Betty Lewis, regularly walked to the small frame church near her country home, opened a window and climbed in to reach the case that over the years had occupied "a cobwebby corner."

It held all that was left of a scattered Sunday-school library, that had been in use two generations before. Queer little books they were, time-yellowed and musty smelling...

So many of them were about unnaturally good children who never did wrong, and unnaturally bad children who never did right. At the end there was always the word MORAL, in big capital letters, as if the readers were supposed to be too blind to find it for themselves, and it had to be put directly across the path for them to stumble over.[8]

Bookworms will concede that something to read is better than nothing, and one can believe that inveterate readers existed among the young public of the past century. Of the 1850 population of the United States, a fat half fell into the under-twenty category. The under-fifteen bracket was doubly important; it accounted for three-fourths of the under-twenty group, and for more than two-thirds of the total population.[9]

What was there, discounting the existence of a school library, in the classroom? Examination of standard readers designed after the century had counted off half its years, shows for the middle classes of grammar school a quite admirable selection of poetry, myth and legend, plus extracts from biographies, essays and fiction classics. Choice appears to have had two principles as base: to provide means of serious learning in all scholastic fields and to teach ethics.

Yet that section of the population also had a growing resource of periodicals. Publishers' keen eyes had long ago spied out the paucity of subject matter and the resulting opportunity to augment it and compete with the Philadelphia religious presses. Thus it was that secular periodicals had been sprouting in largely eastern cities. Some throve or fell away, changed title or merged with rivals; certain among them lived respectably long lives.

The Youth's Companion began its astonishing century-long history in 1827. While not allied with tract societies, its original aim was moral instruction as well as entertainment. Six years after its inception Samuel G. Goodrich, already on stage with his small Peter Parley books compiled for children, set himself up as editor of *Parley's Magazine*. Although a contemporary, he was not competitor to Jacob Abbott by reason of lack of a continuing story line. He carried on editorship of his magazine in the same manner as of his books, which combined natural history, geography and related subjects with broken strands of narrative expanding information on peoples, places and eras. In his endless book production he worked out an arrangement involving assistants. "With his eyesight constantly threatened he employed others (including Nathaniel Hawthorne) to block out work for him, and dictated the final versions to his wife."[10] His intent was to teach and, hoping to get his books into the schools, he had added questions at the bottom of each paragraph-numbered page.

With the passing of a year Goodrich sold *Parley's Magazine*; eleven years later it united with *Merry's Museum for Boys and Girls*, a second venture by Goodrich in 1841, and one enduring into the 1870's.[11]

One cannot but conclude that a certain Bell L. Pettigrew prized her 1851-52 copies of the periodical, for they survived bound in marbled board and leather with her name imprinted in gilt upon the spine.

For the most part a serious tone prevails, which testifies to the solemnity of youthful life and the accent upon acquiring knowledge. During these two years the monthly magazine, at annual subscription cost of one dollar, was a compilation of information on a wide range of subjects from mankind and religion through science, history and geography to legend and mythology, with anecdotes and fragments for fillers. Despite the studious air, *Merry's Museum* presented occasional short fiction pieces of moralistic nature, and irregularly continuing stories entitled "Adventures of Gilbert Go-ahead," treating of travel, and "The Galley Slave."

After reading of places of antiquity such as Ephesus, Nineveh and Persepolis, and of personages exemplified by Croesus, Darius and Xerxes, subscribers might have considered the biography of Napoleon of recent vintage indeed. What is more, children would have found pleasure in the end-pages called "Merry's Monthly Chat with his Friends." These were usually collections of verses, puzzles, and letters from young readers recounting personal experiences and offering praise, particularly for the "adventures."

With the progression of the decades into the 50's, that fiction mirage against the horizon was beginning to assume lineaments of reality. In some cases book-publishers founded periodicals while numerous writers were branching out from novels to magazines, sometimes in editorial posts, often as contributors of brief fiction and serials.

In this interlacing of components a throng of series writers participated. Among other publications sturdy and pleasurable enough to flourish for a span of years was *Forrester's Boys and Girls* (1848-1857) with which William T. Adams (Oliver Optic) had association. *Little Corporal* (1865-1875), thereafter merging with *St. Nicholas Magazine,* based in Chicago, counted as contributors Harry Castlemon and Susan Coolidge.[12] An amalgamation of two earlier papers, *Student and Schoolmate,* introduced Horatio Alger to the public in 1865; its second editor was Oliver Optic.[13] *Our Boys and Girls,* advertised in a back page of The Jutland series as Oliver Optic's magazine, listed Sophie May of Little Prudy and Dotty Dimple series, May Mannering of The Helping-Hand series, and Elijah Kellogg as among "regular contributors."[14]

The name Oliver Optic burst into print with frequency. An 1867 reprint of an 1858 series title has back pages filled with Optic listings but for one devoted to Sophie May; it also touted his *Our Boys and Girls,* which had a life term of nine years. Description of this weekly pronounced it "The Cheapest, Handsomest, and Best issued in America," and promised a "steel portrait" of the editor-author. "Our Boys and Girls for 1867 will contain three stories by Oliver Optic, the price of which would be $3.75. Each number has a handsome cover printed in colors, and is profusely illustrated with drawings made expressly for it. Each number contains illustrated Rebuses, Geographical Puzzles, Exercises in Declamation, Original Dialogues, etc. ...Each number contains sixteen pages, making a yearly volume of eight hundred and thirty-two pages. Terms: Per Year. ...$2.50. Single Numbers— 6 cents...."[15]

What was more, this energetic author wrote that his serialized story, "The Starry Flag," had had such enthusiastic reception on appearance in *Our Boys and Girls* that he "...found allusions to it in at least a hundred letters from young persons..." Although he had not planned to continue with the same characters, he had "...neither the inclination nor the courage to disappoint his young friends...."[16]

Creator of the Jack Hazard adventures and other series, J.T. Trowbridge was one of the editors of *Our Young Folks* (1865-1873) whose pages Louisa May Alcott, Optic, Alger and Trowbridge himself helped fill. It received 20th century historical judgment as having been "bright, amusing, literary."[17] In the 1860's Louisa Alcott accepted an editorial position with *Merry's Museum* and during the same year, answering a request by Roberts & Brothers publishing house for a book about girls, began work on the famous foursome of *Little Women*. Appearing originally in two volumes, it served as leader of the Little Women series.[18]

Horace Scudder was an editor for *Riverside Magazine*, which merged with *Scribner's Monthly*. Elijah Kellogg began, and his wife edited, New York's *Treasure Trove* (1877-93). Publisher Daniel Lothrop launched the periodical *Pansy*, using the pseudonym of the editor, Isabella Alden; her Pansy books made for didactic reading everywhere. However, the favorite child of the Lothrop press was *Wide Awake*, dating from 1875. Foremost among its serials were Margaret Sidney's stories about the Pepper family, while others supplying material included Elizabeth Stuart Phelps, Hezekiah Butterworth and Trowbridge. Edward S. Ellis served as editor for several papers and along with Alger furnished fiction for Frank Munsey's weekly, *Golden Argosy*. Those two, in company with Castlemon and Optic, also wrote for *Golden Days for Boys and Girls*.[19]

By post-Civil War days annual listings of children's periodicals had reached sixty or more. Half were Sunday School publications, and half secular. They had formidable competition in *Youth's Companion*, which put aside its meek ways and took on distinguishing features: emphasis on fiction, introduction of better writers, and an appeal for the family as a whole. Charles Asbury Stephens, Butterworth, Trowbridge and Scudder were names appearing below serial titles. Stephens gathered material through travel, and Butterworth followed that pattern, coming up with his Zigzag series. Of contributing women writers there were Alcott and Phelps. In retrospect, experts cited three reasons for the magazine's popularity: continued stories, interest in family, and a premium list which offered "treasures" of various kinds to those obtaining new subscriptions. Elsie Dinsmore books numbered among the so-called treasures.[20] The circulation was half a million.

Meanwhile came the stellar year of 1873 denoting the birth of the famous *St. Nicholas Magazine* which, while not rivaling *Youth's Companion* for longevity, or subscription list, outshone it literarily. Since several lesser periodicals merged with it, *St. Nicholas* acquired the distinction of being "that voracious devourer of smaller fish."[21]

Its longtime editor, Mary Mapes Dodge, herself a novelist—the most renowned work under the title of *Hans Brinker and his Silver Skates*—said a great many things about the make-up of a children's publication. Not cambric tea, "...not a milk-and-water variety of the periodical for adults," she put it. A child's magazine "...needs to be stronger, truer, bolder, more uncompromising than the other..." It ought to be a place where "...children can come and go as they please..." and find treasures and oddities. There must be "...freshness and heartiness, life and joy."[22]

Here the seventy thousand subscribers, and doubtless their cousins and friends, found names well known to series readers: Trowbridge with his Jack Hazard stories, Laura Richards and her Hildegarde books, Louisa May Alcott with *Eight Cousins* and *Under the Lilacs*, Mark Twain and *Tom Sawyer Abroad*. They were also able to meet in one issue or another Kate Douglas Wiggin, James Otis, Alice Hegan Rice, Ellis, Scudder, Butterworth, Stephens, Coolidge, Phelps and Carolyn Wells. All these series writers were in select company of such people as Rudyard Kipling, Edward Eggleston, Jack London, Noah Brooks, Frank Stockton, Thomas Bailey Aldrich, Frances Hodgson Burnett, Robert Louis Stevenson, Theodore Roosevelt, Howard Pyle, Bret Harte, John Burroughs, Gelet Burgess.

This was a stimulating and no doubt stimulated new world with writers and publishers intermingling as they did to continue that fiction parade that broke loose at times with extravaganza aimed particularly at boys. Short and long stories and whole series stretched as far as an eye could see. Adventure lay everywhere, in the wars, in the West, in marvels of nature, in disclosures of the universe, in the minds of men, even in humdrum everyday life. Nothing was too near and nothing too distant for scrutiny and exploration and transference into fiction. Eventually the subject matter would include fantasy, straight mystery as well, and some writers would dip back into historical reality.

With the story kingdom opening up by intervention of so many elements, the reading child could ascertain the verity of the known and discover the unknown even beyond the seven traditional "wonders." Imagination his companion, he could lose himself temporarily by journeying upon magic carpets woven of words. And woe to thought of speed reading!

Chapter III
The Tie that Binds:
Or, A Series is A Series is A Series

When the question of what constitutes a fiction series arouses controversy, it is wise to define the term against the background from which it emanated. *Webster's New World Dictionary*, in its most pertinent interpretation, calls it "...a number of things produced as a related group; set, as of novels by one author dealing with the same characters...." The words "succession," "sequence" and "chain" hover at close quarters. Yet the specification is deficient for the century that spawned hundreds of groups of books categorized as "series." The concept as applied in this age of wide usage was so flexible, so full of variations, as to defy exact limits.

Expansion of the Webster explanation for the purpose of framing a model series results in this description: a succession of related books delineating the development, by one author, of a cast of characters playing out their roles chronologically through a cycle of time with every volume fitting harmoniously into the narrative.

While excellent specimen of ideal series exist, the concept simply was not bound by fixed rules. Not all writers considered that controlled progression of seasons or years was vital if characters were simply to fly from one great adventure to another. Not all writers felt that a set of books need deal with the same players. One deviation was that of using in each volume a different protagonist with a similarity, say, of circumstances; Alger demonstrated this with his street Arab characters. Sometimes an historic era or geographical background was the connecting link. There were sets lumping together brief series plus single volumes, all by one author. Some of the output of prolific Edward Ellis, as advertised in old book pages, consisted of two-volume "series." A series could be of any length, from that occasional two, frequent three, round numbers of four and six on up to any multiple desired. Publishers took advantage of the pliancy by putting together heterogeneous sets of size, such as Six to Sixteen series or The Young in Heart series, with no inner relationships although a single author's name might, or might not, appear several times. Almost any idea could lead to a set of books bearing the designation of "series."

Thus a second question evolves as to why it became common to cluster books in this fashion. Popular Oliver Optic, whose career began early and endured for decades, did not always carry characters from one volume to the next. In a comprehensive, four-part history of children's literature, Anne Thaxter Eaton noted that "Optic's books were written in series, according to the fashion of the day..."[1] *The fashion of the day.*

Early in the 19th century The American Tract Society, concerned with providing suitable reading material for children, had engaged authors to supply miniature books and classified them as Youth's Biography series and Youth's Narrative series. Yet "...the whole project set its face firmly against fiction."[2] Thus the custom had already begun, and to tolerate the plasticity of the term, even to understand it, is not unreasonable.

Public identification could have been important here, identification between hero and author, author and publisher, series title and either author or publisher. There were visible benefits for all, including the hungry young public.

With society's guarded sanction of fiction-reading, speeding up presses and promoting series seems a natural and fruitful method of supplying the marketplace. An initial volume of prompt popularity could spur continuation as with the serialization used by magazines to engender anticipation and sales. It could lead to a string of closely associated volumes or, again as sales device, assume the same post with less connected books. Having reader appreciation as well as publisher recommendation as being worthy, that pilot would, as a kind of Pied Piper, draw a retinue of readers. For both publishers and authors, ascending reputation and increase of income would follow.

From the point of view of the child, the flow of series must have been significant for more reason than offering pleasurable reading. Consider his rank on that lower plane, a level on which it was necessary to observe such rules of conduct as not speaking until he was spoken to, of living up to adult standards before completing a growth period of learning, of reading censored material designed to fortify Christian moral character, even of dressing as miniature adult in drab garments.

One can envision through the medium of fiction his gradual emergence as a positive human being with a rise in esteem for self and peers. Here were compatriots whose lives developed in the same general fashion as his own but on freer, bolder ground. Here were noteworthy children encountering sometimes splendid, sometimes adverse, adventures and after a struggle coming forth victorious. Furthermore, here was a bonus, a kind of security in frequently accompanying characters from one stage to the next.

That he did want more is evident in the shabby survivals found on shelves today. Flimsy covers replaced some sturdy bindings as publishers brought out cheap reprints of highly admired series. Cracked spines, ragged

Before 1900, small children of the series often came clad in small covers.

corners, successive inscriptions, and occasional British publishing designations indicate wide readership and much handling. Any series found today in near perfect condition usually is a remainder from the last, extravagant days of series, and of trifling content.

Practices of publishers and authors to provide "come-ons" or ties in unrelated series were unashamed. Advertisements appeared in sheaves of back pages, sometimes inside cover boards and eventually on backsides of paper wrappers extolling the books already in print and announcing others in preparation. Individual prefaces gave opportunity to present information, sales results, reader correspondence and reasons for extending series. Final paragraphs of stories prepared the reader for oncoming books, indeed, in some cases furnishing the only link other than repeat performance by one author.

Abbott himself wrote in 1838 that "As the little readers of 'Rollo at Work' and 'Rollo at Play', have done the author the honor to manifest some interest in the continuation of his juvenile hero's history, they are now presented with 'Rollo at School', and 'Rollo's Vacation.' "[3]

In the long continuing expansion of the Pepper series, Margaret Sidney explained at some length the advent of a volume devoted solely to the eldest of the five children. "...So the hosts of readers of the Pepper Series decided, and many of them accordingly besought the author to give Ben a chance to be better known...."[4] In a newcomer to the Rover Boys books Arthur Winfield was even wordier. Addressing his readers as "My dear Boys...," he proclaimed that "...This line of books was started some ten years ago with the publication of the first three volumes. ...At that time I thought to end the series with a fourth volume—provided the readers wanted another. But with the publication of 'The Rover Boys Out West,' came a cry for 'more!'..."[5] A dedication by L.M. Montgomery for a Green Gables book was succinct: "To all the girls all over the world who have 'wanted more' about ANNE."[6]

Finishing off one boy's adventures in a way to place readers in immediate state of anticipation, Horatio Alger wrote, "The next story of this series will be *Paul, the Peddler*; or, The Fortunes of a Young Street Merchant."[7] At times he was more personal. "And now, kind reader, let me hope to meet you soon again with the second volume of the 'Luck and Pluck' series,— *Sink or Swim*: or, *Harry Raymond's Reso*."[8]

Sophie May was less direct in one of the Little Prudy's Flyaway series. "Dear Readers: Horace was scarcely more astonished, when his pocket was picked, than I am this minute, to find myself at the end of my book! I had very much more to tell; but now it must wait till another time."[9]

In his Frank and Archie series, Castlemon alerted his reader with hints of forthcoming action. "These were Archie's first impressions. Before he had been long on the ranche (sic), he discovered that life in California was not so dull and uneventful as he had imagined it to be. He had adventures, and more than he wanted; and what they were shall be told in *Frank Among the Rancheros*."[10]

Elijah Kellogg clearly portended even more calamitous a future for some of his heroes. "Walter and Ned have now become accustomed to hardship, had experience of danger, and incurred responsibility. The next volume of the series, the Cruise of the Casco, will exhibit their capabilities when thrown more entirely upon their own resources, and placed in trust of a large interest under circumstances of deadly peril."[11]

Obviously the specific audience ruled the kind of forecast given. Stories for boys predicted hair-breadth events; those for girls a continuation equally gratifying to them; and those aimed at youngest readers, jollity. Howard Garis in his Uncle Wiggily stories never waited to reach the last page to foretell what might come next. Every little tale ended with a whimsical statement such as "...but if the telephone doesn't talk in its sleep, and wake up the rag doll, so that she cries for a lollypop, I'll tell you next about Uncle Wiggily and the sassafras tea."[12] And when he did conclude a volume, he plainly promised to "make a new book," gave its title, mentioned its general content and spoke a goodbye to last until the sequel should appear.

Chapter IV
Times, Tides and Directions

Once the contrivance of banding books together showed promise and profit there appeared to be no hesitation in promoting its use. The expansion was helter-skelter but it was remarkably successful despite the variation of means employed to make transition from one volume to another.

Abbott's manner of dealing with Rollo in a chronological way was the solid and logical one which many others would adopt. In exemplary way he recounted, with realistic children and settings of home and school, Rollo's growth from the age at which that child learned to speak up through his "philosophy." The second grouping of Rollo Books described advancement through the boy's travel with relatives, to make a total of twenty-eight small volumes. When Abbott brought Lucy on the scene, he did not proceed in that same consistent mode. Lucy's conversations and stories led to experiences at the sea-shore and among mountains. This was genteel treatment for a little girl and the feminine intellect although her creator did speak of "...the gradual progress made by our little heroine in the acquisition of knowledge, and in the formation of character..."[1] In this instance he was using a looser form, connecting the books primarily by character. However, years had passed since his introduction of Lucy. Not surprisingly, she did not make the impact that Rollo achieved.

Series anchored in traditional time setting, with the first chronicle leading easily onward, gave the impression of permanence and reality. From piquant-tempered minx a certain child of Southern accent rose to adolescence and thence to the young woman of *The Little Colonel's Knight Comes Riding*. And the Anne who at age "about eleven" received ungracious reception at Green Gables, conquered Marilla and the immediate environment, went on to Queen's academy, taught, married Gilbert Blythe and started her own family. Such chronology combined with a highly admirable heroine in either case was ideal progression. Martha Finley had, of course, used that method earlier, but her little saint, Elsie, born fictionally at age eight, was a mother by volume five, a widow by book seven, and a grandmother by number eight; yet her name attached itself to nineteen more volumes.

To follow through expanding years a Cinderella kind of heroine such as Anne, or a silver-spoon one like the Little Colonel, was bliss to a girl. Surely the dear-to-the-heart Annes and Jos and Little Colonels, Rebeccas and Gypsies, Pollys and Pattys (did anyone honestly love Elsie enough to classify her with the others?) must have had publishers rubbing their hands in expectation of bumper harvests. One proof was that when Eleanor H. Porter abandoned her Pollyanna, several other writers took over the character but turned out nondescript stories. Similar continuation of series by other individuals or by teams of writers occurred elsewhere, once with a series still highly popular, the Oz books.

Family groups, too, such as the Peppers and Sophie May's collections of cousins and other kin, offered chance for stable manipulation of players in natural succession. More of these would appear later when series reached a peak in quantity but embodied declining sensibility and far less strict design.

Beyond Rollo, a neat pattern with controlled progression through a series did not always serve for young male readers. Here sex differences influenced plots and settings and figures moving through them. Humble day-to-day happenings were not sufficient. Whereas protective conventions, duty and semblance of safety governed the fragile sex, independence, hazards and at times melodrama were in order for fictional heroes. Attainment of an apogee by the masterly sex, after great exercise of wits and perhaps of muscles as well, meant signing off. Nothing more needed saying although several writers liked to sum up and speak prediction.

Pompous Oliver Optic, who early elected the system of combining unconnected stories for groups of books, once finished off in startling manner a sensational tale in which the villain and his companions monopolized far more space than the hero.

While Captain Fairfield—as he is generally called—and his beautiful wife hope the day is far distant which will make him a millionaire, this event in the course of nature, must occur; yet is he richer now, in the possession of a noble character and a true Christian spirit, than he can be made by any *Freaks of Fortune*.[2]

Less inclined to tumult than Optic, but equally inclined to moralizing, Alger, if not announcing the next in line, finalized a hero's victory.

I have no hesitation in predicting for him a noble manhood and an honorable career. In spite of the gifts of Fortune that he possesses, I consider his warm and generous heart, his personal integrity and his manly character to be *John Oakley's most valuable inheritance...*[3]

While the thread of Christian ethics remained strong, luck and pluck were not readily aggrandized by others who wrote for boys. Castlemon and Kellogg, Stephens and Butterworth and Trowbridge sent their boys off to war, to explore the West, to farming or to sea; yet situations were likely to be homelier with protagonists less self-assured than those who, in a single volume, or perhaps two, gained the world. As a result these youths are more believable and since they were unable to guide their destinies with great dispatch, their growth extended to multiple books.

Yet the "going out into the world" for trial runs continued with the break from home, signifying the prerogative of the male creature. While families were backstage, there was usually someone to report to after testing wings. Stratemeyer's Rover brothers had a semblance of a parental generation with father, uncle and aunt usually in obscure position. Young genius Tom Swift, too, possessed a male parent although that person gave the impression of an ancient, but time and place were of small matter when a boy dashed from one thrilling encounter to another.

After all, the crux of series-writing was to capture attention with a *tour de force* as initial volume and inspire enough pleasure that readers called for encores. That guaranteed a certain degree of success, at least.

Irregularities existed even among the relatively sedate literature for girls, and in one of the most famous series. Originally *Little Women* came out in two volumes. Written after a period of time, *Little Men* and *Jo's Boys* continued harmoniously with "the little women" in mature roles and superintending the next generation. By the time that Little, Brown and Company listed in back pages the content of what came to be called the Little Women series, it included as well books not associated with the March family. One, *Rose in Bloom*, was sequel to *Eight Cousins*; the others were orphans. All's fair in publishing, perhaps, and correlated and uncorrelated novels in a single grouping re-emphasize the stretching that was so common to series.

Increasing relaxation of a direct time line became conspicuous as series publication peaked during the second decade of the twentieth century. It could come to a seemingly dead halt, even with a family, when the focus turned on the younger set. That static state shows itself with the Bobbsey offspring, who moved like wind-up children from sea-shore to Blueberry Island to Cloverbank or Cherry Corner. The little Bunkers, six of them, appeared to spend their lives—and pity the kinfolk!—visiting Cousin Tom or Uncle Fred or Grandma Bell. And there was Honey Bunch and her almost inexhaustible "firsts" as she went to the zoo, rode a pony, journeyed to the Great Lakes or wherever. Meanwhile Mary Jane enjoyed her winter sports and summer fun, her jaunts down South or to Italy. The clock stopped while Bunny Brown and Sister Sue, the Bunker kids, Mary Jane, the Bobbseys and other compatriots hopped from place to place like carefree grasshoppers.

Of course the aim was no longer that double one of instruction *and* entertainment. Life was one long holiday. Even the children caught on to that and the custom of spending one's days on the move. Mrs. Bobbsey easily made a decision between having tea and cleaning house upon their return from somewhere.

> "Oh, don't bother now, Dinah," said Mrs. Bobbsey. "Make a cup of tea, first. The dust doesn't matter, and we'll not be here long."
> "Won't we?" exclaimed Nan. "Oh, where are we going next?"[4]

The propensity for groups acting together and heading out at the drop of the proverbial hat in any direction, as did these young families, became a chosen and easy means of projecting a series. Occasionally involving siblings but more often troops bound by interest, expectation or organizational affiliation, these little coveys embraced a philosophy that one did not have to go adventuring in the security of kinfolk, that in any case association with friends was more stimulating.

Less random travel had begun in the 1870's when Horace Scudder introduced it with his Bodley family series. Thomas W. Knox's Boy Travellers filled forty books, while Hezekiah Butterworth chose to guide the Zigzag Club. The *Youth's Companion* associate, Charles A. Stephens, piloted the Knockabout Club as well as Camping Out and Young Yachters series. Under direction of Mrs. Elizabeth W. Champney, the Vassar girls went to roaming in Europe and the Holy Land. Make no mistake about intent in this kind of organized roving; it was serious, and at times the story line fell victim to drowning in facts and figures.

Sober contemplation of travel came to expression through the father of Henry and Harold during their plan-making for a world tour. Mr. Davidson spoke prophetically.

> "...My impression is that the post-graduate course of the future will be educational travel. A student cannot complete his education by books alone; he must know the world, life, men....My belief is that the time is coming when a tour around the world will be an essential part of a young man's education....I should not wonder if such education for meritorious scholars were to be provided for out of public funds. The true schoolroom is the world. Why, I have met old sailors whom I would rather entertain, or have entertain me, than college professors. They knew *life*."[5]

That time was not immediate in its coming. The trend was toward lighthearted adventuring out and away from home, rather than widening of outlook. Barriers were down. Not mountain or cliff, ocean or international border stopped the young generation in fiction. With a multitude of writers hastily devising itineraries, Scouts headed for the Great Dismal Swamp, for Mexico, the Canal Zone, the Philippines. In their rambling they joined the

Horace Scuddler dealt in delicate manner with fancy and family.

Border Boys, Saddle Boys, Bronco Riders, Boy Globe Trotters, Boy Adventurers, Boy Ranchers, Moving Picture Boys, Circus Boys and Racer Boys.

Earlier, Everett T. Tomlinson and Castlemon, among others, produced series pertaining to wars of the past while under impetus of Stratemeyer young Americans had served in the Mexican War, with Admiral Dewey at Manila and under Lawton through the isle of Luzon. Writers with military titles had put cadets through Annapolis and West Point. When World War I shadowed the international scene, out came the Air Service Boys, Submarine Boys, Boys of the Army, Boy Aviators and Boy Allies. They took to patrolling in the North Sea and giving aid in France.

With everyday action left to sisters and cousins and the girls next door, young ladies participated in many a chaperoned undertaking. The Greycliff Girls, Ranch Girls, Meadowbrook Girls and Blue Grass Seminary Girls along with Bluebonnet and her friends had occupied themselves on tennis courts, with sailing, excursions and minor mystery unraveling. One Camp Fire group after another took to the mountains, the shore, the woods and the lakes. Motor Girls, Outdoor Girls, Moving Picture Girls and Motor Maids zigzagged their way from here to there, from this to that, while the Automobile Girls thought nothing of setting out for Palm Beach, Washington or Chicago. One group, with chaperones a-plenty, even made it to Japan. However, at the crucial time a few girls, too, triumphantly invaded Europe. In the name of the Red Cross they met the Russian army, entered British trenches, joined forces with the U.S. Marines, stood on the French firing line and were with General Pershing right down to victory.

With the all-over freedom allowable, a renaissance of old subject matter had come about with the birth of the new century. L. Frank Baum had dared to utilize pure and wild fancy that was earthier than old fairy-tale concepts. This became, of course, the Oz world. Writing his introduction, he made no mention of instruction of any sort but said that the *Wizard of Oz* "...aspires to being a modernized fairy tale, in which the wonderment and joy are retained and the heartaches and nightmares are left out."[6] There is, nonetheless, frank instruction with his incorporation of wickedness and honor and assignment of human qualities to almost every creature. And not everyone would agree that the Land of Oz lacks heartaches—certainly not the small girl who sobbed unrestrainedly because Dorothy, having lost Toto, missed the balloon headed for Kansas and home. Possibly the elements he claimed to omit were to some degree responsible for the durability of Oz.

Here was a rich vein for working. Substitutes followed versatile Baum in producing more Oz tales when, after some years he refused to continue the series. Yet others relished never-never lands. Another imaginary realm combining human and other creatures, although less bombastic in nature, was the creation of Hugh Lofting with the Doctor Dolittle company. Like Baum, Lofting based his stories on those invented for his children.

A few writers revived fable-like worlds in which beasts, birds and even elements operated usually without the intrusion of man. Children read or listened to unlimited supplies of stories furnished by Thornton Burgess and some less able adherents, and one is not at all surprised that the residents of the woods, illustrated with mouths ajar, speak much in the manner of children. "Everybody knows that Grandfather Frog has a big mouth. Of course!..."[7] And off on a ramble goes the narrator with followers at his heels. Against the Burgess backdrop of wide woods and green meadows, no great competition arose except for the preposterous Uncle Wiggily of Howard Garis. When the youngest readers tired of the sweetness of Dorothy Dainty and Honey Bunch and other little dears of gurgling voices and trivialities, they could turn to inhabitants of the countryside.

Although the filament of instruction was often infinitesimal, bland educational series did surface and continue growth with the aid of school use. The academic Our Little Cousin books appeared with the 20th century to move steadily along until presenting almost eighty different cousins over a period of more than thirty years, and with numerous authors and a personal logo. Lucy Fitch Perkins made a similar but less extensive foray into foreign cultures but with distinctive characterization and honest plotting with her Twins series.

With the passing of roughly one hundred years, the great book world, having recorded the developing American scene, was one of free-for-all competition of series now largely recreational in nature, series that would enter and without too long a stay, exit. Along with limited sets building their way to classic proportions, certain newcomers lingered. Titled for chief characters bolting from enigma to enigma and thus from volume to volume, they sold at bargain prices. Swift readers borrowed or traded or gave away the Nancy Drew and Hardy Boys books, bought more and devoured them like popcorn. Episodes of the young investigators sated a hunger manifested at a certain age when reading is mastered and mystification esteemed.

There is a final significant consequence to record. A fully mature individual, dipping back into her own childhood, wrote the first of a realistic and historic series. Laura Ingalls Wilder turned back to the fixed chronological design of Abbott's Rollo to recount Midwestern pioneer life as she remembered it. Despite the vicissitudes of wandering and the inconstant climate, an essence of universality rises like a spring wind blowing across a prairie. The year was 1932, and the sobering theme was in keeping with financial downfall of the nation. Possibly readers, surely satiated with inconsequential series, were ready for sturdier fare. Not that the public would abandon entirely the overabundance of escape series. Hard times demand distraction, too. The fictional riddles would carry on, Tarzan's call would continue to echo, and some new series would appear, the better of them using again the old anchor of family.

The classics, at least their initial volumes, would come out in new, re-illustrated editions and be favored selections for gifts at holiday time, and the animal voices from the choicer tales for listening children would continue to rise and fall under many a roof. Moreover, mention of Kansas-bred Dorothy, Pollyanna, Anne of Green Gables or the magic combination of Meg and Jo, Beth and Amy, would get heads to nodding at mention, and tongues into motion, and dreams unfolded and shaken out in the sunlight like Paisley shawls.

Chapter V

The Authors—
Disguised and Undisguised

Following logically are questions and curiosity as to authorship of the hundreds of fiction series produced in America for youthful readers. The originators seem upon investigation to reach in straggling lines to the horizon over which was appearing the caravan of fiction. They include men and women of historical, social and educational standing, people of influence in editorial posts, clear-cut personages remembered sometimes for texts and/ or adult fiction and non-fiction, individuals written about and often subject to criticism as well as to praise. In even greater abundance are shadowy figures whose characters or moral influence may have outshone their creators. Merging even more into the background are faceless forms, beings as anonymous as any unknown soldier but not glorified in any way.

The lives of those who dreamed up the series are now and then uncommon, often fascinating from today's perspective, often exemplary in retrospect, and occasionally touching. Heroic in the unsung way of many human beings, they might better rate commendation than deprecation. Frequently their biographies even if sketchy make more provocative reading than the fiction they conceived. One can recognize among them impressive achievement along with fortitude and invisible strength. Burdened by circumstances, by personal tragedy, by financial distress or other ill-fortune in a society minus subsidization of any sort, many of them stand out in quiet triumph.

There were clergymen, teachers, editors and journalists, professional writers, occasional businessmen. Ministers felt a "call" to instruct in the department of ethics; teachers claimed the right to communicate knowledge and prescribe and provide proper reading matter. With some others writing was a field in which to try themselves. And of course the born writers needed no artificial incentive.

Women, to whom few avenues were open other than teaching, nursing and any kind of home-service, tested their writing hands. These included girls, widows, maiden ladies, and house-wives for whom management of home and family was not reason enough for being. With those not trained

29

in any specific field, it was not only experience with or management of children that acted as impetus but also lively imagination, sometimes attraction of words and their power as tools, often the need for self-expression and romance as escape from a constricted environment. Some had early learned from journal-keeping the satisfaction gained from exercising pen upon paper.

Demand in the expanding field of fiction existed. The profession was open by trial to all. Perhaps plot-patterns were elemental and repeated themselves regularly and without objection, but the reading public was waiting.

A tantalizing characteristic of this long era was the usage of pseudonyms and possibly this was as much a style as was the compiling of series. The tacking-on of a second title to a novel seems, for a shorter period of time, similarly quaint since some of the beginning *noms de plume* were droll.

At the outset, fiction-writing, like acting, was not one of the more respectable vocations, particularly for a woman. An assumed name, especially if one's gender be feminine, provided protective disguise. One can surmise the consternation following identification as a novelist and, as well, the sense of safety, as with the Brontë sisters, at being sheltered by a pseudonym.

Yet a number of men followed the same practice, with the first of them choosing capricious designations. Though not a fictionist, Samuel Goodrich, known in schools and out of them as one who banded small books in series, clung fiercely to his Peter Parley title and became indignant at its use by several Englishmen of his generation. William T. Adams, widely familiar to youth magazine and series readers, was Oliver Optic throughout a great chunk of the 19th century.

A fictional name added a romantic and/or enigmatic touch or a whimsical element, as in the calling of oneself "Aunt Fanny," for example. It is also conceivable that either women or men would consider an endearing or humorous pseudonym a means of drawing closer to children. Indeed, some true names of extreme homeliness could have benefited by change of almost any sort!

An instance of a two-hundred-word composition devoted to the pen-name of "Aunt Florida" illustrates the potential of the concept. Written to introduce a novel for girls, it served as ploy to quicken interest in both name and story. Supposedly, "a friend" of Aunt Florida was responsible for the introduction; however, one can visualize the sedate authoress herself, hint of a smile upon her face, fashioning phrases in order to excite and puzzle Victorian children.

I fancy some little girl examining this book inside and out, trying to make up her mind whether it be worth the trouble of reading, and saying to herself ..."Who's Aunt

Florida? I'd like to know if that's her real name, and I wonder how she came by it—it's such a queer name for a woman!"

So it is, my young friend, and yet no one can deny that its [sic] a *proper* name; and this (if it call for any explanation,) must serve the purpose.

If I wished I could tell you who she is and all about her; but it would do no good, and might lessen the interest of her story; for little girls like mysteries and mysterious people.

I assure you she's a real live person, and how she came by such a queer name, well,—I suppose somebody's fancy suggested it....[1]

To reinforce possible support, Aunt Florida ended the final chapter with the frank recommendation that if the reader would like hearing more about Phebe and her friends to "...be sure to say it far and wide..." Whether Aunt Florida was Adelaide F. Samuels, who later in the decade was publishing series featuring Travers offspring of other given names, is conjectural.

There was also a practical facet to such camouflage. Particularly productive writers did not care to have their names appearing more than once in a single magazine issue. Writers who turned out better and lesser qualities of work were not always eager to own to authorship of pot-boilers. For a syndicate such as that established by Edward Stratemeyer, pseudonyms were of exceptional value. At times several people supplied stories for a series. One consideration concerned the future; in case of termination of contract by reason of death, disagreement or other factor, another person could pick up a series and carry it along under the old pen-name. There were cases in which writers tired of characters, and others in which material demanded specialists of a sort now and then, or when time and work-load made assistance necessary. Occasionally writers were known to operate as teams.

A number of authors who figure in literary history selected personal appellations and held to them. Wanting to "preserve her privacy," Isabella Alden chose to use her childhood nickname, Pansy, for her religion-slanted stories, while conceiver of the archangel Elsie Dinsmore, Martha Finley, wrote only her earlier books under the title of Martha Farquharson. New Englander Rebecca Sophia Clarke adopted the pen-name of Sophie May for her groups of books chronicling young child-life. The sister of Sarah Chauncey Woolsey had published stories as Margaret Coolidge, and Sarah became Susan Coolidge for the girls who read the Katy Did books, saying that she assumed that name "in fun."[2] When Harriet Mulford Stone reached the point of publication she devised a *nom de plume* from two sources: her favorite feminine name plus the given name of her father, who disapproved of women writing fiction. Thus it was Margaret Sidney who became enshrined in the minds of children following the progress of the little Peppers.

Mark Twain, whose Tom Sawyer books constitute a short series, owned surely the most magical of all pseudonyms. No woman carried so bold a writing name as that. Posing as Harry Castlemon, Charles Austin Fosdick found fame among youths with his five dozen books of war, adventure and outdoor life. Edward Ellis at times turned into Lt. R.H. Jayne and other fictional people, while John T. Trowbridge was known to use the name of Paul Creyton. Early in the 20th century a versatile writer, inventing names to suit the project of the moment, became Edith Van Dyne for the Aunt Jane's Nieces series, and Laura Bancroft and Susanne Metcalf for other series for girls. He wrote as well under several male titles, but under his rightful name originated a series still read, still reprinted, still prominent on bookstore shelves, in libraries and among the possessions of collectors. This was L. (for Lyman) Frank Baum, creator of Oz.

Less prominent individuals, too, varied their pseudonyms from series to series. George Henry St. Rathbone, and what a splendid sound that has, became Oliver Lee Clifton for a Camp Fire Boys series, Herbert Carter for a Boy Scout group and about twenty other imaginary persons in addition. Harry L. Sayler changed to Elliott Whitney for The Boys' Big Game series and to other personages for other series. One John H. Whitson, minister and educator like so many earlier authors, was also Burt L. Standish of the Frank Merriwell series. Conversion became common indeed as the opportunities increased and as, perhaps, the standards began to give way. As a result the reader-investigator-collector begins to wonder if every series author might have been as fictional as work.

It was entrepreneur Edward Stratemeyer who surpassed all others at disguise. Although he wrote under his own name he posed as Arthur M. Winfield for the Rover Boys series and as a host of others as well. That was not the end of it, of course, for he founded a writing syndicate of vast scale and the pseudonyms therein were legion. About fifty additional names served largely-unknown persons who sat at their typewriters or over their blocks of paper and composed new stories about little people participating in infinitesimal excursions hither and yon, of those somewhat more advanced in age adventuring at home and abroad as Scouts, Camp Fire members or other groups. Among the pseudonyms under which these books came out are a good many familiar to one-time followers or to collectors of older series. Typical are Victor Appleton for the Tom Swift and Don Sturdy series; Richard Barnum for Knee-Time Animal Stories; Allen Chapman for Darewell Chums, Radio Boys and others; Alice B. Emerson for Betty Gordon and Ruth Fielding series; Franklin Dixon for Andy Lane, Hardy Boys and Ted Scott Flying stories; flowery Laura Lee Hope for a flock of small-fry family expeditions; Helen Louise Thorndyke for the Honey Bunch experiences; Carolyn Keene for Nancy Drew and Dana Girls mystery stories.

Almost as remarkable as the operation of such a syndicate with pen-names the property of specific publishers, is the record of a certain family closely connected with the Stratemeyer mass-producing business.

Under the syndicate plan Howard Garis first became Clarence Young for the Motor Boys series and thereafter Victor Appleton for the famed Tom Swift books. Even while turning out books for Stratemeyer, beginning at one hundred dollars each and no royalties or claim of any kind, Garis wrote under his own name and collaborated with his wife Lilian on early Bobbsey Twins selections. Lilian Garis herself came to follow the same pattern, acting as one of Stratemeyer's phantom authors but eventually producing on her own the Joan, Connie Loring and Tower Mystery series. In a magazine article, son Roger Garis recounted that so numerous were the series produced by the family and so many the pseudonyms used that the record is fuzzy. He computed that, all told, his father wrote "at least 500 juveniles," his mother "two or three hundred," his sister "about twenty," and Roger himself "perhaps eighty."[3]

The situation is rather confusing for all concerned because if, for instance, Lilian Garis wrote the Dorothy Dale and the Motor Girls series, then she must have been Margaret Penrose. However, this question arises: was the name Margaret Penrose hers alone, or did she share it with other writers? This wide use of pen-names makes suspect numerous unusually euphonious names found among long-gone series and of no particular identification.

At the time that Howard Garis began his alliance with the publishing empire, Stratemeyer provided title, pen-name and "a sketchy outline;"[4] at that point the writer took off. The plan included length such as thirty chapters of about seven pages each. Stratemeyer made no stipulation as to the way one ought to write, Roger Garis recorded, but assumed that story-telling technique was within the employee's ability.[5] After Tom Swift books proved so saleable, Stratemeyer increased payment to one hundred and twenty-five dollars per volume. While still working at journalism, Howard Garis could manage a book in three weeks. As his son stated, the Garis family wrote for the entertainment of a particular reading public and not with the intention of producing "literature."

The pseudonym had quite lost its singularity by this time. That it was common to appropriate one for concealment or practicality's sake, or for the convenience of secret counterparts does not mean that all writers succumbed. By the 20th century it was perfectly honorable, and admirable, for women to write fiction without denying their identity. Individual pen-names such as Mark Twain and Margaret Sidney, Susan Coolidge and Sophie May, even Oliver Optic, continued to draw respect, whereas titles such as Mable C. Hawley, Lester Chadwick or Fenworth Moore quickly became meaningless. With the syndicate's wholesale arrangements, such assumed names were riddles with solutions that floated in the air like dandelion puffs and disappeared.

Lack of distinction often extended to the written word, too. Screened by anonymity, ghost-writers had little reason to accomplish more than the satisfaction of their employer. Readers gobbled up what rolled steadily from the presses and waited for what came next. It was not a yield that induced re-reading. This was not a harmful situation. Not all intellects desire fine writing, and that quantity surpassed quality is no surprise.

Fortunately here and there and now and then other men and women continued to dedicate their talents to composing distinctive series which would survive for several generations. Among them was an occasional writer who turned from adult audiences to try his hand at tickling the fancy of the half-grown. That these special people succeeded is something that well-read beings who were small people decades ago remember.

Chapter VI
What Manner of Men—
And Women—Were These?

Reading an old series today, one may indeed wonder as to qualifications of authors, for style, naivety and sentimentality sometimes give first impressions of limited education and intellect and ability. Yet this was not so. The writers were people of often admirable education and experience, the men usually trained for professions, the women more likely restricted to teaching. In history a century seems brief, but in the mind of an individual it is rather a long stretch of years, and in consideration at the moment is a period lengthier than the customary lifetime.

If Jacob Abbott's (1803-1879) stories of Rollo, Lucy and others seem devoid of liveliness it is because Abbott was instructor before he was entertainer, and yet an early breaker of that old barrier which disparaged anything not relevant to serious instruction. The state of the intellect and its discipline outranked emotional nature and its nourishment, and the reader must gain not pleasure but learning and moral teaching when he sat with book in hand. Welfare of the soul did not extend beyond principles of right and wrong and the goal of salvation.

A New Englander, as were so many of the early fictionists, Abbott was a gentle, tolerant and very young professor at Portland Academy, where Longfellow was among his students, and, at Amherst College, first as tutor, then at twenty-two as professor of mathematics and natural history. It was rather by chance that he turned writer. In Boston he organized Mount Vernon school for girls and on Saturdays spoke to the pupils on the subject of religion, for his specialized training included theology. The informal lectures were successful enough to see publication in book form at request, and thereafter he spent some time each day at writing.

Abbott divided his life into blocks of years spent at a variety of educational and literary undertakings. Approaching thirty, he turned from teaching to serve as pastor of a Boston church, then established himself in a Maine village to spend half a dozen years at two projects: writing Rollo stories and transforming property into so pleasant an area that it became a sort of park and play-place. After his wife's death he joined three of his brothers, also educators, in setting up a girls' school in New York. New Hampshire's White Mountains, scene of the Franconia stories, was the next residence. In late life he returned to his father's old home in Maine and at times taught his grandchildren and a few of the village boys.

As a writer his reputation placed him at the top in influence and popularity during his era. His exercised philosophy was advanced for the day; it was of challenging the young, of treating them as equals, putting confidence in them and responsibility upon them, and allowing them to learn by experience. This involved more than theory, for he was father to two daughters and four sons, one of whom became a magazine editor; from among the grandchildren emerged novelist Eleanor Hallowell Abbott.

Thus it was that Abbott, rather than Samuel Goodrich, gained title as "father of the story series."[1] Goodrich (1793-1860), editor, publisher, even American consul in Paris for a term, was the man answering to the whimsical pen-name of Peter Parley. Lacking his contemporary's understanding of childhood, contemptuous of fancy as an ingredient of youthful literature, he remained a proud dispenser of knowledge for which he employed help in gathering information in the realms of geography, history, travel, natural history and "stories." Underlings supplied material in order that Goodrich could write.

Here I am! My name is Peter Parley! I am an old man. I am very gray and lame. But I have seen a great many things, and had a great many adventures, and I love to talk about them.[2]

In those days of literary pioneering, writers dared to change and lighten the content of reading matter for children, giving them something all their own so that they need not depend upon legend and myth and fairy tale plus religious enlightenment incorporating dreary morals and heart-shaking predictions, and borrow what else they could from what publishers served to adult taste. The Eastern seaboard was at that time origin of most American authors, and the backgrounds of many, at least of the male contingent, were those of school and of church. It was a pattern, and curiously so, as though the ability to speak on paper to an audience depended upon an ability to speak to one orally.

Oliver Optic, alias for William Taylor Adams (1822-1897), one of the earliest suppliers of moral and adventure tales, was a pupil in both public and private schools and by age twenty-one assumed a principalship in Boston. Apparently a principal taught as well as administered, and he spent two decades at this before dropping out and away to write and edit youth magazines. "These twenty years," some unidentified person wrote, "taught him how to reach the boy's heart and interest as the popularity of his books attest."[3] Direct associations with youth and maturity continued as he served on a school board, in the Massachusetts legislature and as Sunday School teacher and superintendent.

No man to exhibit modesty, he evidently commanded audience among adults as well as boys, for he addressed the former within the preface for a book whose hero, a child of eleven, in this instance was really a heroine.

> If any of my adult readers are disposed to accuse me of being a little extravagant, I fear I shall have to let the case go by default; but I shall plead, in extenuation, that I have tried to be reasonable, even where a few grains of the romantic element were introduced; for Baron Munchausen and Sinbad the Sailor were standard works on my shelf in boyhood, and I may possibly have imbibed some of their peculiar spirit. But I feel a lively satisfaction in the reflection that, whatever exaggerations the critic may decide I have perpetrated in this volume, I have made the success of Katy Redburn depend upon her good principles, her politeness, her determined perseverance, and her overcoming that foolish pride which is a snare to the feet. In these respects she is a worthy exemplar for the young.[4]

Newspaper critics praised him extravagantly as ",,,one of the most fascinating writers for youth..." and as "...perhaps the favorite of the boys and girls of the country..." The imprint of his benign bearded face appears on covers of some of his books.

Certainly he was of gaudier image than John Townsend Trowbridge (1827-1916), who was born in a log house in western New York state and not in a position to advance far in formal education. However, literature and language caught his attention early. Fascination for a foreign-phrase list in his spelling book led to self-teaching of French from books left him by a cousin. He applied himself similarly to Latin, and by first adolescence began to write poetry. After working as a farm laborer and, briefly, at school teaching, he determined to become a writer and in 1848 went to New York City and thence to Boston, the literary center. There he found his way into the editing of periodicals, including *Our Young Folks*. His popular Jack Hazard series, based on boyhood memories of the banks of the Erie Canal, began as a serial in that magazine. Other contributions appeared in *Atlantic* and *Youth's Companion*. Yet Trowbridge's fiction, including forty volumes, he considered "high-class hack-work"[5] and inferior to his poetry. Ironically, it was the fiction which endured.

Reviewers wrote more quietly of him than of Optic, but with solid praise for his ability. Possibly other series, Silver Medal, Tide-Mill, and Start in Life, too, influenced a superior critique of Jack Hazard appearing in some issue of *Scribner's Monthly*. Since a cyclopaedia of biography quotes a single comment from it and gives credit to John Burroughs, one may safely attribute to Burroughs the longer excerpt taken from that critique and used by John C. Winston for advertising filler in back pages of a Castlemon novel.

"Trowbridge knows the heart of a boy like a book, and the heart of a man, too, and he has laid them both open in these books in a most successful manner."[6] Elsewhere in the *Scribner* review are lines perhaps more telling. "Neither as a writer does he stand apart from the great currents of life and select some exceptional phase or odd combination of circumstances. He stands on the common level and appeals to the universal heart, and all that he suggests or achieves is on the plane and in the line of march of the great body of humanity."[7]

Today's reader finds a thoughtfulness in his narration a searching treatment for human sensibilities, a wistful element of sadness common to human nature and thus a subjective ingredient unknown to writers such as Optic and Alger. An historian of the present century pronounced that with the five-book Jack Hazard series Trowbridge "...raised the level of writing for young people."[8]

Nor was the image of Elijah Kellogg (1813-1901) of the Elm Island and Forest Glen stories a flamboyant one. Son in a Maine parson's family, the boy "...ran away to sea at thirteen to spend three years before the mast in Maine sailing vessels."[9] Attendance at Gorham Academy and work, including a year's indenture as a farm laborer, preceded Bowdoin College, for which he earned the means and from which he was graduated at a mature age. The year was 1840. Thereafter Kellogg spent three years at Andover Theological Seminary and, ordained in 1844, began his ministerial life among the fisherfolk of Harpswell in Maine. He swam, sailed, fished and farmed with boys of the parish, and it was to Harpswell that Bowdoin faculty sent problem boys to spend a few weeks with Kellogg.

When electing to concentrate upon writing, he was in his fifties. Although now serving at the Mariners' Church and with the Boston Seaman's Friend Society, Kellogg used the old locale and subject matter known to him from earlier days: New England frontier life with marine background, Indian lore, dependence upon both land and sea. His likeable "country boy" heroes displayed strength, pride in manual work, and practical business sense as well as exuberance and ingenuity for adventure. The stories are lively, with no sparing of interaction between youth and adult, meaty with information; action and crises are well enough solved, and with a kind of disguised glorification of the human race as if every worthy human being were a modest hero in his own way.

Financially successful, Kellogg turned over his earnings to charity and tried to persuade others to do the same and, as biographers phrase it, "died a poor man." His philosophy he expressed plainly as in announcement of a volume to follow in the Elm Island series: "...the effect of putting weight upon youthful shoulders, and the rapidity with which character develops under pressure and the spur of necessity..."[10]

Long-revered Horatio Alger, Jr. (1832-1899) reached a finale similar to Kellogg's so far as finances were concerned. Oft-told and with sometimes contradictory details, the story of the enigmatic writer who attained physical stature of only a bit more than five feet, differed from that of any young hero such as Tom, Tony, Ben, Dan, Dick, Herbert, Hector, Walter, Jack, Jed or Luke, Paul or Phil, or any of the other newsboys, office boys, train or telegraph boys or bootblacks of the Alger series. Yet his influence, like that of educator William Holmes McGuffey with his famed readers, spread out over several generations in this expanding nation.

Alger's beginning was unportentous. Son of a Unitarian clergyman whose ambition included his namesake's following in the religious profession, Horatio was sickly, and parental training was such that someone bestowed upon him the nickname of Holy Horatio. Yet at age eight he began Latin study and went from district schools to Gates Academy in Marlboro, Mass., and on to Harvard, specializing there in languages and displaying prize-winning scholarship. Five years of journalistic connections with Boston newspapers defrayed expenses at the Cambridge Theological School. An inheritance gave him the chance to break away, and he went to Europe for a year. In 1864 came his ordination for the Unitarian church in a Massachusetts town, but a year and a half later he established himself in New York City and began a study of street Arabs.

Already he had begun writing, and after *Ragged Dick* came out serially in Optic's *Student and Schoolmate* magazine, A.K. Loring of Boston published it and contracted with Alger to write a six-volume set of similar stories. Identifying with the management of the Newsboys' Lodging House in New York, Alger acted as sympathetic and generous friend and idealized the boy-heroes for the stream of books in which rewards were inevitable results of honesty, effort and persistence. Some said that these rags to-riches heroes served as compensation for timid and weak qualities and an ailing conscience. Whatever the mystique of personality and the hints of multiple love affairs, so say biographers, Alger gave over-generously, and some of his protégés imposed upon him. Reportedly he adopted two impoverished boys and a niece as well and, still a bachelor, died in a sister's home.

Alger received recognition in his own day, although the greatest sales among the "leaders" of his books came after his death at a time when his series were issued in paperback. Frank Luther Mott gathered up opinions of Alger in a single expressive paragraph.

To criticize Alger today is to challenge the widespread and loyal Order of Old Fellows Who Read Alger When They Were Boys. They are apt to forget their author's banality, his typed characters, his bad writing, and his copybook moralities, and to remember only their boyish response to his getting-ahead thesis and their breathless interest in his rapid story-telling. Alger's name has become a by-word for the boy's success story, and that is no mean fame.[11]

The saga of an Alger contemporary, that verbally robust folk-hero Samuel Clemens (1835-1910), reads like romantic fiction, as indeed it could have been. This possessor of extravagant and ironic humor and of tall-story-telling talent was also a man of tragedy for whom the spectre of death diminished family, deliberate blow by blow, beginning with small son, then eldest daughter, wife, and third daughter, until only a single child remained in his lifetime. The fortunes and misfortunes of Mark Twain and his place on the American literary scene have provided subjects for theory after theory, criticism after criticism, for debunking as often, it seems sometimes, as for even moderate glorifying. As every native or adopted Missourian, scholar and devoted reader knows, his formal education was minuscule, and as he emerged from the great throbbing Mississippi vein of the nation he remained a barbarian of sorts, irrepressible at home and abroad.

By contrast relatively staid, lacking the legend of the great Missourian who was not, after all, primarily a producer of series, other men still made meritorious contributions to American youth by means of journalistic endeavors and adventure-spinning of one kind or another.

Friend and correspondent of explorer Henry M. Stanley, Thomas Wallace Knox (1835-1896) was perhaps the best qualified of the small group writing of faraway places. Left an orphan while very young, he was working on a New England farm by age ten. Saving a bit of money, he went to school when able, studied on his own, and by twenty-three was principal of a Kingston, N.Y., academy. Living adventurously in the manner of Clemens, he felt the lure of Colorado's gold discovery, worked as a reporter in Denver, then as city editor. During the Civil War he acted as volunteer aide through two campaigns and became war correspondent for the *New York Herald*, thereafter accompanying an expedition intent upon establishing telegraphic communication lines through southern Asia. This meant sledge and wagon transportation across Siberia. Experiences and observations from traveling the world over resulted in fifteen volumes of Boy Traveller series, and Knox won admiration for descriptive powers and style. Today the heavy volumes, complete with end-page maps and a wealth of illustrations, are such compendiums of factual information strung together with story line slight enough to be disappointing to a reader. However, he incorporated a wealth of historical adventure in other books for older children.

The practice of presenting travel material in methodical detail extended to other series published in an era when foreign-travel books for youths followed the popularity of such volumes written for adults. Abbott, incidentally, had done this a good deal earlier when he sent Rollo off to Europe in a family group.

The Rollo Books were in vogue during the childhood of Horace E. Scudder (1838-1902), Bostonian, who attended Williams College and taught privately in New York. It has been written that the primary reasons for the appearance of good literature for the young during the final quarter of the 19th century were the *St. Nicholas Magazine* under the editorship of Mary Mapes Dodge and the editorial efforts of Horace Scudder in Boston. Growing up with half a dozen siblings in a home where there was opportunity to acquire interest in the arts and particular literary taste as well as standards, he was qualified to introduce into children's magazines articles concerning books for the young. Scudder became editor of *The Riverside Magazine* which, for its four years of existence, 1867-1870, carried some Hans Christian Andersen stories never before published, ballads and famous verse, good illustrations and stories written by the more talented authors of the time. It was his belief that one should present classic literature to children and he came up with the idea of the Riverside Literature series which included entire works rather than such fragments as appeared in readers. When thirty-four he began a long association with Houghton, Mifflin Company, at that time known as Hurd and Houghton. At age fifty-two he assumed editorship of *Atlantic Monthly*.

Perhaps Scudder's gifts lay more in editorial work than with the creation of literature, but he did put out eight volumes concerning the peregrinations of the Bodley family, the first rather curious but endearing, a whimsical compilation of stories and stories within stories, of long poems, some by known authors, and the reactions of the little Bodleys. The *Boston Daily Advertiser* called *The Doings of the Bodley Family* "...one of the most charming of all volumes for children.... The publishers have spared nothing to make the book a perfect treasure...."[12]

Even today this seems true, from cover design through end pages, large print, illustrations, content. The likeness to an early magazine or bound volume of sequential issues is evident, although the same little creatures pop in and out of every section: Nathan (Thanny), Lucy and Philippa (Phippy). Scudder made of the Bodley family a strictly private affair with fancy and emotion coloring the text. And, oddly, Thomas Nast did some of the illustrations.

Still another New Englander, this one of astonishing name, Hezekiah Butterworth (1839-1905), wrote of historic Indian days with imagination and appreciation of nature. His contribution to the supply of travel series for adolescents was Zigzag Journeys. Although growing up in a farm home he differed from the expected robust country youth. A biographical sketch terms him "...a nervous, timid, superstitious boy, with a love for ghost stories."[13] The plan was to attend Brown University but health proved a handicap to extended formal education; the compromise was study under the direction of a Brown professor.

Acquiring an appetite for journalism, Butterworth wrote articles on self-education for *Youth's Companion* and found a place for himself in that magazine. His association covered a quarter of a century. While his travels were not so extensive as the seventeen volumes of zigzagging suggest, he did visit Europe and South America. Known as a patriotic writer of religious tone with a large dash of sentimentality, he, too, ended up as a district school teacher and local editor. Yet this man with the "transparently good face" wrote poetically of pioneering days, contributed to such distinguished magazines as *Atlantic, Harper's* and *Century,* and composed the poem used at the opening of the 1893 Columbia Exposition's peace and arbitration congress.

Filling out this coterie of travel authors was Charles Asbury Stephens (1847-1931) from Maine. Completing Bowdoin College in two years and earning all expenses at the same time, Stephens came under the influence of Professor Elijah Kellogg and turned to authorship. In his college days he began contributing to *Youth's Companion* and so pleased the editors that a sixty-year alliance began. Stephens wrote exclusively for that magazine, and as many as six of his stories appeared in one issue under different names. Traveling in the Americas and in Europe, he was resourceful at gathering information and absorbing color to blend in adventure stories. His Camping Out series had various settings while the Knockabout Club reflected experiences and observations. *The Knockabout Club in Spain,* for example, carries surprisingly gaudy and graphic covers and end-pages but its contents comprise a mostly sober travelogue with occasional ironic twists. Stephens did perform well in straight fiction as an all-around writer who combined sturdy plotting and realistic characterizations with descriptive style, controlled sentiment and intellectual appeal. In mid-life he went through medical school and then built a laboratory for research of cell life, adding a second profession and writing about theories and experiments. Surprisingly enough, at one time he visualized "a floating university."[14]

In another way Harry Castlemon, in reality Charles Austin Fosdick (1842-1915), was equally singular. Son of a public school principal, he left Buffalo's Central High School for Navy service when the Civil War exploded. As a Mississippi squadron member he served on seven different gunboats until 1864, then removed himself to Illinois and worked in a country store. There he embarked upon a career as an exceedingly popular writer of adventure stories for boys.

Castlemon was exceptional in that while he lacked the advanced education of many fellow-writers, yet he produced some of the liveliest and most complexly plotted and ingenious series of the era. His boys are independent, satisfactorily admirable but yet believable, sometimes impulsive, impatient and daring. Stated morals are few, and when they appear, are direct and sensible. Of course there are villains to fire continuing action, to bring about crises and heart-pounding moments.

Boys wanted adventure, not "fine writing," Castlemon believed.[15] That was certainly what he gave them—high adventure—and while one is not likely to come upon writing of strictly literary quality there is little to find fault with in direct or indirect expression, in narration or in conversation, if one excuses an occasional summing-up to move on into the next situation.

Through the character of Frank Nelson of the Gun-Boat series he presented personal war experiences. There followed the Sportsman's Club, Go-Ahead, Rod and Gun, Roughing It, Boy Trappers and other series. Some of them saw as many as thirty editions. Legend goes that no other author was a greater favorite during the second part of the 19th century than Castlemon for his naturalness and vivacity. Today, anyone investigating the writers of that period can without hesitation accept this judgment. If the names Horatio Alger and Oliver Optic seem more familiar to those with interest in literary epochs, one can only believe that readers have not, for some unknown reason, come across a sampling of Castlemon books.

There were others, too, who emphasized early American backgrounds. Ohio-born Edward Sylvester Ellis (1840-1916) was among them. His first energies went into teaching. Graduate of a New Jersey state normal school, he became vice-principal of a public school while still in his teens. At nineteen he wrote a best-selling dime novel, *Seth Jones*, but for a decade his writing was of juvenile series involving frontier life, Indian wars and like adventures. John C. Winston recorded in some of its reprints of well-selling series that Ellis' father "...was a famous hunter and rifle shot..."[16] and that in all likelihood some of his exploits and stories led the son to write of those historic days.

Professionally he was an active man, serving as teacher at a state normal, as city superintendent in New Jersey's Trenton, as editor of a weekly paper for young people. He wrote for newspapers and he wrote textbooks, building up a reputation as a captivating schoolmaster and wholesome fictionist.

Journalist-author James Otis Kaler (1848-1912), known under the shortened name of James Otis, had no inclination to follow his father's hotel business in Maine. At seventeen, having finished public school, he left home with the intent, as the old hand-me-down tales have it, to make his way in the world. He wrote for Boston and New York newspapers, at one time composed sermons for syndication by a Philadelphia house, held an editorial post on Frank Leslie's *Boys and Girls* magazine and wrote stories in off hours. Restless in nature, he wandered about the country with a circus as publicity man and at one time served as editor for an American paper based in London until that business collapsed.

In 1880 *Toby Tyler*, his first book, appeared on the children's literary scene. The characters from his circus days re-appeared soon thereafter in *Mr. Stubbs' Brother*. Before the third volume arrived, thirty-two years had passed and Otis had turned to a field in which numerous other writers began; he became a school superintendent in South Portland, Maine. His companions knew him as a convivial man who enjoyed outdoor life and youthful company. Readers knew him through the pages of about one hundred and fifty books, mostly written for the young, and through *St. Nicholas* and *Youth's Companion*.

There was also Everett T. Tomlinson (1859-1931), a New Jersey man of many hats. Clergyman, school-administrator, editor and writer, he seemed successful in all fields entered. Educated at Williams College, he acted as a high school principal in New York state, as headmaster of the Rutgers College grammar school, prepared Greek and Latin textbooks, edited the classical department of the *Boston Journal*. During long service as a Baptist minister he began writing stories with historical settings, the Four Boys and the Blue and Buff series. Yet Tomlinson seemed bent upon dispensing detailed history lessons. Heroes of *Young Continentals*, acting almost as early detectives, got into and out of scrapes without mysteries ever seeing solution in one volume. He was too much the teacher, perhaps, to become an absorbing fiction writer.

Certain authors fall into uncertain categories since they sampled one thing and another before finally arriving at a definite stage of authorship, unknowingly working their way into that state in quite roundabout manner.

Probably George W. Peck (1840-1916) of the preposterous Peck's Bad Boy fame was the only series-writing governor known. His work began with apprenticeship at age fifteen in a print shop after which he went out as journeyman for Wisconsin papers. He was a hotel clerk before enlisting as a private in the cavalry during the Civil War and returned home a second lieutenant, there to alternate establishment of his own newspapers with engagement in police and political affairs. His Milwaukee-based *Peck's Sun* became his first real success and after ten years Peck acquired the reputation of one of the most original and entertaining writers in the country. First elected mayor of Milwaukee in 1890, he soon had the Democratic nomination for governor and held two two-year terms. Thereafter he revived his newspaper and continued the series featuring that gross "bad boy."

The record for the 19th century is no less than imposing, but let no man dare to believe it composed entirely of those representing his own sex. Restrictions limiting the activities and opportunities for women need no essay of explanation today. One could call the feminine writers near heroic for daring to compete with the favored sex. In their own ways they were equally impressive, and it may well be that their collective courage was superior. Certainly some of them were remarkable for their valor and character.

Boston-born Mary Gray Phelps (1844-1911), only daughter in a family of minister-father and minister-grandfather who became associated with the Andover Theological Seminary, was also child to a woman who supplemented ministerial income with her own writing. The early death of this parent prompted Mary Gray, called "Lily" within family walls, to adopt her mother's name, Elizabeth Stuart. This was a death-haunted home; following the father's re-marriage to a sister-in-law of delicate constitution, the first stepmother, too, died, and another took her place.

This child of many names attended private schools offering girls the same curriculum as boys, and it included some theology. Resolving to become a writer, she held three precepts: to use contemporary subjects, to make her heroines daughters of simple New England families, and to employ plots involving ordinary affairs.

An adult novel, *The Gates Ajar*, written to calm "...the grief she had felt upon the deaths of both her mother and stepmother and that of her fiance, killed at Antietam,"[17] she wove with a religious theme and expressed unorthodox notions of heaven and life after death. It found many readers and she followed up with three sequels. Her girls' books were another matter. Delightful Gypsy Breynton, half-grown personable heroine, broke the old mold of proper, prim little lady and attained the author's precepts. Published in 1866, the first volume of the series preceded by two years Louisa May Alcott's similarly humanized Jo March of *Little Women*.

In 1895, writing a preface for a fresh edition of her Gypsy books, Mrs. Phelps tried to recall her vision of that young person.

I see a lively girl in pretty short dresses and very long stockings,—quite a Tom-boy, if I remember rightly. She paddles a raft, she climbs a tree, she skates and tramps and coasts, she is usually very muddy, and a little torn. There is apt to be a pin in her gathers; but there is sure to be a laugh in her eyes. Wherever there is mischief, there is Gypsy. Yet, wherever there is fun, and health, and hope...there is Gypsy, too.[18]

On the same occasion, attempting to visualize Gypsy as a woman, she found herself asking many questions as to whether Gypsy chose a profession or became wife and mother. She could not reach a decision.

Only one thing I do know: Gypsy never grew up to be "timid," or silly, or mean, or lazy; but a sensible woman, true and strong; asking little help of other people, but giving much; an honor to her brave and loving sex, and a safe comrade to the girls who kept step with her into middle life....[19]

Elizabeth Stuart Phelps could have been a woman of the current era. Although she had vowed never to marry, she became, in middle age, wife to another writer, Herbert D. Ward, who was much younger. The marriage was not a happy one, biographers report, and Gypsy's mentor became an invalid and died at sixty-six.

As for Louisa Alcott (1832-1888), another fiercely independent individual, the long-loved story of *Little Women* is not truly the story of the Alcott family no matter how readily the reader is willing that it be so. The truth is that the family of six, depending upon its loving members for security, moved countless times and lived in continuing financial uncertainty. After Bronson Alcott's Temple school in Boston failed, he never had courage to found another. The Alcotts became recipients of "donation parties"[20] of the kind accorded ministers' families; good friend Ralph Waldo Emerson contributed money from time to time, and relatives supplied used clothing and made loans. And all the while the Alcott parents practiced "practical Christianity,"[21] giving not only time and effort to others but even sharing scanty food and firewood.

The child Louisa's apprenticeship began in early childhood with the requirement of maintaining a journal open to parental examination. The expectation of learning to "be good" by following exacting Christian tenets no doubt aided the stormy and rebellious girl in building self-discipline, but it also fettered her.

Closeness of the family provided the spiritual support, seeing the members through crises. Eleven-year-old Louisa was little concerned with man's nature at the time of the disastrous attempt at an idealistically conceived life at Fruitlands and community-living on a small scale. Her happiest years came during early teens in Concord, the heart of the Alcott world which alternated between that town and Boston. Except for one year she had lessons at home with her father, and these she augmented with incessant reading and with access to Emerson's library. Later she was to write of Emerson that "...he is the god of my idolatry...."[22]

By age sixteen she and her older sister, Anna, realized the necessity of helping support the family. (Educator-philosopher-Transcendentalist Bronson Alcott seemed to be leaving that up to God.) The two tutored and taught, sewed and companioned, and Louisa, who worked for a term as "second maid," thought in terms of earning through writing. Both had collaborated on plays produced at home, and had written sentimental stories designed upon those in popular weeklies. Louisa's yen was to let the imagination ride free and far with romance and tragedy. Eventually, with drab made-over garments and twenty-five dollars earned from writing, she went off to Boston to work and write. According to descriptions she was only a bit under six feet in height, had thick "chestnut" hair, olive complexion, eyes full of purpose and face lit by intense expression.[23]

Successes, small and hard-earned, continued to be combined with uninspiring labor, but in January of 1864, a review of the past year showed professional earnings of almost six hundred dollars, of which she had used less than one-sixth for herself.[24] At last, answering to requests from the publishers Roberts Brothers for "a girls' book," Louisa wrote Part I of *Little Women*, using for pattern the old Alcott household. Triumph was instantaneous, and the following year, 1869, she wrote Part II. Originally she had envisioned the novel's title as *The Pathetic Family*, a phrase that rather pierces the heart.

As mainstay of the Alcotts, she paid off longtime debts, satisfied family needs in every direction and acted, too, as encourager, confidante, surrogate help-meet, defender. While confessing hatred for sequel-writing, she worked at it to assure her goal and periodically turned out "rubbishy tales"[25] since they brought in more money. The idea of bundling books together seemed to come later. Beyond the famous Little Women series of eight volumes, were lesser ones.

In reality she was somewhat of a tragic figure, this author with the flowery name. Almost all of her years she stifled her own longings: the early "stage-fever" which never vanished, the desires to break out and away on her own and to enjoy privacy. While glorying in family relationships, Louisa found herself unable to work well at home and frequently went elsewhere for periods of time. This need to escape endured through the years. Yet primary goals remained those of providing ease for parents, continuing education for the youngest Alcott, aiding the family of the widowed sister and, near the end, providing for the niece bequeathed to her. The resolution to gain comfortable independence for all was her reason for being and also reason, by cause of long, demanding work hours, for the break-downs in physical and spiritual welfare. Her second year in Europe—the earlier had been as traveling companion to a semi-invalid—she gave to herself in order to accompany her sister May and the friend who sponsored May's trip. It resulted in spurts of light-heartedness overflowing in extravagantly descriptive letters home. Here was another Louisa, vibrant and impulsive as during the best hours of childhood.

Of course the girl-reader can almost forever cherish the fancy of good Professor Bhaer and Jo, so long as she keeps her distance from biographies. In the real world there was, and alas to that, no kindly professor for Jo. Nor was there a Laurie; his source was a young Pole met during that first year in Europe. The fictional Jo is indeed a more comfortable image than that of a careworn author who, suffering headaches, nervous ailments and other disorders from early adulthood, took morphine for sleeping. Ironically, Louisa and Bronson Alcott died within a few days of each other, Louisa only a few months past her fifty-fifth birthday and her father almost ninety.

Readers also made acquaintanceship with another spinster of that era, Rebecca Sophia Clarke (1833-1906), known as Sophie May, who showed upon the literary scene earlier than Miss Alcott with young characters of engaging qualities. During almost forty years of publishing, Sophie May presented half a dozen series of six volumes each, using nieces and nephews as models and sometimes actual names from old town records. They are often charming, these small creatures, and not at all devoted to piety as some debunkers have intimated. In spite of names and their possible implications—Dotty Dimple and Prudy (after all, Prudence is a respectable name for New England, and who would not shorten it to Prudy?)—the little Sophie May girls were just as likely to show ill humor or to behave with anything but their Sunday-best manners as small people of any period. That moral standards of behavior were of importance in households was a fact not disputed by anyone; that the Sophie May children were captivatingly natural is also a fact to anyone possessed of a fondness for the very young and their uninhibited propensities and of an ear for their imaginative phraseology.

Someone termed Sophie May "the Dickens of the nursery."[26] Preparation for this role began at home in Norridgewock, Maine. Educated in classical languages by tutors, this fourth of six children comprising the family kept a diary from her ninth to eleventh years, recording therein the debates, lectures and sermons attended. A female academy rounded out her education and at eighteen Rebecca Sophia Clarke went to teach in Indiana, where a sister lived, but a hearing infirmity soon sent her home. (Not too surprisingly, *Dotty Dimple Out West* has an Indiana setting, but the year was 1868 and, as with the author, home locale for Dotty was Maine.) The first stories appeared in the magazine *Little Pilgrim*. Boston publishers Lee and Shepard, a name prominent with series, collected the stories. Sophie May did for young children what Elizabeth Stuart Phelps and Louisa May Alcott did for older ones, depicting them realistically with all their mischievousness and their imagination and humor.

Grave and pious subject matter did not lack reader interest, however. Isabella Macdonald Alden (1841-1930), authoring the Pansy books with their religious themes, was proof of that. Her father, an educated merchant of New York state and an earnest Presbyterian, tutored Isabella and sent her to three upstate boarding schools: a seminary and two "institutes." She subsequently taught primary classes at the seminary. In the 1860's she won first place in a contest with a book qualifying in terms of an interpretation for children of "God's plan for salvation."[27] As second wife to one who had prepared for the ministry, she fulfilled a regime of religious writing, editing, organizing, and household management and produced seventy-five books. An autobiography in progress at the time of her death saw completion by a niece, writer Grace Livingston Hill.

"Pansy" was not alone in intensive promotion of Christian virtue in form suitable to Sunday School libraries. Poor, pitiful Elsie Dinsmore's portrayer, Martha Finley (1828-1909), growing up in Ohio and Indiana, went eastward at age twenty-five. Both mother and physician-father were dead, and she hoped for a livelihood based on teaching and writing. For a church board of publications she composed stories with titles such as *Lame Letty: or, Bear Ye One Another's Burdens*; these were paperbacks appearing under the name Martha Farquharson.

Approaching forty, she retreated to the Midwest and supposedly made a study of components necessary for a popular novel. In 1867 out came the first of twenty-eight Elsie books with the theme of "...a child's struggle for virtue in a wicked world."[28] Although the audience for tear-gushers, which in some respects could certainly rival today's soap-operas, ballooned to a reported twenty-five million in America and England combined, *St. Nicholas* and *Youth's Companion* did not solicit her stories, and critics seemed to consider her invisible. Reading of any Elsie or Mildred book will reveal multiple reasons for non-solicitation. A reprint of *Elsie's Holidays* with the following inked inscription is almost unbelievable for its date: "Merry Christmas to Gladys with love from Mother and Daddy Dec. 25th 1938."

A Finley custom was to head almost every chapter with from one to as many as four quotations from British and American poets and from the Bible. An example is: "O, what a state is guilt! how wild! how wretched!—Havard."[29]

Life was sunnier for Ohioan Sarah Chauncey Woolsey (1835-1905), the Susan Coolidge responsible for the Katy Did series. She was part of a large and loving family brought up comfortably with formal education completed at the Select Family School for Young Ladies in Hanover, New Hampshire. The family moved to New Haven when Sarah was twenty; it is incidental that an uncle was president at Yale. As did Louisa Alcott for a brief period, Sarah Woolsey performed hospital work during the Civil War.

It was not until 1870 that she really began her writing. Adult literature brought her praise, but the Katy Did books, built partly upon childhood happenings in the Woolsey household, were favorites. Settling down to a literary life, she wrote, acted as editor for Roberts Brothers and as manuscript reader for Little, Brown and Company. Quick of wit and tempestuous in the manner of her fictional Katy, Sarah was a woman of size and of lively manner. It was William James who described her as "a cross between an elephant and a butterfly."[30]

Harriet Mulford Stone Lothrop (1844-1924), too, emerged from a sizable family of comfortable background. Her childhood day-dreaming in New Haven concerned the countryside and small brown houses, and on excursions she watched for the latter and began to assemble characters and stories. It was not until the 1870's that this graduate of Grove Hall Seminary found places for poems and fiction. Sending a story entitled "Polly Pepper's Chicken Pie" to *Wide Awake* magazine, she received a request for more. One about Polly's sister Phronsie followed, and the publisher asked for a dozen tales about the Peppers.

To those engrossing themselves in the fortunes and misfortunes of that brown-house family, the author was forever Margaret Sidney. It was in January of 1880 that the first chapter concerning Polly appeared in *Wide Awake*; by year's end the stories appeared in book form. The Peppers generated more than a broad reading public. Widower Daniel Lothrop, founder of the publishing company, stopped off in New Haven in order to meet their originator. Marriage was the end result, with some happy years, before Lothrop's death, in the Concord house that was one time home for Hawthorne and, earlier, for the Alcotts.

For some years Margaret Sidney managed the publishing firm, continued to write and to give time to historical and patriotic organizations. Of more than forty books, the Pepper series was the group to bring her fame. The last of them came out in 1916, almost three dozen years after the first. The only child of the marriage was a daughter, who became a professor at Stanford University. Before her death in 1924, the author was still inscribing Pepper volumes, as she did for a Palo Alto child, writing name, date and the phrase "With the love of Margaret Sidney."

A third Ohioan needs mention, at least, for reason of becoming competitor to the men who were writing travel series. This was Vassar-graduate Elizabeth Williams Champney (1850-1922), who began her literary efforts in childhood and first saw her own adult writing in print in *St. Nicholas* with a dialect poem. Eventually she was able to satisfy literary ambition with travel experiences accepted by *Harper's* and *Century* magazines. The series published in the 1880's, Three Vassar Girls, concerns foreign travel of older girls, while the Witch Winnie series of the following decade deals with art-student life. Residing much in Europe, she wrote books for adults as well, using historical, art and foreign backgrounds; her husband, J. Wells Champney, usually furnished the illustrations.

Probably fiction written for the more sophisticated ages faded into obscurity sooner than that aimed at younger children and subject to frequent re-reading. And probably the novels depicting struggles that needed realistic battling of circumstances and/or stony-hearted adults who seemed never to have known the sometime griefs of childhood remain in memory the longest. Thus while pleasant tales make good reading, they are not likely to set afire the sensibilities of compassionate young readers. Even though certain classics involving girls who began as real Cinderellas had not yet been written, the conception of entertainment as primary intent of writers (with a modicum of moralizing, of course, still a vital ingredient) was growing noticeably.

Laura Richards (1850-1943), born Laura Elizabeth Howe, was a developer of this theory. The fourth of six children born to eminent parents Julia Ward Howe and Dr. Samuel Howe of the Perkins Institute for the Blind, Laura went to rhyming for nursery and for nonsense and to writing mini-stories for easy reading and finally to the Hildegarde, Margaret and Captain January series. All this came in time.

With equally inventive siblings Julia, Florence, Maud and lone brother Harry (one brother did not survive), she enjoyed a childhood termed, when writing autobiographically in the early 1890's for *St. Nicholas,* as bright and happy and carefree. Indeed, relating sometimes the activity of the group in the manner of author Kenneth Grahame in *The Golden Age,* Mrs. Richards described adventures in fields and garden, orchard and house and of play with the children at the Institute for the Blind. The young Howes, annually celebrating August 1 as "Yeller's Day," assembled after breakfast on a hill-top behind the summer home and yelled, shrieked and howled until hoarse and from time to time during the day resumed the expressive procedure. Theirs was a life including many teachers at home, partly, she wrote, because "...our father was constantly overrun by needy foreigners seeking employment. He was a philanthropist; he had been abroad and spoke foreign languages. That was enough!...."[31]

It was after marrying Henry Richards, after becoming a mother seven times over, after the children grew older, that she acquired a reputation as writer of books for girls. Hildegarde herself is so well endowed with comforts that one cannot summon the sense of identification and the sense of indignation that a Rebecca or Anne or Polly calls forth. However, there is lively storytelling and surprise plotting of early mystery even while the heroine is relatively pastel in coloring. L.E.R., as Laura Richards was known in her Maine home termed The Yellow House for its use as center of literary, artistic and public affairs of the community, received a Pulitzer prize in 1917 for the biography of her mother. Until the last year of her long life she wrote, retaining as aims those which her mother had held: "To learn, to teach, to serve, to enjoy."[32]

And then there was Annie Fellows Johnston (1863-1931) whose girls, conceived sometimes as gently as those of Laura Richards, somehow struck chords of depth because of obstacles that needed overcoming.

Here there was no illustrious background. Annie Fellows Johnston did have access to her dead father's theological library in the Midwestern home and to a Sunday School library as well. Brought up with her sisters amidst a bevy of cousins, Annie joined the group in storytelling, in a sharing of everything read. After district school and a year at a university where an uncle was a professor she began a varied life of teaching, office work and travel. She married a cousin, a widower with three children. By now she was contributing occasionally to *Youth's Companion,* and with the husband's death came need for managing the family's livelihood; she adopted writing as a means for that, using experiences away from home as sometime inspiration. The first book, *Big Brother*, had for basis a trip on which she and a sister had seen a carload of orphans being transported to homes in another state. It was her habit to make use of environment, whatever it happened to be. In Kentucky's Pewee Valley she encountered a child and grandfather, an old Confederate colonel, who prompted the Little Colonel series, this in 1895. Several years after the publication of the first story she went to live in that Pewee Valley. When it became necessary to make a home for a delicate step-son in desert country, the volume *The Little Colonel in Arizona* materialized. Her books are varied and many. This series, peopled with gentle story-book characters dear to the spirits of the romantic, extended to a dozen titles read and re-read by generations of girls and remembered longer than the Cozy Corner stories or Georgina of New England background. Here the wistful tone is prominent; the yearning to capture the heart's desire— and the desire is seldom unreasonable—concerns circumstances and friendships and that sweet sentiment of untarnished love.

To finish off the triumphs of 19th century series-writing in some splendor there was Joseph Alexander Altsheler (1862-1919), a writer rather special for the unusual qualities in his heroes and for his often poetic phraseology. Chronologically he belongs to the 20th century, as the 19th was reaching its finale when his first book came out. Yet in spirit he was a 19th century man because he wrote romantically of a still virgin and unspoiled country.

Altsheler grew up in Kentucky and his child-mind fed upon oral recollections of pioneer-and-Indian adventures related from generation to generation in his mother's family, and upon recitations by Civil War veterans from both Union and Confederate armies. These impressions, subject to re-play by his own imagination, formed a foundation for the serious tales written with inspiration fortified by the writings of Francis Parkman.

As a child he had gone off into the woods to lie on his back and dream of recounted adventures. This was his nourishment, together with scarce books, Scott, Dickens, Thackeray and Cooper, read and passed by friends and neighbors from one to another. After Liberty College in Kentucky, and Vanderbilt University in Tennessee, he began a career on the *Louisville Courier-Journal*, working his way from reporter to specialized slots to editorial position. At thirty he moved on to the *New York World* and made his way to the editorship of the thrice-weekly magazine edition. When it needed a boys' story and none was available, Altsheler himself decided to write one. At thirty-five he published his first book and wrote an average of two per year for the remainder of his life, a matter of little more than two decades.

An adult can read him today and feel somewhat awed and full of wonder at his disciplined eloquence, admiring of his ideal hero, and then speculate as to whether he was not a writer's writer. Yet in 1918 he was judged by vote as "...the most popular author of boys' books in the public libraries of the country."[33]

Investigation of a well-stocked children's library which seems not to retain a number of old books which might well be of interest to some young readers or, at least, suitable for occasional historic display, netted the observation that acclaimed classics of the series still rate shelf space and that even a row of Altsheler books stood among the A's. Yet inquiry resulted in the information that children seemed not to draw the Altsheler volumes, that they "looked too forbidding."

What a pity! Perhaps someone will rediscover Altsheler yet—not for television but for editions with illustrations and new bindings.

Chapter VII
What Manner of Men
—And Women—Were These?
After 1900

The rage for series was peaking in the same old haphazard way that it had begun. What was not apparent was the circular fashion in which it was moving; the finale would find the beginning of a series as simple and enduring as Abbott's commencement, a series that would attract both adult and child attention and start a steady build-up into an American classic. What was more, additional writers, with the decline of the shallowly entertaining, would furnish more substantial groups of books.

During the long and uneven development to the point of the past century's close, a number of authors had already attained or almost attained what would come to be called the best-seller level devised by Frank Luther Mott in his study of book sales from the 17th century halfway into the 20th. (Excluded were texts, Bibles, dictionaries and similar volumes.) According to his reckoning of the several centuries, a book, to qualify, must have enjoyed "...a total sale equal to one per cent of the population of continental United States (or the English Colonies in the years before the Revolution) for the decade in which it was published."[1] Only American editions and American sales came under consideration.

Between 1867 and 1885, six children's books had reached this golden goal: Alger's *Ragged Dick*, Alcott's *Little Women* and *Little Men*, Mark Twain's *Tom Sawyer* and *Huckleberry Finn*, Sidney's *The Five Little Peppers and How They Grew*. Runners-up would stretch the inclusive years from 1865 to 1896 and admit nine more titles: Sophie May's *Dotty Dimple*, Finley's *Elsie Dinsmore*, Alger's *Fame and Fortune* and *Tattered Tom*, Trowbridge's *Jack Hazard and His Fortunes*, Alcott's *Eight Cousins* and *Jo's Boys*, Peck's *Peck's Bad Boy and His Pa*, and Johnston's *The Little Colonel*. As usual, the quality is somewhat uneven, but the record seems remarkable.

Required sales had ranged from 300,000 to 625,000 during those four decades. For the first decade of the 20th century a sale of 750,000 copies of any one title was necessary to rate the descriptive best-seller terminology, and for the 1910 to 1919 period, 900,000.

Before the great series era should end, half a dozen more flames blazed. The phenomenon of the new century with the outburst of syndicate publishing was sight of a few gargantuan fictional figures rising amidst the hordes of Lilliputian forms. Almost needless to say, "factory" writers did not number among the Gullivers.

The market was a bustling place catering to a voracious appetite for fiction whether it be served up in forty-nine and twenty-nine, fifteen and ten cent reprints or in fine editions. Reading of fiction had become quite respectable, even on Sundays once churchly obligations were fulfilled. The notable older series blended with ease, holding place for a long measure of time. Too, adventure tales had crossed the Atlantic in both directions, furnishing an exchange; Americans had been reading the British Mayne Reid and R.M. Ballantyne, W.H.G. Kingston and George Alfred Henty in American bindings, while the British made acquaintance with Yankee authors. There were sharp-sensed business men as always, eager to supply the expanded appetite. Educators came to the foreground in the manner of Goodrich, with geographical and sociological fictionalized series, attempting to persuade children to examine the world more fully but adding stronger story lines than had Peter Parley with his bushels of little books.

A variation is noticeable at this point, that of more frequent appearance of writers from regions other than the Eastern seaboard with its concentration of population and publishers.

Responsibility for the tremendous augmentation in run-of-the-mill series with use of collective pseudonyms, lay with Edward Stratemeyer (1862-1930). Posing as Arthur M. Winfield, he had already begun the rollicking Rover Boy series. Under his own name, furthermore, had appeared such series as Old Glory and Soldiers of Fortune, with still others ascribed to the pen-name of Capt. Ralph Bonehill. Daughter Harriet was one day to relate that her father could "...tell an original story at a moment's notice."[2]

His German-immigrant father had arrived on the American shore just in time to join the rush to California, but the family home that Father Stratemeyer established was in New Jersey, where he became a tobacconist. Son Edward, educated in public schools and by a tutor as well, used a hand press to print original stories for friends. Reading Optic and Alger, he resolved to become a writer for youth, and this he achieved gradually during some years of self-employment and as an editor for Street and Smith. By the end of the century as he neared age forty, writing was his full-time employment.

In 1904 he formed the Stratemeyer Syndicate, planning and then farming out to various writers the plots and outlines for stories and series. And this entrepreneur wrote concluding chapters for an Optic book and completed several stories left unfinished by Alger. Along the way he himself authored many a book while the syndicate total, by 1930, was computed at more than seven hundred. The most popular series, Tom Swift and the Bobbsey Twins, claimed a sales record at that time of more than six million copies each.[3]

Fortunately, readers had more than syndicate fare. To a curious extent events in the lives of two highly successful men, the older of them a contemporary of Stratemeyer, ran on parallel lines although two decades separated their births. These were L. Frank Baum and Edgar Rice Burroughs. Growing up in comfortable homes, both showed early interest in writing. Baum's abilities occurred in greater strength than Burroughs', but Burroughs possessed an added facility at sketching. Baum attended a military academy for two years and was miserable; Burroughs spent five years at one, with disciplinary problems affecting his status but ended with instructing for a time. Both tried their sons at like academies.

The two were restless individuals with roving instincts, moving, impulsively or not, from one field to another. And both went halfway through their lives before discovering exactly for what their particular talents suited them. Then came definite success, and rather quickly, and the two left the Midwest to establish homes in southern California, Ozcot and Tarzana. Despite prosperity, or in the midst of it, both made rather extravagant investments that terminated in financial predicaments so that they looked in all directions for means of increasing income. Baum declared bankruptcy in 1911. Burroughs tried changing his mode of living. And both grew weary of their famous characters.

The first-born of the two, Baum (1856-1919), lived in upper New York state and at age twelve started the *Rose Lawn Home Journal*, publishing it monthly for three years, setting type and doing the printing. His young manhood was unsettled. There were years filled with New York reporting, with print-shop work and editing, with composing verse and articles for periodicals, with management of an opera house, even with the writing and production of a play. Comedy and Irish melodrama were particular interests, and apparently there was family backing at times, for his father had prospered in the development of Pennsylvania oilfields.

After marriage and reverses in the family business, Baum appeared in South Dakota's Aberdeen with Baum's Bazaar, a variety store, and when the bank foreclosed, he began to publish the *Aberdeen Saturday Pioneer*, for which he wrote verse, editorials and a column. The town already had multiple newspapers, and another "pioneer" in that prairie land went under. With his wife and four sons he moved to Chicago and to short careers as reporter, department store buyer, and traveling salesman for a crockery firm. By 1897 some of his stories saw publication and a Chicago firm put out his *Mother Goose in Prose*, the first book illustrated by Maxfield Parrish. During the same year he became editor of a technical magazine and made the decision to earn his living as a writer. *Father Goose*, illustrated by W.W. Denslow, initial illustrator of Oz, was next, and then came that ageless *The Wizard of Oz*, runner-up on the best-seller list. The year was 1900, the dedication was to "...my good friend & comrade, My Wife," and there was no uncertainty about the direction of Baum's professional life from thereon

The following year the Wizard, based partly on stories Baum told his sons, appeared on a Chicago stage, raising to the realm of theatrical stars a pair of unknown performers, Fred Stone and Dave Montgomery. A friend of Baum, F.K. Reilly, took over the publishing of almost forty additional Oz books (which have the imprint of Reilly & Lee). Baum wrote fourteen of them; after his death Ruth Plumly Thompson wrote a good many more, and others, including Oz illustrator John R. Neill, furnished additions.

Baum tired of Oz, and in 1910 when he moved his family to the West coast, he announced by means of *The Emerald City of Oz* that his land of fancy no longer had means of communication with any other world. Several years later, when resuming the series with *The Patchwork Girl of Oz*, he stated that with the development of wireless telegraphy, communication was again possible. Still versatile, he was writing series featuring Aunt Jane's Nieces, Boy Fortune Hunters, and others, under some of the pseudonyms he used. And he pursued an elusive goal never reached, writing and/or collaborating successfully on dramas.

Despite criticism of lack of distinctive style in Oz, the books entranced and continue to entrance generations of the young. Biographers for *Twentieth Century Authors* drew a verbal portrait of Baum by use of photographs. The telling adjective for a weary and reflective face with its thick mustache and eye-glasses is "quizzical." His was the reputation of making careful answers to letters children wrote him and of using their ideas when possible.

His counterpart, Edgar Rice Burroughs (1875-1950), was born in the city-jungle of Chicago, the youngest in a family of boys, and an unmotivated student who early enjoyed dealing with written words, rhymes and cartooning. At fifteen he joined a brother sent to rural Idaho for his health and there experienced cowboy life. Attendance at Phillips Academy ended with school-requested withdrawal, and he spent a total of five years at Michigan Military Academy. Burroughs went through years of short-term work with his father's battery company, with a gold-dredging concern in Idaho, as a railroad policeman in Utah, with a mail-order house, an advertising agency, a salesmanship course. His move for turning to authorship was not "sudden perception" but a sense of desperation.[4] The beginning was the story "Under the Moons of Mars," published in *All-Story* in 1911, and the big break-through came three years later.

It was in 1914 that he triumphed with the first of a long series whose hero, Tarzan, placed in melodramatic situations, joined legends while the name entered the American vocabulary. *Tarzan of the Apes*, too, appeared in *All-Story* before reaching book form as a best seller. In Dr. Mott's phrasing, it was "...a typical pulp-magazine serial in the extravagant imagination..." with "good story-telling" and with "mediocre writing."[5] As it turned out, Tarzan burst into incredibly big business. Promptly the following year he "returned;" the stories were syndicated for newspaper use and the first related movie came out in 1917. Johnny Weissmuller was number nine in the line-up of Tarzan players.

One judge of books of sky-rocketing sales and readership opined that Burroughs worked under the influence of Kipling and H. Rider Haggard while Burroughs claimed that the story of Romulus and Remus had inspired him. The same reviewer phrased well the symbolism of the character. "In the eyes of contemporary man, huddled in large cities and frustrated by a restrictive civilization, Tarzan was a joyous symbol of primitivism, an affirmation of life, endowing the reader with a Promethean sense of power."[6]

Burroughs, loving father to three children, never visited Africa. In his zeal to maintain financial success he became a corporation, Edgar Rice Burroughs, Inc., ERB, Inc., for short. His wish was to be known as an author and not simply as the author of Tarzan.

Notwithstanding likenesses between Burroughs and Baum, personal ambitions differed. At heart a playwright, Baum, after the success of the initial dramatization of the Wizard, had set his heart on a career in the theater but never achieved it. Burroughs' wishful thinking related to the military. He had served a short stint in the army and his father managed to extract him from a disagreeable station. The desire to attend West Point had come to naught; however, in association with the Illinois reserve militia he trained troops during World War I, and despite his age by the era of World War II, he served as correspondent. A dissimilarity also existed in readership of the two men for Tarzan's appeal and that of his compatriots was to older youths while the country of Oz had a direct lure for fairy-tale lovers.

Ironically, long-lived Oz, rating but a runner-up position at the time of first publication, barely preceded the 20th century's first best seller, which today is practically unknown but for its place-name. This was *Mrs. Wiggs of the Cabbage Patch*, which came out in 1901. Its sequel, *Lovey Mary*, did not reach equal rating, a common outcome for almost any series. Author Alice Caldwell Hegan (1870-1942) of Kentucky background attended Miss Hampton's private school in Louisville. Teaching a boys' Sunday School class at a city mission when she was sixteen, the young girl became familiar with an impoverished section known as—have you guessed it?—the Cabbage Patch. A good deal later Louisville's authors' club, which included Annie Fellows Johnston, encouraged the writing of this first novel. Miss Hegan honored a parent in the dedication. "This little story is lovingly dedicated to my mother, who for years has been the good angel of 'The Cabbage Patch.' "[7]

The story not only brought to general attention the situation of slum-living but effected great changes in the life of the writer. In the following year she married Cale Young Rice, a poet; in 1903 came *Lovey Mary*; in 1904 Mrs. Wiggs took to the stage in an adaptation of the story; after establishment of the Cabbage Patch settlement house in 1910, Mrs. Rice served as member of the board. One would like to relate that the whole story ended happily, but that was not to be. Her writing during the depressed 1930's hinged on financial need, and after her death the grieving husband committed suicide.

Today the pictorial designation of "Cabbage Patch," flung into the unknowing world of children and their parents by manufacturing entrepreneurs, seems to bear no other significance at all. Nor did this best seller and its sequel remain on visible shelves in the manner of some others. Why? Probably because the real heroine was a grown woman. Possibly because the background of near-South embraced more definitive class-consciousness; Mrs. Wiggs was of low social status while the romantic pair figuring in the story belonged to the upper stratum giving assistance to the less fortunate. What Mrs. Wiggs would say to the commercial use of the place-name is problematical, but it stands to reason that she would have been cheerfully philosophic about the matter and would have felt some compassion for those "orphan" dolls, pudgy dumplings that they be.

One looks eastward again for the second of the acclaimed writers of this small block of years, for Maine was the home state of Kate Douglas Smith (1856-1923), author of best seller *Rebecca of Sunnybrook Farm* and its companion, *New Chronicles of Rebecca*, which answers "What else?" if not a continuing "And then what?"

She remembered a childhood of simple living, many books and a chance meeting on a train with Charles Dickens. Already familiar with many of his novels, she participated in a private two-hour conversation and in 1912 wrote a slim book about it. By age seventeen she had had a year at a female seminary. Because of her step-father's precarious health the family crossed the continent to the western coast and Santa Barbara. Kate found fifteen-dollar-a-month employment as church organist, but parental death and enduring financial stress sent her off for kindergarten training. In Santa Barbara she worked as private instructor before heading north to take charge of the famed Silver Street Kindergarten in San Francisco and to found the California Kindergarten Training School. Somewhere in the Santa Barbara interlude she had placed with *St. Nicholas* a three-part story based on seminary experience. A check for the munificent sum of one hundred and fifty dollars had seemed equal to a pot of gold.

Yet it was her profession which spurred writing not only in the furtherance of kindergarten training but also for helping fund such institutions; the sentimental little tale, *The Birds' Christmas Carol*, first came into print to benefit her kindergarten. Kate Douglas Smith became Mrs. Samuel Wiggin in 1881. Widowed early, she began to broaden her activities, building up an extraordinary mode of living that included writing, travel, support of various child institutions, and public "reading," usually of her own stories, sometimes in support of charities, sometimes in support of self. Gradually she came to hobnob with luminaries of the various arts both abroad and at home, and was not timorous at acknowledging such associations in her autobiography. Although remarrying, she retained the writing name of Kate Douglas Wiggin.

Her early juvenile novels are pale by comparison to the famous young New England girl; the return to the childhood environment for background brought clearly-defined characters to the Rebecca books. *Rebecca of Sunnybrook Farm* (1903), born of day-dreams about a gypsyish little girl riding in a stage-coach, turned into play form; Mary Pickford starred in a screen version. Along with its translations into European tongues was a Rebecca dictionary for use in German schools. The novel was also among the five Wiggin juveniles published in "raised" type for the blind.

Another girl of distinguished proportions was the literary child of one who, while not a citizen of the United States, meets classification as a North American, a position strengthened by the ardor of her readers. Grandparents brought up motherless L.M. (Lucy Maud) Montgomery on Canada's Prince Edward Island in a home eleven miles from a railroad and twenty-four from a town but only half a mile from a beach. Like her Green Gables' Anne, L.M. Montgomery attended district school and went on to college for a teacher's credentials, then followed the old pattern of teaching and writing. Searching for an idea to fulfill a Sunday School paper request for a short serial, she found an old notation of "Elderly couple apply to orphan asylum for a boy. By mistake a girl is sent them."[8] When the plotting worked out to more than a brief serial, the author made better use of the idea, and in 1908 the famous Anne entered both the imaginary and real worlds of American girls and became a best seller. She was a favorite child of Mark Twain.

Anne married a doctor, but Lucy Maud, in her thirties, settled for a Presbyterian minister and another setting. Yet she used her loved Prince Edward Island for almost every fiction scene. This quiet lady apparently lived a quiet life, but Anne went right on providing material for a whole row of books coming out in one impression after another and carrying her well into marriage and middle-life although in the reader's mind the uncertain Anne who arrived at Green Gables that memorable night remained forever youthful. Somewhere along the way a special Mary Miles Minter edition came out with scene-illustrations from the motion picture and with Miss Minter's portrait in color on the jacket. With a strong talent at characterization, L.M. Montgomery peopled all of her stories with admirably-hateful yet grudgingly-admirable figures by the score, particularly among adults of both sexes. She gave another version of Anne to the girls of the world during the 1920's; this was Emily, who possessed a similarly indefinable spark during a shorter series.

The fourth winner among heroines concerned a particularly sunshiny young lady called Pollyanna. Her creator lacked the accomplishments of a Lucy Maud Montgomery to sustain a steady interest in the gradual unfolding of a life. Eleanor H. Porter's (1868-1920) background itself elicits limited attention for lack of definitive details in biographic sketches. Hers is a recital of a New Hampshire childhood with a druggist father and sickly mother, of ill health that caused the girl to give up high school and to resume study in private when able. Yet she had training at the New England Conservatory of Music, married, lived here and there. There were no children of the marriage but the invalid mother lived with the couple. Reportedly, Mrs. Porter "gave up" music in her early thirties and concentrated on writing. Following some adult novels, Pollyanna brought the little-known author a good deal of fame.

Three years after *Pollyanna*'s 1913 publication, the story was dramatized for the stage. By 1920 Mary Pickford played the role in its first filming. Forty years later Pollyanna again came upon the screen "as big as life and twice as natural," shedding sweetness and light a-plenty. *Pollyanna Grows Up*, a runner-up on best-seller records (and one can conclude that only the first volume could be responsible), came out in 1915. That was the end of it from Eleanor H. Porter's writing hand. After her death Harriet Lummis Smith and Elizabeth Borton were among those continuing the Glad Book series which, like some others with instantly-popular first volumes, slid very much down hill. Critics have questioned the popularity of Porter heroines, adult and juvenile, but this was still a day of village virtue and sweet optimism.

While it is well to give attention to the achievements of women, productions by the other sex must also come in for plaudits. Burroughs, whose books reached translations into thirty-two languages including Braille, was not alone in glorifying the year 1914. Of men turning out statistically-related classics in this decade and a half, there was as well an author of adult fiction who turned now and again to write engagingly for a younger audience.

Christened Newton Booth Tarkington (1869-1946), the creator of Penrod Schofield could be called any ambitious writer's idol in that publishing triumph came to him fully and after not too long a term of trial and rejection. Educated at Phillips Exeter, this Hoosier "finished" with the Princeton class of 1893 but received no degree since he had excluded Greek from his academic program. With two fields to choose from, writing and drawing, he began with commercial art but after due attempt abandoned that for fiction. Early novels were *Gentleman from Indiana* and *Monsieur Beaucaire*. Once established, he focused an easy, breezy style and perceptive eye upon small people.

Thus it was that best-selling *Penrod* faced the public from bright blue hardback covers in 1914 and that the name of Tarkington zoomed to a prominent position among youthful readers. Two additional volumes completed the series, but children, including girls, highlighted other of his novels. In 1918 and again in 1921 Tarkington won Pulitzer prizes with *The Magnificent Ambersons* and *Alice Adams*, and many other literary plums fell his way. Much of his work underwent translation, and some novels were dramatized. It was said that Tarkington possessed a "...gift of gratifying popular taste without writing down to it."[9] Strangely or not, he never learned to use a typewriter so that when afflicted with blindness for a time, he dictated to a secretary. His record during this century was about one novel per year.

It is for Penrod and other Tarkington-conceived children that some readers remember him. When a sophisticated near-teen child of voracious reading appetite said, upon making Penrod's acquaintance in the present era, "That's the funniest book I ever read," an adult can accept the appraisal with respect.

The big names outshone the lesser ones, of course. Potential rivals had not much chance of keeping up with the most popular. There was but one Tarzan and one Penrod, while endearing Cinderellas numbered four. However, characters of lesser magnitude were legion.

Carolyn Wells (1862-1924) was in the running for much-read, and then forgotten, series during 20th century years with her Patty, Betty, Marjorie and Two Little Women books. Coming from a "mellow" Protestant household with "...stern and rock-bound ancestors,"[10] as she herself phrased it, she read at three, wrote her first book at six, attended public schools, had three summers at Saveur School of Languages in Amherst, Mass., and was an extensive reader. "I do not say that I am highly educated, but I know a lot."[11] Her work as a young adult was in her home-town, Rahway, N.J., with the Library Association. Her work as a writer encompassed one hundred and seventy titles, eighty-one of them mystery or detective novels, many others in the field of humor, the best-known being *A Nonsense Anthology* (1902). A "literary factory" in herself, she gathered admiration as a humorist and nonsense-verse composer. It was her statement, despite increasing deafness resulting from childhood scarlet fever, and a late marriage interrupted by death after a year, that she "...looked forward, steadily forward, and never back."[12] Literarily she did look back in one way, however, by reason of ardor for rare books.

The focus swings easily from this prolific woman to the Stratemeyer Syndicate whose factory output is also a matter of impressive numbers but of multiple writers. Known or anonymous, they dominated the run-of-the-mill market. Scratch the surface and you are bound to come up with such pseudonyms as Victor Appleton, Laura Lee Hope and Clarence Young. These were among names doled out at times to the Garis family.

Surely the most prominent in the Stratemeyer stable was Howard Garis (1873-1962), but not for what he turned out under *noms de plume,* beyond the initial Tom Swift series. A particular association is with the Uncle Wiggily series although that was not the only group bearing his true name. One could argue the popularity of the Tom Swift books, under the Victor Appleton signature, but they are more dated than the animal tales and were aimed at an entirely different age bracket. If Carolyn Wells was a "literary factory," Howard Garis was surely a rival for that title. His son Roger called him "a fiction machine."[13]

When Garis, earlier a reader of the Rollo books, left the Syracuse, N.Y., home for Stevens Institute of Technology to study mechanical engineering, he flunked out except in English and elocution. He tried a trade school for type-setting, and a business college, and ended up a journalist. Roger believed the year to be 1905 or 1906 that his father, at that time a staff member of the *Newark Evening News,* began his association with the syndicate. Not only did stipulations deny royalties, Garis could not claim authorship or use syndicate pseudonyms.

As time progressed, Garis, using his own name, turned out the series of Rick and Ruddy, Curly-tops, Happy Home, Buddy Books and more. In 1910 he had begun supplying, at the request of a newspaper publisher, brief animal stories, these at the rate of six per week, a stint that continued for half a century. Here, then, was the birth of Uncle Wiggily, a single character cannily dominating endless recountings, outgrowing newspaper corners and ending up in hard-cover books, in radio readings, story-telling tours, games, phonograph records and toys. Howard Garis was a natural spinner of tales, either by voice or by typewriter, by nature and certainly by habit, judging from the reminiscences of his son. Fabrications extended from fiction to reality and back again. Sometimes it was his wife or his family at whom a story took aim, to cause wonder or to extricate the storyteller from an awkward position. Endless times the airy stories involved Uncle Wiggily and his associates, and the finales were almost pure nonsense.

In this period animal stories for the very young were daily offerings in newspapers, and small libraries of books, composed of woods-animals speaking in the manner of human creatures and frequently possessing more common sense, came into existence.

The most famous collection ever was the work of Thornton Burgess (1874-1965), who loathed the business-office career begun by necessity since his widowed mother was a semi-invalid. He was born in the old glass town of Sandwich on Cape Cod. Attending school in the village, he worked outside of school hours at whatever offered itself but spent spare hours in woods, fields, marshes and on the beach, thus early and unknowingly collecting materials that would be so vital in his adult life. A year of commercial college was all that was possible but within two years, with the lure of writing guiding him, he took an office boy job in a publishing firm, working up to reportership on a weekly and writing for several farm papers. When his company took over *Good Housekeeping* magazine he became one of the editors. In 1910 his first book, *Old Mother West Wind*, came out. This was the beginning of the "How," "Why," "When," and "Where" stories, the Bedtime Story Books, and all the other nature tales. By 1912 Burgess was syndicating *Bedtime Stories* in newspapers of the United States and Canada and, like Howard Garis, gave radio talks and platform lectures.

His narratives are somewhat in the tradition of the Uncle Remus tales, seeming to bear upon myth and legend and traditional explanation of the ways of animal and fowl. There is a flavor of folk-lore, a steadiness and dependability with small morals worked into outcomes so that young minds could sense cause and effect and satisfaction at minor disaster or reward. Burgess' illustrator, Harrison Cady, supplied the same authentic and comfortable believability through the many books.

New England born Albert Bigelow Paine (1861-1937) also enjoyed an effective if less extensive partnership between animal-adventure writer and illustrator. He was fortunate in rating clever J.M. Condé for his Hollow Tree and Deep Woods tales.

Transplantation of Paine, biographer and journalist, to the Middlewest took place in his infancy. He attended a one-room prairie school and an academy near Xenia, Ill., and thereafter assisted his father in a general store and on the farm. By the time that he went to St. Louis to learn photography he was writing "rhymes" and went on to prose, some of which *Harper's Weekly* accepted. New York lured him but partnerships in newspaper ventures failed. For a year he was children's editor of the *New York Herald*, and for nine years League editor of *St. Nicholas*. His books numbered about forty, among them biographies of Thomas Nast and Mark Twain; the latter has borne the term "gossipy." His most unusual book was a six-copy biography of a banker published only for that family. Critics, while describing Paine as dignified and scholarly in appearance, also called him pompous and somewhat condescending, with pride in his acquaintanceship among the rich and the great.

One who dealt in a wholly different way with the animal world, sending characters on far travels and using a human being as central figure, was Hugh Lofting (1886-1947). Whimsical enough to join the kingdom of so-called lower animals, Doctor Dolittle went his tranquil way, sometimes encountering fanciful conceptions of the author's composition. A gentleness pervades all, along with quiet humor, while subtle touches in speech and behavior appeal to the adult who may be reading aloud to the young.

Lofting, whose caravans of animals, domestic and wild, ranged the world with Doctor Dolittle, came to the United States in the early 1900's and attended the Massachusetts Institute of Technology. Although he returned to England to complete his training, in 1912 he married and settled in the United States. In 1916 after enlistment in the British army, he began sending self-illustrated letters and stories to his children; thus began the series that came to be translated into a dozen languages. At the time of his death another Doctor Dolittle book was in progress.

Lofting despised the term "Juveniles," considering it an epithet, and declared that there ought to be a classification of "Seniles" to balance it. The idea of setting off children as "a separate species" irritated him. "For who shall say where the dividing line lies, that separates the child from the adult?" he asked. "Practically all children want to be grown up and practically all grown-ups want to be children, and God help us, the adults, when we have no vestige of childhood in our hearts."[14]

Every effective writer of fiction for children surely has in his spirit that young and unspoiled quality of which Lofting spoke. Lucy Fitch Perkins (1865-1937) had it even while bent on education of a sort as one reason for writing. She was a vigorous woman who combined roles of writer and illustrator, as did Lofting. Background for her Twins series, too, was the world itself, and the well-plotted books became the most interesting and best projected group designed to introduce children to the young of other lands.

For Mrs. Perkins the world opened in Indiana "backwoods;" both parents had been teachers, and work, thrift and respect for learning were home standards. She was not limited to her backwoods, for the family made long visits to the earlier home near Boston. Some of her cartoons appeared in a local newspaper during residence in Michigan when Lucy was an adolescent, and kinfolk made possible her training at the Boston Museum of Fine Arts. She went back to teaching and illustrating because of the 1893 depression and her husband's illness. For the Prang Company she taught in Chicago, lectured, illustrated and painted murals in school rooms. Two thoughts took focus: the need for understanding and respect between nationalities in this melting-pot country, and sympathetic presentation of this idea to catch interest. One school familiar to her enrolled children of twenty-seven nationalities.

The Dutch Twins appeared in 1911 as first of the series of twenty-six volumes written over two and one-half decades. Illustrations first sketched from a kneeling position gave Mrs. Perkins opportunity to capture a child's perspective. And neighborhood children termed "the poison squad" passed on her stories. So successful were the books that Houghton Mifflin published school editions as well as the more luxurious ones of larger size.

The continuing Twins bear tribute as one of the last notable series of the century's history. With presses rolling feverishly and names forgotten along with books, professional writers in adult fields yielded to the attraction of the juvenile market but failed to come up with a Penrod or Pollyanna. One of these was Michigan-bred Clarence Budington Kelland (1881-1964) who earned a law degree but became a reporter and political writer. Later, as editor of the magazine *American Boy* and lecturer on children's literature, he was no doubt better equipped than some to make the venture. A series beginning with adolescent Mark Tidd's adventures in business, was his first fiction attempt, after which he wrote stories causing wider ripples than young Mark, those of the Yankee promoter Scattergood Baines and the one used as basis for the film *Mr. Deeds Goes to Town.*

The flurry during the Twenties in lavish publishing of new series leaves little to remember. Today, the left-overs look like intruders in old-book shops and like forlorn souvenirs in thrift stores and at large rummage and library sales. Triple Spies, Honey Bunch, Pee-wee Harris, Bomba the Jungle Boy, Mary Jane, Jerry Todd, Don Sturdy with the old Stratemeyer pseudonym Victor Appleton and with a spine medallion imprinted with "Author of Tom Swift Books." Sports, mystery-delving, high jinks, all blithe and airy, all in tune with the times, and taking the place of Alger and Castlemon, Elsie and Tom Swift, and Tom, Dick and Sam Rover.

In their pristine days they were not alone but stood in better company, that of the big sellers lately preceding them, and the classic carry-overs from the last century. The animal tales and family stories for little people endured; the serene voice of Doctor Dolittle murmured on, and two by two, the Twins appeared. Tarzan, never knowingly out of Burroughs' hands, flourished, while other writers supplied Oz books. Yet a general diminishment was in the offing.

Upon Stratemeyer's death in 1930, his two daughters, earlier barred by their father from his business world, took over the syndicate. Because of the depression and, later, the shortages brought about by World War II, the syndicate reduced its number of series.[15] The same situations would have affected all publishing.

Wellesley graduate Harriet Stratemeyer Adams (1894-1982), who retained the reins, stated that her father "...founded the syndicate to supply...stories for boys and girls. He outlined and edited all of the works himself."[16] This is not in exact accord with Roger Garis' account of the method used by his father, who "...would write the books, sometimes following the outline, and sometimes not."[17]

Extending the most popular series, The Bobbseys and scientist Tom Swift, rescuing sleuth Nancy Drew, and creating another mystery-loving pair with the Dana sisters, Mrs. Adams demonstrated the Stratemeyer business acumen, and in time would update the older volumes. She in turn prepared outlines, chapter by chapter. "Scientists and other specialists wrote from these," she reported. Employing the pseudonyms Carolyn Keene for the girls' mysteries and Franklin W. Dixon for the boy detectives of the Hardy family, she herself supplied more than one hundred books, working from outlines and dictating into a machine. Secretaries did the transcribing and Mrs. Adams and staff members edited.[18] Thus the syndicate title count continued to grow.

"Everything passes, everything perishes, everything palls."[19] The time had come; the cycle was nearing completion.

That the finale, however, should not go without evidence of some ultimate, lucent stroke was due to a then-unknown woman, Laura Ingalls Wilder (1867-1957) who, late in her years, stepped quietly into the altering scene and began to recount the story of her childhood. It began simply, this autobiographical family saga which surely represented the history of many a pioneering group. The actual recording began, very much later in time, within the pages of school tablets.

One learns of an individual life by reading of a family's gradual trek through Indian country and the newly opened western Middlewest. Child-dependency was relatively brief; Laura began her prairie school-teaching at age fifteen, married at eighteen and agreed to trial farming. Climate was the primary enemy: dust, burning winds, drought, prairie fire, and long, long winters; such trials were not new to her. To top off such conditions there was the 1893 recession, and Laura Wilder worked a daily twelve hours at dress-making for one dollar per day in order to help finance a wagon-journey move to rural Missouri. Eventually she and Almanzo, her husband, completed all that they had planned, from clearing land and setting out apple trees to building a home with resources from their own property, stone for foundation and fireplace, and oak for the rest of it.

Mrs. Wilder had some journalistic experience on farm papers, and daughter Rose Wilder Lane, journalist and novelist, encouraged the autobiographical project. Thus an astonishing lady in her mid-sixties, who had been the clear-eyed Laura wandering gladly first with parents and sisters, then with husband and child, began the precise, admirably simple and graphic account for all to read. One wonders as to the general reception of *Little House in the Big Woods* in the Great Depression year of 1932. It was a blue-bound volume with sizable print and Helen Sewell illustrations all in modest black and white but for the frontispiece, which was of shades of winter night-time blues with touches of brick-red.

However, the prime consideration is that an illustrious future lay ahead, for Laura of the Little House books, like Rollo, would find a prominent role in literary history for the young.

Chapter VIII
The Sorrows and Successes of Orphanhood

Beneficial to a discussion of young protagonists is a look into the society which their life-counterparts occupied, and a determination of what influenced writers in their adoption of character models. Especially is it needful to show reason for the wide usage of the orphaned state.

Often sizable to begin with, the family formed a strong, supportive unit. Frequently a household was an extended one, to use today's term, but in a more natural way. Highly useful widowed grandmothers and maiden aunts in residence shared responsibilities, adding to security and the furtherance of strict Christian mores. At times a relative might assume a parental role, for death, not divorce, was the greater divider. Countless aunts, uncles and cousins living nearby, or making long visits, figured prominently in young worlds, as did close neighbors, longtime friends and hired help.

Young children fared well under the umbrella-like protection of the enlarged family. Intermingling much with adults of several generations, they had a plenitude of mature molds upon which to pattern themselves, while school and church acted as reinforcement to home-training. Such comprehensive stability, even while constraining in one sense, was deep-rooted. Today's institutional officials request the presence and assistance of grandparent figures in day-care centers and grammar schools; they arrange associations of child groups with convalescent homes, and promote organizations providing big sister and big brother positions to help fill the voids in the nuclear family.

Other-day writers recognized such values. In their often scanty biographies one finds indications, particularly with women, of steadfast households and recountings of near blissful days which came into creative use. Even though men's biographies may lack mention of childhood beyond note of parental solicitude or ambition, reasons given for leaving home indicate financial need for employment, or the adventurous urge to get out into the world, a male prerogative. Pleasurable tales could ensue; yet sometimes singularity was missing.

The other side of the picture reveals manifestations of misfortune imposed by death. Abbott himself became sole parent to his six children. Young Sam Clemens was but eleven when his father died. Elizabeth Stuart Phelps was child to her natural mother and, in turn, to two step-mothers. Kate Douglas Wiggin's father died just after the beginning of her memory, and eventually a kin of some degree took his place as step-father. Thomas Wallace Knox was a complete orphan at six and began working at age ten. Annie Fellows Johnston's mother was a widow, and the author herself married a widowed cousin and became step-mother to three sons. Grandparents brought up motherless Lucy Maud Montgomery. Thornton Burgess became fatherless and worked as well as attending school.

The various fates of the writers affected outlooks and series production. Books were inclined to be reflections of the authors' situations and experiences of both child and adulthood. Nearly all of them were voracious readers; occasional men engaged in journalistic work and knew the grimy side of life; the teaching profession, and thus regular encounters with children of all conditions, was common among both sexes. All of them were acquainted with the calamities of their environments and incorporated misfortunes in their fiction: death, dread disease, accident, penury. With the more thoughtful writers, these were not melodramatic but were common conditions.

Particularly among the women, limited in boundaries, home situations cast shadows upon young lives. Gypsy Breynton's friend, Peace Maythorne, suffering spinal injury, expected to live not too long. Frail Beth March, ill with a debilitating fever in volume one of *Little Women*, succumbed in volume two. A heart condition hampered Sophie May's little Flyaway. Katy Carr had an invalid cousin and Katy herself was confined to bed for a grueling period of time after the swing gave way. There was fear that Polly Pepper might lose her eyesight after a bout with the measles. Jimmy Wiggs up and died and Chris Hazy stumped around the Cabbage Patch on a peg-leg. From age three, Pinkrosia, country friend of Hildegarde, was bound to a wheel-chair. And so it went. Still, relatives and friends, including ministers, teachers and doctors, helped weather disasters.

For the isolated, lone protagonist, safeguard other than self did not exist. Such children emerged from among the homeless, or near homeless, whose lowly state was well enough known during the 19th century. If the use of the orphan, the most adverse position of all, became another characteristic of series, it still had solid basis in reality.

Missions and asylums were prevalent. There were "poor-houses," and the "paupers" residing therein included children. Christian-educated women and men acted in parental manner to aid family remnants, not always, perhaps, with wholly Christian intent. A child (especially a boy) could be of help in almost any setting. Expected from him was thankfulness, although to bear oneself with humility and to express gratitude for deliverance from a base status over which he had no control and for which he bore no blame is rather more than a child is equipped or inclined to handle.

In 1883 one George C. Needham wrote of his investigation into the plight of the desolate both in Great Britain and the United States. While his book with its weighty religious tone examines the problem of "unnatural parents or vicious guardians," it explores particularly the strait of the child and the heavy utilization of emigration from population centers to rural reaches of the West. Needham contended that "...*child reclamation* is a more important consideration than *adult reformation.*"[1] Indeed, one chapter is titled "Save the Children."

Defining "street Arabs" as those young individuals resourceful enough to look out for themselves, and "gutter snipes" as those too impotent to do so, Needham devoted several pages to Ragged Dick, one of the boys from Alger's "fascinating pen." He gave more space to "a very interesting article published in *St. Nicholas,* from the pen of Mr. Brace, entitled 'Wolf-Reared Children.' "[2] Pickety, the little "street-rover" described, ended up with others among the homeless in a house where the boys helped pay their way by means of small jobs until such time that they should be sent to Christian homes in western agricultural areas.

More than once *St. Nicholas* informed its readers as to the destiny of that stratum of society. In 1888 the magazine dedicated seven pages to an illustrated article concerning Philadelphia's Girard College financed by philanthropist Stephen Girard for "poor white male orphans" and governed by detailed instructions as to buildings and the welfare of boys. Constructed between 1834 and 1846 for about 1400 occupants, the institution was not a college in the current sense, but yet a school designed to educate its residents academically and technically, and included library, chapel and playing fields as well as dormitories and classrooms. Boys entered between ages of six and ten and could remain until age eighteen.[3]

Charitable societies, publishers and people like Needham documented social evils and remedies, including emigration of children and that movement's success. Author Johnston saw a load of orphans in the midst of their travel for such transplantation and wrote a book inspired by the experience as well as using lone children in her series. Author Wiggin in her autobiography recalled a childhood pastime of fashioning, along with other paper dolls, sets of "orphan" dolls all dressed alike and supplied with a guardian matron. She, too, in casting characters, chose children deprived of family.

Again the treatment of such individuals varied according to the sex of the authors. With a boy the permitted range was wider both in action and latitude, and this liberty extended to the youth lacking parents. He participated in bold expedition, ventured abroad by any means of transportation, committed errors, employed slang, and spoke his opinion unasked. Adults even at times entrusted him to carry out projects. These boys, possessing a certain independence or enterprise, did not rate or need tender sympathy; neither did Tom Sawyer, who had to tolerate Aunt Polly and a hateful half-brother, Sid.

Both Alger and Optic cast the lone girl-child in street-Arab role, but unconvincingly. It was not a natural position for the girl of that era, and she fit awkwardly into that image and was tormented by male competitors. Society demanded a restrictive place for her, no matter her social position, and who knew better how to handle her in that narrow world than the women authors? Feminine series writers did not experiment so readily with like characters until later, even though the bereft young girl, already familiar through fairy tales as a Cinderella, came to hold a shadowy place in fiction. Her great blossoming as protagonist came after 1900 in both series and singles.

One forgotten writer, however, Adelaide F. Samuels, perhaps researching the fiction field, even as Martha Finley, may have held the premise that if one orphan be key to popularity, then several dozen might lead to world renown. In *Daisy Travers; or, The Girls of Hive Hall* (1876), good Grandfather Milly, having saved Daisy and her brother, by adoption, from heaven knows what horrors, acted in accordance with Daisy's wishes. When she reached age sweet sixteen, he established twenty-five children from miserable poorhouses in a fine home. There the orphans, well-fed, well-dressed, well-instructed and counseled by adults and Daisy, suffered some travail brought about by jealousy and earlier experiences. At story's close, several of talent were marked for distinguished futures. It is not a spirit-warming tale.

Women had already aroused public compassion by writing of homes crippled by death. Of fatherless flocks, the almost destitute Pepper family was prime example. Being motherless, the six little Carrs of the Katy Did books had to endure the presence of Aunt Izzie as a mother-figure. Solitary children appeared in a number of the Alcott books. Alice Hegan Rice and others used forlorn folk, and of course there was Finley's choice, after her study of ways to turn out desirable fiction, of motherless Elsie Dinsmore.

Yet the big three were products of the early 1900's: Rebecca, who rode the stage to Sunnybrook Farm; Anne, who went by error to Green Gables; and Pollyanna, who left a paltry home of missionary barrels to head happily toward Miss Polly Harrington's palatial home. They transcended other wistful nobodies and endeared themselves to readers along with coveys of like creatures brought to life by means of pen and ink to elicit sentiments of compassion.

There are positive advantages to the casting either girl or boy orphans as protagonists. Fictionally they were usually valiant children of sharp sensibilities, endowed with the will to persevere, and the character to attain some small height. With them there was only one direction to proceed, and that was upward. Adversity, a condition offering challenge and demanding vanquishment, fostered spirit, ambition and self-development. The rank of orphan, that being standing alone and unwanted, moved the reader's heart and strengthened his commiseration when any mean adult spirit set additional obstacles before the child.

What was more, the character, defensive traits already present, was likely to be quick of tongue, to possess "spunk," and to show a readiness for risk. The condition invited a wider and more tantalizing sweep of plotting, and the combination was almost unbeatable. It is small wonder that castaways are highly visible in the history of series.

If the boys appeared first, that was but a natural state of affairs. If the feminine authors waited until feeling bold enough to act entirely on their own, that was to be expected. When the time came, they were doubtless unastonished that their star players had too many rivals to enumerate quickly. After all, the orphan, when handled with skill, was an obvious winner.

Chapter IX
As for Heroines

It is no shock to discover that the memorable girls of the series, like the women who conceived them, should require particular fortitude to survive in a society rating them as inferiors. That gallant heroines were not immediately forthcoming is no surprise. After all, they had to work their way out of a repressive background. That so many of them should find special niches in literary history is a tribute to the writers disadvantaged by their sex.

John Stuart Mill put the position of women entering this profession in plain enough words. "It is but of yesterday that women have either been qualified by literary accomplishments, or permitted by society, to tell anything to the general public. As yet very few of them dare tell anything, which men, on whom their literary success depends, are unwilling to hear."[1]

However, Mill went on, "Literary women are becoming more freespoken, and more willing to express their real sentiments."[2] That they did so in series is a verity more for later viewing, for the first prominent writers of such works were male in gender, and what they did with their girl characters is nothing to praise to heaven.

Mill would testify, too, to general ignorance on this subject. "It is only a man here and there who has any tolerable knowledge of the character even of the women of his own family. I do not mean, of their capabilities; these nobody knows, not even themselves, because most of them have never been called out. I mean their actually existing thoughts and feelings."[3]

One would have to include Jacob Abbott of being at least close to these "few," even though he accepted readily the condition of the day, the gross inequality of the sexes. Eventually he came to portraying girls of greater signal character. As the first in line, he established the basic image. With progression of years, variations would come into view, with additions or deletions, some with incredible features, some with humanistic elements enough to endear their owners to readers for several generations, some embodying such compassion-drawing force as "misfortune's child" to radiate immense popularity, and many, of course, assigned stock-character parts with individualization fixed largely by the authors' say-so.

Author-educator Abbott gave thought to the determination and development of the human constitution. For the Franconia series, which grew out of boyhood memories and the experience of raising his own six children, he used a common preface. It reads in part: "The development of the moral sentiments in the human heart, in early life—and every thing in fact which relates to the formation of character,—is determined in a far greater degree by sympathy, and by the influence of example, than by formal precepts and didactic instruction." Speaking of the stories themselves, he explained that "They present quiet and peaceful pictures of happy domestic life, portraying generally such conduct, and expressing such sentiments and feelings, as it is desirable to exhibit and express in the presence of children."[4]

That series came later in time than some of the Lucy stories and presented more natural individuals. Described as "a very still, gentle and obedient girl," Lucy is unalluring, and her primary occupation seemed to be that of digesting information. Verbal and behavioral interplay between the sexes, livelier in the Franconia books, was foreshadowed earlier in *Rollo at School*, in which naughty little Dovey Brome is quite the most interesting among the children. Yet Dovey and her heedlessness became subject for a little talk by Miss Mary, the teacher, who put the matter before the rest of the class in the pleasant way of the author.

Abbott's model was far more likeable than one which followed, a child weighted down with piety as heavy as the most compact steamed pudding. Age did not count here; it might be anything from five into adolescence, and presence in the Sunday School library was likely the goal.

It was not enough that Martha Finley endowed her best-known heroine with all that Abbott might wish in a child and more. Heiress Elsie Dinsmore was dutiful, diligent, respectful and kind, gentle, patient and truthful, but she possessed one trait in overabundance enough to give a reader mental as well as physical indigestion. Elsie was the holiest of the holy. At age eight, believing that she had not been forbearing enough with the household of inconsiderate kinfolk (here the extended family was a handicap!), Elsie knelt before an open Bible and made confession of "sins and sorrow" to the Saviour, begging to become more like Jesus, while her tears fell upon the pages. Martha Finley embroidered in every stitch and color known to Victorian womanhood a being beyond belief, a child who tells her father, "You must love Jesus better, my own precious papa."[5]

Speaking "with a touching mixture of true humility and holy boldness," this child had moments when, under question, she instructed her father and his friends in the true path. However, in between these infrequent victories she spurted showers of tears. Perhaps all this self-watering was of benefit. The pious tone running so deeply through the initial volume also streaks through later books, while a few saintly characters balance off plots in preposterous adventures with some wholly evil souls and many not yet "saved." The series could qualify for endless soap-opera installments. Yet occasionally one of today's old girls speaks with nostalgia of having read the series. Elsie is hard to bury.

It is not easy to accept "Sabbath-school books," limited as they are in blood, bone, muscle and nerve. Their dimensions are cramped. Reason for being, as well as to entertain primly, was to instruct the young and lead them along a shrunken route of righteousness.

Five-year-old Bessie Bradford, with her sister, worked throughout one volume toward the accumulation of a joint five dollars, half the sum needed to provide a Sunday School library for children "far out West" where people were ignorant and "...don't know much about God or how Jesus came to die for them."[6] With two friends the small Bradfords hoped to provide a box of books to accompany the Sunday School teacher about to wed a missionary. Being the older by two years, Maggie played spokesman.

"...and I am afraid Miss Winslow wont [sic] be comfortable out there, mamma, 'cause they don't have nice houses like ours, but just rough ones made of logs, which they call log cabins. You know Miss Winslow is a lady, and I am afraid she wont like to live in a place like that."

"Miss Winslow has thought of all that, my darling; but she is willing to put up with these hardships for the sake of carrying the glad message of salvation to those poor people."[7]

Thereupon the two mites work at such despised tasks as hemming tea-towels in order to earn money, and trying truly to make their boot-laces and gloves serve longer in order that funds customarily spent for replacements may go for the library project.

Circumstances are entirely different for sixteen-year-old Julia Ried, daughter in a destitute and death-ridden family, who acts as first-person narrator for a chronicle meant to be a "Sabbath-school book." The conviction that the moral duty of any Christian of whatever degree is to bring all associates to Jesus colors the atmosphere. Yet Julia, who found prayer meetings "thrilling," questions the belief that a life-story such as hers, designed for a library shelf, "...should utterly ignore two great questions that have to do with human hearts: love and marriage."[8]

Obviously this kind of recounting does not make for exciting reading at any age. The break from narrowly stereotyped heroines to those with more natural inclinations was a gratifying improvement. Not that regard for duty, scruples and church-affiliation was discarded from the demure protagonist Abbott inaugurated, but that overblown sanctity of Sunday narratives should be dropped and, one would like to think, with that worn old phrase "a sickening thud."

Yet at the same time fresh air began blowing through rooms housing young fictional girls, for writers with more talent and wider horizons opened windows and doors, some timidly and others almost recklessly. None discarded the model of the reasonably sedate child entirely until the arrival of the bulk of ordinary writers and heroines of this century, but perception expanded the inner eye and gave the protagonist some liberty to perform in a human manner. It was not in the male nature, though, to let girls be "themselves."

Chronologically, Bessie and Maggie could very well have played dolls with some of Sophie May's little girls, but would have done so only if the latter comported themselves in totally Christian manner. Despite the synonymity of names such as Prudy and Dotty Dimple to characteristics now scorned, Sophie May was not nearly so sanctimonious as some critics have indicated, nor did she attempt verbal flights at the stilted elegance which was the aim of some. If her children's world was small, it was still a real world and of fitting size, and peopled with delightful and delighting individuals who were as human and at times as intractable as small people everyone knows. Her characters displayed naturalness and ingenuity.

"Well, I've nothing to tell, any way, but just thoughts," said Grace, pocketing her orange, and taking Cassy's hand again, while they each hopped on one foot like happy little robins. "I've a great many thoughts whizzing in my mind all the time, Cassy. I've been thinking lately I mean I've been wishing, for ages and ages, that I'd been born a boy; but it's silly, and so I never say it."

"Why, Gracie Clifford, I've heard you say it five hundred times! I'd as soon be a girl, because I *am*, and there's the end of it."

"But to grow up and be a woman!" said Grace, with a shudder. "Do you ever think of the wrinkles, and the cross kitchen girls, and the children that have to cut their teeth? And you can't sleep nights, and then they won't let you vote!"[9]

Constructing, for the Katy Carr series, a household with a demanding Aunt Izzie in charge, Susan Coolidge, too, recognized the need for advancement from the staid child and announced it early.

Aunt Izzie had been a gentle, tidy little thing, who loved to sit as Curly Locks did, sewing long seams in the parlour, and to have her head patted by older people, and to be told that she was a good girl; whereas Katy tore her dress every day, hated sewing, and didn't care a button about being called "good," while Clover and Elsie shied off like restless ponies when anyone tried to pat their heads.[10]

Other spirited girls were curtsying to the young public, too. Gypsy Breynton and Jo March were tomboys, a term not often heard today, and no doubt shockingly unladylike at a time when slang was the property of the male sex. Both tried the patience of their families and got into "scrapes."

Like Katy Carr both were captivating because they stepped out and away from the genteel Victorian-girl likeness.

Rolicking, frolicking Gypsy appears as spontaneous and refreshing as if just brought to life. Her brother Tom, fond but critical and joke-playing, claimed that she had no "system," and was "...like a toad that's always on the jump." Mrs. Phelps did not delay in presenting a hoyden so aptly nicknamed.

Gypsy climbed out of the window without the slightest hesitation, and walked along the ridge-pole with the ease and fearlessness of a boy. She had on a pretty blue delaine dress, which was wet and torn, and all stuck together with burs; her boots were covered with mud to the ankle; her white stockings spattered and brown; her turban was hanging round her neck by its elastic; her net had come off, and the wind was blowing her hair all over her eyes; she had her sack thrown over one arm, and a basket filled to overflowing, with flowers and green moss, upon the other.[11]

Jo March, older than Gypsy, thought that it was too bad indeed to be a girl "...when I like boys' games and work and manners!" She was unconventional in speech, and colt-like. Reproof made her rebel even more.

"Jo does use such slang words!" observed Amy, with a reproving look at the long figure stretched on the rug. Jo immediately sat up, put her hands in her pockets, and began to whistle.

"Don't, Jo; it's so boyish!"

"That's why I do it."

"I detest rude, unlady-like girls!"

"I hate affected, niminy-piminy chits!"

" 'Birds in their little nests agree,' " sang Beth, the peacemaker, with such a funny face....[12]

One must admit other "knowns" into this select group, even if their adventuresome qualities did not lead them to revolt. At least cherished dreams and desires elevated them to a plane above ordinary girls, and those made for remembrance.

Among them is Polly Pepper, prone to scheming means of enhancing the dull days, and envisioning better times, comforts for Mrs. Pepper, gingerbread more often for the ever-hungry brothers, possession of two hundred candles to set aflame all at the same time and thus furnish sufficient light during one evening, at least. During spare moments she drummed atop the bare table, pretending that she sat at a piano and, to bring some elegance to the household, devised the title of "Provision Room" for the shed "tacked-on" to the house and used for kitchen storage, for " 'twas a good place to keep provisions in, even if we haven't any; and besides,...it sounds nice!"[13]

Popular heroines: Rebecca, Anne and Pollyanna, Gypsy, Jo, Katy

Laura Richard's Hildegarde and Johnston's Little Colonel who, too, expressed their feelings, belonged to this group for reason of Tennysonian atmosphere that could blend perfectly with a summer's day and with slipping away to a solitary spot to read and day-dream over attainment of the impossible, that of becoming idyllic heroine. While as "only" children, they were recipients of much adult attention in relatively luxurious settings, the two faced and fought obstacles relating to their own development. This princess role, at a little distance from reality but yet believable, was as necessary to a child's collection of heroines as any other.

On the other hand, girls among Mrs. Perkins' Twins sets were practical creatures given to candor when questioning position and defending their own gender. Small Take argued the case with her father.

"...but you are a girl.   It is not your fault.... We cannot all be boys, of course. But to the keeping of the Sons is given the honor of the Family...."

"Don't I do anything at all for the honor of my Family?" asked Take.

"When you are grown up you will marry and live with your husband's family and serve them in every way you can....Now, you must just be a good girl and mind your Father and Grandmother, and Mother, and your brothers."

"I'm just as old as Taro," said little Take, "and I think I know just as much. Why can't he mind me some of the time? I think it would be fair to take turns!"[14]

Being part of a family of girls, young Laura Ingalls did not have to do battle in this respect. However, she often found herself defiant toward stringent family rules governing behavior and speech. And she was alone, other than her father, in liking the gypsyish wandering.

"Don't speak with your mouth full, Laura," said Ma.

So Laura chewed and swallowed, and she said, "I want to see a papoose."

"Mercy on us!" Ma said. "Whatever makes you want to see Indians?..."

"They wouldn't hurt us, would they?" Mary asked. Mary was always good; she never spoke with her mouth full.

"No!" Ma said. "Don't get such an idea into your head."

"Why don't you like Indians, Ma?" Laura asked, and she caught a drip of molasses with her tongue.

"I just don't like them; and don't lick your fingers, Laura," said Ma.

"This is Indian country, isn't it?" Laura asked. "What did we come to their country for, if you don't like them?"[15]

There were degrees of devotion to varying protagonist parts; there were degrees of quality, certainly, classes to test and rate and choose from, and out of all the reading and re-reading, judgment resulted not overnight, not with impulsive conclusion but with exercise of head and heart, tangibles and intangibles, balancing and re-weighing of sober considerations that held up forever after. When all was done, Everygirl came up with the favorite prototype. Much as she loved others and dramatized them in play and in fantasizing, she placed her first loyalty with the young character who, alone, faced a hostile universe which she must conquer in order to survive in spirit.

This heroine, aged ten, eleven or twelve, adored, dreamed about, both pitied and envied, was nobody's child, a veritable weed possessing little but a knowledge of and experience at work, ability to compromise, to improvise, and equipped with wits sharp enough to accomplish this.

On initial appearance onlookers saw this lonely child, sallow or sickly, freckled, plain at first glance in outgrown or handed-down garb of dreadful taste, as a being not yet in permanent form, as a burden and little else. They expected her to be meek, mild, humble, grateful for and worthy of food, shelter, and moral instruction. And she was not. Her tongue was likely to be tart, even unruly, and she might be painfully honest. She challenged ideas and customs and, horror of horrors, she even challenged adults. Eloquently and often she displayed dangerous streaks of imagination, originality and perception. Individuality sustained her; day-dreaming or diary-keeping or solitary games helped her to endure.

This darkly delineated Cinderella was not peculiar to the series. Perhaps she did not really belong in that category of fiction at all, for how could sequels stand up to that first volume in which she was bound to make a place for herself, a permanent niche equal to those owned by more fortunate counterparts from birth? Yet the reaction to a successful drama of this kind was a plea for more, and in some cases the plea was answered.

Faced by an ogre of sorts (usually in the form of a woman), faced by critical situations, by inevitable mishaps exactly when desiring to display best form, betrayed by tongue or temper or impulse, the Cinderella somehow found her devious way, learning painful lessons as she advanced. Integrity saw her through; secret or non-secret friend renewed her courage; fortune covertly aided at rescue because of her very toughness and suffering. Meanwhile, the aunt, guardian, benefactor, first seen as villain, gradually diminished the rigidity of her spine and came to an acceptance of her charge's effort and charm. Thus a communal transformation ensued.

The Anne who went to Green Gables by error already viewed herself as being too homely ever for a marriage proposal unless it issue from a missionary to foreign parts. Marilla, who did not care for talkative children and who did not want a girl orphan, would have agreed.

> Marilla came briskly forward as Matthew opened the door. But when her eyes fell on the odd little figure in the stiff, ugly dress, with the long braids of red hair and the eager, luminous eyes, she stopped short in amazement.
> "Matthew Cuthbert, who's that?" she ejaculated. "Where is the boy?"[16]

Supersensitive to atmosphere, Anne did not wait long to express her emotion.

> "You don't want me!" she cried. "You don't want me because I'm not a boy! I might have expected it. Nobody ever did want me...."[17]

At Sunnybrook Farm, the reception for Rebecca Rowena Randall, who at least had a mother and half a dozen brothers and sisters at home, was barely less glacial on the part of the domineering one of the two grandaunts. And Miranda, who came to think of Rebecca as a "black-haired gypsy," was not slow to inaugurate household rules.

> She...put the bunch of faded flowers in her aunt Miranda's hands, and received her salute; it could hardly be called a kiss...
> "You needn't 'a' bothered to bring flowers," remarked that gracious and tactful lady; "the garden's always full of 'em when it comes time."
> ...
> "I'll take you up and show you your room, Rebecca," Miss Miranda said. "Shut the mosquito nettin' door tight behind you, so's to keep the flies out; it ain't flytime yet, but I want you to start right; take your passel along with ye and then you won't have to come down for it; always make your head save your heels. Rub your feet on that braided rug; hang your hat and cape in the entry there as you go past."[18]

Blonde, freckled Pollyanna, wearing a red gingham dress when she should have been in black because of her father's recent death, made a sympathetic impression on Nancy, the kitchen maid who awaited her at the station. First encounter with rich Aunt Polly, who had an attic room prepared for the unwanted addition to the household, was the contrary.

Miss Polly Harrington did not rise to meet her niece. She looked up from her book, it is true, as Nancy and the little girl appeared in the sitting-room doorway, and she held out a hand with "duty" written large on every coldly extended finger.

"How do you do, Pollyanna? I———." She had no chance to say more. Pollyanna had fairly flown across the room and flung herself into her aunt's scandalized, unyielding lap.[19]

All received graceless receptions but made the best of their situations. Pollyanna had quickly introduced her Glad Game to Nancy and went on to acquaint others with it. Anne named the dells, ponds and glades and was *glad* again and again for the beauties of the region. And Rebecca fortified herself with the thought that reward for tolerating Aunt Mirandy would be the formal education and thereafter the ability to earn and help pay off the mortgage on the home farm.

These were the big three of the Cinderellas belonging to the series. Lovey Mary, protégée of Mrs. Wiggs, did not share such limelight. The Dorothy who blew from Kansas to the whimsical land of Oz was an orphan but not friendless. Bluebonnet of Texas lived in an atmosphere of caring people, and Betty Lewis came under the wing of the Little Colonel's mother. In the more ordinary series from this orphan popularity period, those characters lacking parents were on equal footing with members of their particular coteries and were rendered, by friends, the compassion otherwise expected from the reader.

Jolly girls in flocks, not all pretty but usually all attractive for one quality or another even if handicapped, were stock characters. Their writer-parents identified them at the start: one clever of speech, one serious or scholarly, one careless but so obliging and good-natured, one romantic, one a specified leader. In the light-paced series they acted in groups, vacationing together in spots brimming with modest adventures, finding their combined ways to the heart of some enigma, undertaking a project to raise money, playing at romancing. The story, no matter how trivial or outlandish, was foremost.

This was Anygirl, U.S.A., illustrating almost anonymity, and she had a counterpart of Anyboy in like story. Often the paper characters were of one dimension, and a name implied little; one would do as well as the next. Barbara, Joan, Betty, Ruth, Jane. Take your pick, and never mind characterization below the skin. Put the girls into a group, official or casual, and return to the first pages to check on which is from which family or place. Not that it made much difference. Factory-produced, rather than hand-fashioned, Anygirl is seldom memorable.

In one series, the young woman consenting to take office as guardian for a new Camp Fire group, assessed the members.

Babs, she thought to herself, was going through life with both hands held eagerly out for whatever it might yield to her....Marjory was akin to her, but she had more reserve. Rosalie's timidity would cheat her of many good times...and Gladys would plunge into everything thoughtlessly. Clara's dainty aloofness rather set her apart from the others. "Not a good mixer," Phyllis thought. "Well, Camp Fire will change that."[20]

The garden variety was a perennial, making steady appearance year after year under varying names, and probably dismissed from mind when a new book came to hand. Yet with her companions she provided entertainment, showing up in droves during the Twenties.

Feminine freedom of movement and of decision reached an epitome with the intrepid Nancy Drew, born of the Stratemeyer Syndicate when the national financial glory of the country was beginning to dissolve. The fictional American girl of the lightweight class came of age with this mystery-solver who, knowledgeable and logic-minded, followed "hunches" which usually proved productive. She "pondered" problems, visualizing resolutions and outwitting villains. Wise, just and philosophic, she led the way, often in her "snappy little roadster," with less perceptive companions and adults in attendance. Banker Raymond Hill, in one adventure, called her reasoning "marvelous" and proclaimed that Nancy possessed "...the best-ordered mind and keenest ability to put two and two together of any person I ever met."[21] In Nancy's world of endless enigmas, isolated houses boasted secret compartments hiding vital messages written in invisible ink, loose bricks or stones concealing treasures. Skulking strangers invaded private grounds, and individuals of obscure backgrounds needed rescuing. The wonder girl's keen sleuthing forever resulted in reunion and revelation, with identities and riches discovered and properly bestowed. The respect accorded her by almost everyone with whom she came into contact surely elicited admiration from her half-grown readers.

Nor can one overlook the handling by men authors of feminine roles even though no particular individuals rush to the foreground for attention. Of course there was Baum's famous Dorothy, but the Oz fantasy overwhelms characters. Paradoxically, despite the flights of imagination, Baum seemed a realist close to earth, feet firm thereupon, for he dealt with casts of players and their frailties with ease and honesty. Wearying of make-believe land, he wrote girls' series under assumed names, putting together companies of girls with a human touch, balancing them off with clusters of boys for some romance and building up of modest sentiment. His girl "detective,"

Josie O'Gorman, following her dead father's profession in the Mary Louise series, is more believable than Nancy Drew, whose incredulity at times falls into comedy.

Baum had come a long way, both in years and conception, from the earlier male-devised young ladies inclined toward shrieking, coquetry, sweet pouting fits and willingness to remain docilely in the background and allow the other sex to handle delicate situations.

In producing his Bessie, Optic brought forth a simple creature "...too gentle and affectionate to take advantage" of her parents' indulgence. With her adoring father as protector and companion, Bessie went out to enjoy ocean waves.

> A great billow immediately "tipped her over;" but she sprang to her feet again, leaping and shouting with childish delight. Another great wave rolled up, and again she was lifted from her feet like a piece of cork....
> "This won't do, Bessie," said Mr. Watson, shaking his head.
> "Why, pa, I think it's delicious," replied Bessie, in a silvery scream....
> "Be very careful then..."
> "There isn't a bit of danger, pa, not a bit," replied the sylph, as she extended her agile form upon the water, and began to beat blue brine with her delicate little feet.[22]

After the tenth wild wave swept her out and away, hero Levi, in his dory with a load of dog-fish, saved her from disaster, thus opening the way for additional rescues and for romance.

Optic made a try at female protagonist with Katy Redburn in *Poor and Proud*, and Alger, certainly remiss at including budding feminine stars, attempted the same with Tattered Tom, who eventually turned out to be one Jane Lindsay. Both girls fell into the category of street Arabs, and both failed their proper roles and their own sex, for they spoke and conducted themselves primarily as boys.

Stratemeyer used run-of-the-vine girls to bring crumbs of romance among the Rover brothers, but they were less fragile than Bessie of the silvery scream, more of a gingham fabric nature. When Dick kissed Dora's hand one evening in farewell—and this gesture itself was non-typical Rover behavior—Dora's reaction typed her.

> "You're terrible," she murmured, but it is doubtful if she meant anything by it. Girls and boys are about the same the world over, and Dick's regard for Dora was of the manly sort that is creditable to anybody.[23]

The truth was that male authors and boys alike seemed to have little time for girls. Can one wonder? What young heroes preferred was high adventure, and this in company of their own kind and consequently not subject to restrictions. In addition to that, the authors were likely to be uncomfortable with girls. What one biographer said about Optic could very well apply to many of his sex and is a reflection of Mill's judgment of men in general. The conclusion was that Optic "...knew little about girls, who are distinct supernumeraries in his stories, the good little sisters who stay at home until their brothers return to tell them the history of their adventures, and on whose prayers for their safe return the brothers can always rely."[24]

Yet women *had* been "called out;" they had shown themselves indeed capable, capable of constructing a fictional world based on what they believed and on the patterns of their own lives, revealing now and again dissatisfaction with their status. Support for success in their demonstration of their talent appeared statistically in the *Golden Multitudes* records, seven titles winning inclusion as against five by male authors and, in the runners-up listing, six titles, outbalancing by one the performance of men.

Chapter X
As for Heroes

Rollo himself was rather a subject than a hero. Largely he was a means of projecting learning: history, science, morals and behavior, religion, travel. A reader's sympathy, relatively slight, nonetheless is sufficient to the point of feeling relief when Rollo regrets misconduct and makes the state of affairs known, and of mild rejoicing when Rollo reaches a correct decision.

Provided with consciences and ordinarily aware of this invisible equipment, the low-key Abbott characters with their quaint, sometimes quite charming ways, did not always follow those inner voices; here boys were more lax than girls. However, by first teens, disposition was set; adolescents exercised judgment and were capable of handling independence and trust. Even some of the girls came to make and execute plans with competence and to take responsibility for those of lesser age. It was customary that older children counsel the younger but from a neutral position.

Curiously, despite their limited years, employees in several households, Jonas, August and Beechnut, played big-brother roles and gained respect for know-how, general kindliness and ability to entertain with storytelling. Antoine Bianchinette, known as Beechnut and described as "about thirteen," was a special figure. In addition to working at whatever needed doing in the Henry establishment, he carried out commissions in the city for his employers, accompanied the young on excursions, and had instinctive rapport with children. Obviously he is Abbott's model character, and acceptable but for so tender a term of years.

A shy child, thrown into a state of terror amidst a mixed party of young people, responded to none who would comfort her other than Beechnut.

Beechnut...walked up and down the yard, carrying her in his arms.

"I like you *very much*. You are an excellent girl. I am very glad that you are here. I will take care of you. These children shall not hurt you at all...."

Augusta lay with her head upon Beechnut's shoulder, sobbing a little now and then, but gradually becoming more composed....

Presently Beechnut sat down upon a seat in the corner of the yard, and took Augusta down into his lap.

"How old are you?" asked Beechnut.

"Three years old," said Augusta.

"Why, how old you are!" said Beechnut. "Once I knew a girl who was only two."[1]

Expansion of the male character from Abbott originals proceeded in much the same manner as with the female. There was an exception. That was the adoption (earlier than with girls) of the orphan as bound-to-win protagonist. It is true that disaster more often confronted adolescents in 19th century days of briefer life expectancy than today, when agencies give assistance. A boy, and by birthright he was the one expected to assume in some part the responsibility for financial support, became a "man" by circumstances if he had to work rather than attend school. One is not enlightened as to family status of Abbott's singular youths, but well before women writers introduced orphans in great abundance, several men seized upon the plight of the forsaken individual as natural object to summon pity and interest, and bolstered him up with large applications of piety. It was not so much that protagonists voiced sanctimonious phrases but that the all-powerful narrators interceded in ministerial manner to make Christian announcements. This method differed from that practiced by women and needs a brief examination extending to non-orphans as well.

In almost any instance a boy made a brave show partly because of higher rank, an unearned qualification. Too, as with wild birds, the male was more inclined to color than the female. Even while modest he tended toward valor of a physical and sometimes a moral kind. The modesty did not conceal potential strength; the youth performed under the glow of the sun as well as in the dark of the moon. Thus he deviated from his mismatched counterpart, who was bound in speech and action by humility. She had the makings of a lady but needed some disciplining; her awkwardness and her tongue needed refining. Heart was not lacking, but hers was the duty of service to humankind at large: apprenticeship for the universal and educated housewife and mother. On the other hand, the bright-plumed hero, whether cultured or not, was out to shape a high place for himself among the fearless of the universe.

Authors Optic and Alger presented stock heroes to accomplish this in jig time. Never flinching at danger or wavering before temptation, they emerged from any experience as unspoiled beings. Possibly one of their kind should have courted Elsie Dinsmore were he not too gauche to play her suitor.

Levi Fairfield would not have passed muster in the drawing-room of wealth and fashion, or even in the humbler parlor of the Cape Ann nabob....It is quite true that his clothes consisted of as many patches as his sail...and they were daubed...with dogfish slime, to say nothing of numerous dabs of paint and pitch, tar and grease. But underneath his garb of unseemly cut and doubtful unity were iron muscles and a heart of steel.[2]

Cheated by a greedy uncle, this orphan drew approval for "...his mild eye, his gentle bearing, and his noble conduct." Opposites were opposites and there was little in between. Right and wrong, good and evil, white and black were rigid. Valiant qualities increased in contrast to the villain, Dock Vincent who was "...all that is gross, and vile, and wicked." Too, there had to be someone for deliverance, someone helpless and threatened by the evil element. At volume's climax, when Levi appeared beyond the shore with Bessie of the silvery scream, in this instance saved from vicious Dock, joy swept the watchers on the pier.

A deafening cheer rose on the air...Men swung their hats and women their handkerchiefs, and the wave of rapture to the heart of the multitude was mightier than the swell of the sea beneath them.[3]

Hail—the conquering hero came!

Climax of an Alger story, likely to be less dramatic, ended with a flat summing-up. From the first, the Alger boys were of a kind, manly of spirit, blessed with clear eyes and quick wits albeit they were untutored, clumsy of manner or clad in rags and tags. Ragged Dick had not the slyness of some acquaintances, but "a frank, straight-forward manner that made him a favorite." "A bright, intelligent face and fearless look" described Ben Bruce. Tom Thatcher was "a sturdy boy of sixteen with bright eyes and a smiling, sunbrowned face."

With a good share of steadfastness and willingness to strive, customary Alger protagonists were also simple and trusting, revealing private affairs, ready to accompany a stranger anywhere. They shared patient fortitude and the belief that endeavor and uprightness, being superior to "gifts of fortune," would undoubtedly overpower calamity, poverty and obscurity. And in the Alger novels endeavor and uprightness did just that. It was all so easy provided that a boy was of qualifying dimensions. Occasionally an irregularity occurred as in *Sam's Chance*, in which the mission was to "cure a boy of radical thoughts." To accomplish this, Alger placed one of his more fortunately-endowed youths in Sam's environment and supplied opportunities to overcome disabilities and cure faults.

Fates of lucky, plucky Alger youngsters dwelt often upon coincidence, accident, chance, good luck. Sometimes it was the occasion of saving a child from mishap, or returning a watch or envelope of money found on the street or in the pocket of a gift-coat. Rewards for such integrity involved a lump sum of much-needed cash, often a job, sometimes the immediate and total trust of a man of means.

Again, as with Optic, there was some villainous figure for opposition and temptation. "I have got my own way to make," a boy would tell at least himself, "and I want to rise in the world." Or, "I won't despair; I will trust in the Lord." Naturally, possessing a "proper spirit," the protagonist won out. It does seem that such tales were incredibly naive; this condition was, perhaps, typical of an expanding new nation.

A more believable component entered boys' series with the growth of a coterie of more literary men whose aim paralleled the unfoldment of the realistic heroine. Does one imagine that the fashioners of characters with greater fidelity to the human image were intellectually inclined? They were of the same stuff, educators, churchmen, journalists and editors, but they brought naturalness into plots and into the make-up of the human spirit. Theirs were not stick figures but beings exuberant over minor successes, troubled with self-doubt and guilty of self-recognized errors. And they could be serious, giving time to thought and contemplation of their world. Exploits of those in this homelier mold were not of gigantic size, not showy, and evil-doers were not so villainous nor crises so melodramatic even though holding a fatalism from which there was no easy escape. Morality was still strong, but it entailed a struggle against which the untroubled protagonist of simple victory did not have to contend.

Although Butterworth, Knox and Stephens were didactic in their travel series, they displayed more readability in other books. Kellogg fashioned rural boys less prone to consider heroics than to carry out projects conceived on their own or set out by their elders. Unpretentious goals demanded a good deal of labor, physical endurance and sometimes guidance. Beset by the uncertainties of adolescence, these boys learned by doing. Decisions were often their own, ambitions were practical, involving forest and farm, hunting and fishing, all of the occupations that Kellogg himself knew and encouraged.

Witness the appealing reaction of Charlie at the offer of being "headboy" of three who would operate the island fields during the summer absence of his father. Verbal rejoicing in itself was not enough.

"O, wouldn't I?" cried he, jumping to his feet; "won't we raise crops, and have things; won't we make business ache, and tear things up by the roots?"...and he went out of the house capering, and singing "We three young farmers;" and up he went to the old maple, and clambered clear to the top, to sit down on the platform, digest the good news, and lay plans for the future.[4]

Trowbridge characters, too, revealed themselves by comportment and dialogue rather than by bald statements set forth by the author. Youths absorbed in struggle, physical, moral, intellectual, which constitutes the act of living, had little time for grand gestures. Consider two schoolboys, caught in floodtide and finding refuge in an orchard tree, trying to analyze the situation in which their close friendship was ensnared and to puzzle their way out.

For boys, adventure was the pulling power.

"I remember what you said to me that Saturday in this very tree!" Worth broke forth again, but now with less anger than grief. "You could never bear to be separated from me; and if I went away from home, you would go too. You were picking apples from the end of that very limb over your head."

"I remember it," said Chase.

"And now see what you have done! See how we are separated!" said Worth... "We are in the same tree again, but thousands of miles apart. If we had remained friends, and I had gone away, and the whole round earth had been between us, we should still have been nearer together than we are now..."

The emotion...made him eloquent. In reply to this outburst, Chase could only say,— "How could it ever have happened? I don't know!"[5]

Once the relationship was on the mend, the author sent the boys out toward the old sugar-camp for clearing up of the last mysterious occurrences, thus rounding out the story by posing the two against a serene setting.

They entered the spacious woods. Quails and squirrels started up before them, rustling the dead leaves; crows cawed musically afar off in the tall tops. The wild fragrance of woods in early spring filled the air. The forest was like a mighty harp to the sweeping wind.[6]

Like other perceptive portrayers, Altsheler peopled his books with any number of sturdy, down-to-earth examples. Yet he did dare to idealize one of physically heroic mold, Henry Ware, who, however, does not give impression of being faultless.

The leader's head, propelled by the powerful strokes of the arms below, came within a yard or two of the *Independence*, and some stray rays of the moon, falling upon it, brought it from dusk into light. It was the face of a young river god, strong features cut cleanly, a massive projecting chin, and long yellow hair from which the water flowed in streams.

The head was raised from the water, the hands grasped the edge of the boat, and the figure sprang lightly on board, standing perfectly erect a moment, while the water ran from his fringed hunting shirt, his moccasins, the knife and tomahawk at his belt, and flowed away over the boards.[7]

While acting with self-discipline, this youth engrossed himself in stages of learning to meld with the environment, of equaling dexterities of a superior Indian warrior, of discerning the spirit of wild life and of the elements. Like testing required for a coming-of-age rite, his experiences in a primitive land became exalted. The story exudes the flavor of legend or myth.

On the other hand, Burroughs, a writer of another kind, swiftly created, against an exotic background, a totally splendid hero, Tarzan, who attained age ten by page fifty-six and eighteen in fifty additional pages.

The young Lord Greystoke was indeed a strange and warlike figure, his mass of black hair falling to his shoulders behind and cut with his hunting knife in a rude bang upon his forehead, that it might not fall before his eyes.

His straight and perfect figure, muscled as the best of the ancient Roman gladiators must have been muscled, and yet with the soft and sinuous curves of a Greek god, told at a glance the wondrous combination of enormous strength with suppleness and speed.[8]

Add to that magnificent portrait such appurtenances as bow, arrows, scabbard and, about the throat, on a chain of gold, his mother's locket richly ornamented with diamonds.

The brute strength, clever brain and self-determination could be the envy of Anyboy, while the appearance (would Anyboy note that diamond locket?) could certainly incite admiration in one already thrilled by the echoing Tarzan call.

Castlemon, another believer in adventure as foremost demand of his readers, did not give his characters grandeur or depth. His ordinary boys were nonetheless personable. Possessed of obliging male kin willing to endure young company in the early West, two reckless youths of Civil War vintage could fling themselves during one volume into more precarious situations than most males experience within a lifetime. Cautious but indulgent parents seemed aware of the spirited immaturity but seemed also to conclude that boys were going to be boys.

"But remember," said Mr. Winters, "you are to be governed entirely by Uncle James; for, if you have no one to take care of you, you will be in more fights with bears and panthers."

The boys readily promised obedience, and, hardly waiting to finish their breakfast, went into the study to talk over their plans.

"Didn't I tell you there was something up?" said Archie, as soon as they had closed the door. "We'll have a hunt now that will throw all our former hunting expeditions in the shade."[9]

At times Castlemon did confine his characters to a closer environment for their exploits and, interestingly enough, in *Our Fellows*, took time to sketch ably the neighbors composing the band.

Duke Hampton, tall, dignified, handsome and a leader, was the best rider among them. Mischievous Mark surpassed the others in wrestling. Curly-haired Herbert, despite his nicknames of "Chub" and "Duck-legs," was a high-jumper and fast runner. Sandy, scholarly but awkward of tongue, was large, strong and the best shot, while narrator Joseph, owning the finest dog and the swiftest horse, was a champion hunter.

This 1872 characterizing was a form that others would follow but in less pronounced way, to distinguish the grouping that came into wide usage among the commoner series issued in great numbers. Stratemeyer's attempt at it for the Rover series is less explicit. His verbal photograph of the "lively, wide-awake, fun-loving" brothers verges on the dull.

Of the three Rover boys, Richard, commonly called Dick, was the eldest. He was sixteen, tall, slender, and with dark eyes and dark hair. He was rather a quiet boy, one who loved to read and study, although he was not above having a good time now and then, when he felt like "breaking loose," as Tom expressed it.

Next to Richard came Tom, one year younger, as merry a lad as there was to be found, full of life and "go," not above playing all sorts of tricks on people, but with a heart of gold, as even his uncle and aunt felt bound to admit.

Sam was the youngest. He was but fourteen, but of the same height and general appearance as Tom, and the pair might readily have been taken for twins. He was not as full of pranks as Tom, but excelled his brothers in many outdoor sports.[10]

With their father so stricken by his wife's early death that he must move restlessly about and then disappear for a time, the Rovers chafed at life under guardianship of aunt and uncle. Feeling unable to deal longer with the boys, the kinfolk sent them off to school; this situation existed as the first volume opened, and made way for a string of expeditions through book after book.

Nor was there a mother in the Swift household as set up by Victor Appleton, an alias assigned to Howard Garis. Tom Swift was the boy inventor endowed with precocity in the realm of science and with an "aged" inventor of a father who allowed the boy-wonder to go on his own persistent but self-effacing way from airship to submarine to electric rifle to wizard camera and on and on. But not without villainy, mystery and occasional failure, one must add, and not without near-escapes from hot wires, explosions and spies. An advertising blurb in a back-of-a-book page states that "These spirited tales convey in a realistic way the wonderful advances in land and sea locomotion. Stories like these are impressed upon the memory and their reading is productive only of good."

As often with young heroines featured in death-affected series, youthful heroes continued in roles of conveniently parentless or one-parent setting. For boys, death and/or plain disappearance could be advantageous, generating more power and an increase of freedom, a not-so-sad-at-all situation.

In case of living parents, the author could always place the boy far from home to escape supervision. Castlemon followed this route regularly, and Ellis used it as well. His young scouts Ned Clinton and Jo Minturn were forever falling into enemy clutches from which Lena-Wingo, the Mohawk, rescued them.

"Young scout big fool tell him make no noise, then he make noise—when he should make noise, then he make no noise."
And so it was Lena-Wingo! Ned shook off the overwhelming terror that had pressed him down...and spoke in a matter-of-fact voice as he took the hand of the red scout.
"I wasn't quite clear that it was you, and I wanted to wait till I could find out before I showed where I was."
"Next time think of that before whistle."[11]

Heightening the tribulations of the bumbling pair was the now and again presence of Rosa, Jo's sister, who displayed more common sense than the scouts, an unusual touch for a man writer.

While not bestowing prodigious physical prowess on their male characters, the more talented women writers constructed them with more skill than some of their masculine colleagues.

In the first place they did not attempt the boldness of Optic and Alger to give the opposite sex supreme position. A few cast a good many boys of relatively gentle mold in second-place positions. Alcott showed a distinct liking for them and for their traits, as frankly indicated by Jo March, and she felt at ease in dealing with them. Laurie carried a vital role from the start of *Little Women* and on through follow-up volumes. Alcott ventured forth with bands of boys in several books but also gave them the company of girls. While Margaret Sidney finally named separate books after the Pepper sons, she still featured the family as a unit, and Polly and Phronsie as continuing characters of note. Lucy Fitch Perkins' twins, always robust boy and girl combinations, shared the spotlight according to traditional male and female positions.

Heroes and lesser boys conceived by women bore the qualities of sensitivity, gallantry and honor and came in for detailed description. Sometimes they were a bit girlish, which is not surprising. Given names tended toward romanticism, either in sound, association or by means of shortening to nicknames: Laurie, Gilbert, Teddy, Geordie, Jamie, Tommy, Teddy, Prince Charlie, Jasper, Alex and Rob. Sidney presented Jasper King as the young friend of the Peppers whose consideration and courtliness endeared him, and she gave Ben a resolute heart as befitting the eldest son of a fatherless brood. Gilbert Blythe of the Green Gables community had similarly commendable traits, as did the youths of the Little Colonel's sphere; yet now and then a hero transcended reality.

Virtually all were susceptible to the influence of mother, home and heroine figures. An appeal from Mrs. Jo invariably swayed even so rebellious a fellow as Dan of *Little Men* and *Jo's Boys*. Mothering the neglected boys who became pupils at Plumfield, she advised first upon childish affairs and, as the children progressed, upon worldly pleasure and love interest, preparation for profession and, always, on moral standards.

This had all begun early with the prime Alcott hero, Laurie, who received compassionate attention from the March family. Jo, naturally, had been the first to further acquaintanceship with this boy-next-door when she had the opportunity at a party.

...Laurie's bashfulness soon wore off; for Jo's gentlemanly demeanor amused and set him at ease, and Jo was her merry self again, because her dress was forgotten, and nobody lifted their eyebrows at her. She liked the "Laurence boy" better than ever, and took several good looks at him, so that she might describe him to the girls; for they had no brothers, very few male cousins, and boys were almost unknown creatures to them.

"Curly black hair; brown skin; big, black eyes; handsome nose; fine teeth; small hands and feet; taller than I; very polite, for a boy, and altogether jolly. Wonder how old he is?"[12]

Green Gables' Gilbert Blythe, academic competitor of Anne, invited disaster when he teased her. Anne openly ignored him for several years and almost three hundred pages.

...It was Gilbert, and the whistle died on his lips as he recognized Anne. He lifted his cap courteously, but he would have passed on in silence, if Anne had not stopped and held out her hand.

"Gilbert," she said, with scarlet cheeks, "I want to thank you for giving up the school for me. It was very good of you..."

Gilbert took the offered hand eagerly.

"It wasn't particularly good of me at all, Anne. I was pleased to be able to do you some small service. Are we going to be friends after this? Have you really forgiven me my old fault?"[13]

With women, the implication was that while boys might hold more prominent place in the world there was need of feminine counseling and companionship. Men writers, innocently or not, inferred another, unspoken philosophy. They sent their boys expectantly in all directions and left the girl friends, sisters and mothers in limbo. This seemed agreeable to the male section of the population. As a father of two young sons told his wife in a pleasant family-life series when she worried aloud over the danger of a boy-built "rollercoaster" construction on a sharp slope:

"Boys have to take risks, and try experiments, Madeline...It is a sort of miracle that any boys live to grow up, considering all the risks they continually take. But such things help make a boy manly, and give an outlet to his energies..."[14]

As girls' stories moved more and more into romance of varying kinds, so did narratives designed for young male readers become more and more daring. And while romance needed a name, a face, a dream, poetry or a diary, a best friend with compassionate ear, a rival for a while, perhaps, until the knight came truly riding, boys' undertakings demanded audacious action, the more accelerated and the more complex, the better. Thus the plot must be primary and the characters secondary.

By simple statement an author assigned to boys vaguely general qualities of leadership, stamina, some kind of loyalty to the group, and blurred good looks. He built up small heroics with successions of incidents, outrages, mysteries and contests fomented by false and fabricated means if necessary and with the aid of evil-doers. Events built up to peaks of suspense and some kind of triumph. When rate of movement slowed, youths assisted by instigating plots of their own or simply played pranks that might or might not lead to something portentous.

Mark Twain and, in turn, Booth Tarkington, were particularly cognizant of a certain stage in male life, an interlude so adroitly implied by one Sir Francis Doyle and quoted in a volume devoted exclusively to the life of a child in American Colonial days. "It is the intention of the Almighty that there should exist for a certain time between childhood and manhood, the natural production known as a boy."[15]

Certainly the two distinguished rascals of their creation fitting so well the above terminology, stand apart from those young heroes manufactured by the dozen. Irrepressible Tom Sawyer, not disposed to suffer too much, usually managed to circumvent any hazard, while the lesser Penrod Schofield, burdened with sister and parents, left lighter footprints in a close-to-home setting of a more refined epoch. (Peck's "bad boy" is far too gross for inclusion here.) The scrapes of these masters of invention were of their own planning and they devoted their life's blood to the execution. Tom, more than a century old now, has gained virtual immortality. Balancing off his heedlessness, the more serious Huck Finn, marveling at Tom's notions and knowledgeability—and sometimes doubting both—became narrator for the balloon expedition of *Tom Sawyer Abroad* and for *Tom Sawyer Detective*.

How could anyone hope to match this Tom, even though ranging through woods, over plains into mountains and caves, and overseas, afoot, on horseback, by canoe or ship or "speedy little monoplane," by train, dog-sled, horse-cart or any other conveyance discoverable? No trick or scheme or "yarn" could parallel his.

Certainly there was small resemblance in his make-up to Abbott's responsible characters, although now and then Tom Sawyer did accept a little religion at a critical moment. Yet the sober protagonist of Twain's own period, the youth beset by ethical decisions, demand of compromise and tearing away of illusion, vanished from the scene. This non-hero, wistful at moments, perhaps approached the reader too closely. Possibly the delicate nuances in relationships caused unease in adolescence. Mayhap rougher material became more acceptable than the refined, and the coasting-along of characters less exacting to the spirit than the dropping away from grace by individuals like himself.

At, say, fifteen, a boy's face often possesses a poetically dreaming expression not often visible except during private moments or at an instant when caught by professional camera. (Here is the image most used by women writers.) This may be the point from which the possessor begins to depart from the state of sensitive protagonist. After all, the male child was long taught to cultivate the qualities of a man, and the term "man" symbolized so much. It implied stature, visible and unseen, sturdiness, and abundance of strengths and control under almost any condition. The less muscled, the delicate in appearance or temperament indicated, supposedly, less aptitutde at performance in that superior role.

Larger-than-life heroes could draw the reader with the secret acknowledgement that this would be the only way to experience bold and free conflicts with dashing action, startling turns of contests, close succession of exploits with pauses too brief for brooding or reasoning or evaluation. Escapes to vast dreams of glory were possible with gargantuan figures and, after all, the oldest dream had source in first history of the human race.

Tarzan was, of course, of this ilk. Burroughs placed his super-hero in an aboriginal African setting to personify primeval man who hunted and fought in order to survive. Yet Tarzan was not the hairy, animalistic creature in keeping with the delineation of early man. Unclouded eyes reflected astute intellect which with physical powers and comeliness molded him in a semi-deified image.

But the day of the glorious hero faded, too. Youths, leaping their joyous way in limitless land of make-believe, acted together in their high jinks or turned to robots, flying labs and astronauts, cycloplanes and atomicars and other wondrous scientific manifestations.

The realities came in for up-dating, too; Tom Swift, Jr., had a mother, a sister, and a father who was no longer "an old man." Grouped together, brothers and father of the Hardy family operated on a less personal scale than did the Rovers. After all, wasn't the outlook both national and international as the boys assisted their parent after school and during vacation periods in unraveling mysterious crimes and attempts at crime? Meanwhile, alas, it was the same old story for the other sex in boys' books: the mother and aunt remained at home to sew and cook!

Chapter XI
Fanciful, Fictitious and Fabulous

If romance really be, among other things "a fictitious tale of wonderful and extraordinary events, characterized by much imagination and idealization" of "the quality...of excitement, love and adventure found in such literature," all very well. What reader would want to limit it to love? Nearly all fiction, less it be doggedly realistic, is romantic in at least some small way: in atmosphere at moments, in setting, foreign or not, in physical character or individual enterprise, in dramatic situation, confrontation or plotting, in relationships between two or more people, in unanticipated success, in fantasy or in the handling of one of these.

No matter the form in which it appears, romance is the desirable element, the element that provides escape from a world demanding certain standards and certain performance and that gives chance for sailing swiftly away on a magic carpet borne by small visions someone's inner eye has viewed in an instant and captured. Romance is a primary reason for reading.

To the very young, almost everything veils itself with romance, the orange school bus that grinds powerfully around the corner, the grey squirrels making use of a power line as their freeway, the old lady across the street taking her careful constitutional with a broom worn down to a nub serving as staff, the great camphor tree humping roots like the backbone of some recumbent beast and called by the child, for reasons of his own, "the elephant tree," "*my* tree," and "the umbulla tree."

Those who write well for children know intuitively of this aura upon what seems commonplace to the ordinary adult eye. Those who write for children have usually associated with them in school room or library or semi-recreational organization and/or have had direct hand in their rearing as parents, aunts and uncles or grandparents. The first-rate among them have retained as part of their make-up the chimeric eye of the child, the imagination, the fleeting revelations that come and go like candle-flames in the wind. Along with that they have thus retained natural right of entry into that never-never land from which fiction emerges.

Even Jacob Abbott was not beyond an occasional romantic touch although one must watch for such manifestations. Formal education for the small girl of the Lucy Books began with attendance at a "family" school, one conducted for children of a particular household but gathering in a few others as well. In the school above the gardener's quarters, children had leave to move about and converse quietly until the teacher gave a signal for attention, and during recess they could run about the gardens so that a day at school was a pleasant and pleasurable time. There was one rule that the children observed, however, and the symbol was "a large plume, made of three or four peacock's feathers." Lucy learned the first day of the significance of so fanciful a device.

Marielle told Lucy that when the plume was lying down, they might all talk, but, then, when the teacher put it up in its place, at the end of the table, then it was study hours, and they must not talk at all.[1]

This romantic "notion" was at least a start. One hundred years thereafter, Mrs. Wilder's plain pioneering tales were not too distant from that cultured New England scene in that they enacted themselves on a simple plane. In her case the environment was romantic for its isolation and danger; yet an innocence often lay over a landscape, an innocence as luminous as Laura's fingers would appear were she to hold them up to clear sunlight.

Laura and Mary stayed near the wagon...They looked at the prairie grasses swaying and bending, and yellow flowers nodding. Birds rose and flew and sank into the grasses. The sky curved very high and its rim came neatly down to the faraway edge of the round earth.[2]

Well after Lucy's time and long before Laura's, Horace Scudder was treating young children with extraordinary delicacy. In the Bodley family, Nathan was brother to lively Philippa, who was Phippy at home, and to an even smaller and sensitive Lucy. When the Mouse Castle and its two white inhabitants came from Aunt Lucy's home for Nathan's birthday, the children were entranced.

"Father," said Nathan after supper, "I do believe that these mice like music. I have been singing to them, and they stood still, close together, right here on the Pavilion. I could see their hearts beat."

"Oh play the bagpipe to them, papa!" cried Phippy....

"Oh," said Lucy, softly, and looked at her father rather anxiously.

"Well, Lucy," said he, "shall I play it?" She came close to him and whispered in his ear.

"I don't believe I'll play the bagpipe," said Mr. Bodley. "These mice are city mice, and I don't believe they ever heard such queer music..."[3]

A household on another plane, as that sustained by Mrs. Pepper for her five children, could have—indeed needed—brushes with romance. When a family had nothing but affection plus potatoes and bread enough to stay alive, there was only one way to go. An author was bound to introduce good fortune a crumb at a time without ever overdoing it. That Phronsie should be lost was a shocking misfortune but that Jasper King should rescue her brought romance to the situation and the beginning of advancement for the group. There was the mutual adoption, person by person, to begin with, and finally of entire families, to give a steady turnabout to the well-being of the brown-house residents and a sense of family to the King father and son. There was also the mutual adoration of old Mr. King and Phronsie and the growing devotion of Jasper and the Whitneys, his sister's family. Kind Dr. Fisher came to marry Mrs. Pepper and, as if that were not all romance enough, add the discovery that Mr. Whitney and Mrs. Pepper turned out to be cousins who had lost sight of each other several decades earlier.

A writer could pile high occasionally and over a period of time, this thing thought of as one kind of romance, and still not spoil the original goal. Margaret Sidney did that when allowing Polly and Ben and their mother to make "a real Christmas for the children," and then heaping on further surprises thanks to the Kings and the neighbors.

> Down the stairs they went with military step, and into the Provision Room. And then, with one wild look, the little battalion broke ranks, and tumbling one over the other, in decidedly unmilitary style, presented a very queer appearance!
>
> And Captain Polly was the queerest of all; for she just gave one gaze at the tree, and then sat right down on the floor, and said, "OH! OH!"
>
> Mrs. Pepper was flying around delightedly...there were the laughing faces of Mrs. Henderson and the Parson himself, Doctor Fisher and old Grandma Bascom...
>
> "It's Fairyland!" cried little Davie, out of his wits with joy...[4]

The readers wanted more for the Peppers; they wanted all that was possible, and they participated, somehow, in the giving as well as in the worry of mishap, because the Peppers so deserved something good. Longing for it, waiting, they became as breathless as Polly when Christmas and that "fairyland" arrived.

A confrontation of the Little Colonel, an only child, with her haughty grandfather was a down-to-earth kind of romance. Theirs was a case of family relationships marred by pride, with the high-tempered old man living in the pillared mansion at the far end of a road, and the child and her mother residing in a cottage not distant. The set-up was right for clashing, and the old colonel roared out his wrath in those early days.

> "What does your mother mean?" he cried savagely, "by letting you run barefoot around the country just like poor white trash?....I suppose it's some of your father's miserable Yankee notions."

...The same temper that glared from the face of the man, sitting erect in his saddle, seemed to be burning in the eyes of the child who stood so defiantly before him. The same kind of scowl drew their eye-brows together darkly.

"Don't you talk that way to me," cried the Little Colonel, trembling with a wrath she did not know how to express.

Suddenly she stooped, and snatching both hands full of mud from the overturned pie, flung it wildly over the spotless white coat.[5]

Such an act of challenge as this flinging of the mud finds joyous acceptance in the heart of the young reader. It could be girl or boy, in case of the very young, who feels pleasure from open rebellion in instant reaction. Such, too, is the case with whimsy of the kind that men, more than women, interestingly enough, built up in stories to relate to their children, and preferably with the use of a whole repertory of suitable voices. Such impromptu recitals likely include incredible action and violence, but small children not only accept but relish either quality.

Bruno Bettelheim maintains that the fairy tale communicates vital information to a child: "...that a struggle against severe difficulties in life is unavoidable, is an intrinsic part of human existence—but that if one does not shy away, but steadfastly meets unexpected and often unjust hardships, one masters all obstacles and at the end emerges victorious."[6]

With fantasy and its varied crowd of beings not limited by real boundaries, almost every detail of plotting verges on romance and out-of-this-world ingredients. The prime example in series is that site somewhere over the rainbow where the Land of Oz exists.

Baum was that story telling father operating by car, so to speak, inventing anew from moment to moment, spinning out details captivating to a child, with imagination leaping from here to there and back again and then off on another tangent. The illogical is perfectly logical when it concerns diverse creatures from wizard through superhuman being to Tin Woodman, from witch to winged monkey, from hairy beast to wooden saw-horse brought to life. In the land of make-believe, unlikes live in harmony or battle each other with wits and fantastic forces.

While the father represented by Baum tells marvelous tales at an idle hour or during a long drive across country, Baum wrote his. And after a while children sent him their ideas, and he wrote that the children were his assistants, that their ideas were often clever and worthy of incorporation in Oz books. Everything under the sky became animate under Baum's pen; astonishing situations abounded, and magic and wickedness a-plenty spiced the action.

Now the Wicked Witch of the West had but one eye, yet that was as powerful as a telescope, and could see everywhere. So, as she sat in the door of her castle, she happened to look around and saw Dorothy lying asleep, with her friends all about her. They were a long distance off, but the Wicked Witch was angry to find them in her country; so she blew upon a silver whistle that hung around her neck.

At once there came running to her from all directions a pack of great wolves. They had long legs and fierce eyes and sharp teeth.

"Go to those people," said the Witch, "and tear them to pieces."[7]

Hugh Lofting was the same kind of yarn-spinner, but Doctor Dolittle's exploits appear rather pale set next to Oz activity. His characters were largely gentle and of pleasant water-color tinting. There were lions and monkeys, too, as well as such domesticated friends as Polynesia the parrot, and Jip the dog. The realm of Doctor Dolittle, lacking the spine-tingling violence of Oz, has a sunny charm all its own which opponents of Dr. Bettelheim's theories would approve.

...A fine rainy mist lay on the sea like a thin fog. And the wind was soft and warm and wet.

As soon as Jip awoke he ran upstairs and poked his nose in the air. Then he got most frightfully excited and rushed down to wake the Doctor up.

"Doctor!" he cried. "I've got it!...The wind's from the West and it smells of nothing but snuff. Come upstairs and start the ship—quick!"

So the Doctor tumbled out of bed and went to the rudder to steer the ship.

"Now I'll go up to the front," said Jip; "and you watch my nose—whichever way I point it, you turn the ship the same way. The man cannot be far off——with the smell as strong as this...."[8]

As the child progresses in age he may come to prefer something nearer reality so long as it is not beyond his achievement, knowing that while fantasy figures experience what is out of his reach, the accomplishments of beings like himself can always be focus of hidden desires. Of course Baum brought reality into Oz, too, when the seekers finally discovered that the wizard was but an apologetic man who revealed that they already had within themselves the very things they hoped he would supply.

Although girls were partially in the background, the fictional sky was still relatively unclouded by discrimination because of the clear division between books written for children who had reached an easy reading stage. And imaginary characters did not *have* to go afar for adventures; it was hardly feasible if they were of tender age. It was even possible to draw into the home-scene, drama splendid enough to the eye and mind for in-between groups of readers by the use of day-dreams.

Tarkington's Penrod trailed imaginary clouds of glory occasionally with a mythical audience of pretty Marjorie Jones, but Tom Sawyer ventured beyond that. Mark Twain utilized a host of romantic elements: exploration on island and river and in cave, night-time excursions, court scene and church drama, graveyard, witching, charms and a villain, hidden treasure, lost children, elementary girl-boy alliances, battles of wit and day-dreams enacted in play and in truth. The result is a sort of compromise between the generations, a give and take, and a settling upon ways to have the best of several worlds. Tom's fantasizing carried him far from his confining environment and, not surprisingly, each ensuing volume sent him out and away, though not exactly as he had dreamed.

But the elastic heart of youth cannot be compressed into one constrained shape long at a time. Tom presently began to drift insensibly back into the concerns of this life again....What if he went away—ever so far away, into unknown countries beyond the seas—and never came back any more! How would she feel then!...No, he would be a soldier, and return after long years, all war-worn and illustrious. No—better still, he would join the Indians, and hunt buffaloes and go on the warpath in the mountain ranges and trackless great plains of the Far West, and away in the future come back a great chief, bristling with feathers, hideous with paint, and prance into Sunday-school....But no, there was something gaudier even than this. He would be a pirate!..."It's Tom Sawyer the Pirate!——the Black Avenger of the Spanish Main."[9]

It is somewhere here that expectations of romance in fiction parted company, with boys heading in a direction of variegated topography of a half-known world, and girls for some serene, less distant landscape in direct harmony with what lay behind them. (It was not until World War I stories that girls ventured across the ocean on their own, and then the mission was likely to be that of ministering to the other sex.) The divergence was in keeping with the ranks thrust upon them by dissimilarities of sex, both physical and emotional, and the anticipations of society that they continue in assigned roles.

The male position was foremost and the female stood but in its long shadow, reaping little more than a reflection of that romantic status and potential. After all, man had always been first, and the belief stood that woman was incapable of physical feats by reason of delicacy and lack of aggression, and that her intelligence was also less able.

Primed for some sort of grandeur, the male mounted a mythical hill for a view. The prospect encompassed dimensions that swept from mountain to jungle, primitive land to city, continent to continent, with opportunity for ingenious and astounding exploits. Romance lay free for encountering hazards at any point of the compass, and there was promise of treasure or laurel leaves, challenge of strength and resulting grandeur.

The earlier authors of boys' books transformed their protagonists, providing that they were God-fearing, with the aura of extravagant personal success leading to their becoming ships' captains or astute men of business. Alger dealt with the romance of such success gained by reason of industry and Christian principles. It was his formula, used forever with changes of names and conditions and sometimes old-time melodrama, although the finale was usually tame. His sixteen-year-old Tom Thatcher, shoe-factory employee at fifty cents a day and supporting mother and sister, spent several months making his way from east to west coast in an attempt to locate his father, who had disappeared eight years earlier. Good men, recognizing immediately Tom's purity of spirit, assisted at freeing him from scoundrels' clutches, restoring the father's gold "fortune," and ascertaining the whereabouts of Mr. Thatcher, who had suffered memory loss after being beaten by his partner. After all the trials, including a term spent as Indian captive, Tom brought his father home, where the villain's identity was revealed. Alger pronounced the finale in customary low-key style.

> It is not certain that Tom will remain long in Wilton, or in his present business. He has a handsome offer from Samuel Perkins, of Pearl Street, New York, whose papers he restored, and as he would like a larger field of action, he may remove to New York and become a commission merchant.[10]

Tom Swift, being Tom Swift, had the talent of turning out almost any amazing invention that came to mind and was accustomed to success, which he accepted with unassuming modesty. He could and did divert flooding waters about to burst a dam by flying off in the Humming Bird, his trusty airship, to get the necessary powder for his giant cannon. The cannon had already proved its prowess in testing.

> Tom rushed from the bomb-proof, dropping the electric button. He caught sight of his gun, resting undisturbed on the improvised carriage.
> "Hurray," he cried in delight. "She stood the charge all right. And look! look!" he cried as he pointed the glasses toward the distant hillside. "There goes my projectile as straight as an arrow. There! By Caesar, Ned! It landed within three feet of the target! Oh, you beauty!" he yelled at his giant cannon. "You did all I hoped you would. Thirty miles, Ned! Think of that! A two-ton projectile being shot thirty miles!"[11]

Score another victory for Tom Swift, naturally. Later, depraved spies notwithstanding, Tom triumphed with a demonstration of the cannon for "the entire ordnance board" of the United States government.

> "We shall certainly recommend your gun, Mr. Swift," declared the Chief of Staff. "It does just what we want it to do, and we have no doubt that Congress will appropriate the money for several with which to fortify the Panama Canal."[12]

Tom's spectacular deeds overshadowed Castlemon's light-hearted young fellows whose patriotic instincts led them to enlisting or who set out eagerly on other expeditions for excitement. Romantic escapes could occur at a furious speed. At one point Frank Nelson himself caught up and reviewed experiences just to wonder at their number and variety.

> What astonishing adventures had been crowded into the short space of ten hours! Frank's mind was in a perfect whirl; and, if he could have freed his hands, he would have pinched himself to see if he was really wide awake. But, after all, he knew that

the events of the day were no dream—his aching limbs and throbbing head assured him of that. The fight with Old Davy, Archie's mishap, and his mysterious disappearance at Don Carlos' rancho, the death of the trapper, and the unexpected encounter with Pierre Costello—all were realities. It was no dream, either, that he had been bound to a tree and left in those dark woods; and it was equally certain that he was not the only living thing there. He heard a stealthy step on the leaves, and a moment afterward, saw a pair of eyes, which shone like two coals of fire, glaring at him...[13]

By contrast, adventures of the Rover brothers seem humdrum. However, Stratemeyer occasionally managed a flash of girl-boy liaison. When it was Tom's turn for that kind of compact, there was Nellie. After his rescue at the close of the Alaskan adventure, in she walked again.

"I just had to come," she said, and then she caught Tom and held him tightly. The tears were streaming down her cheeks, and the others had to turn away. "Oh, Tom! Tom!" she murmured, over and over again.

"Oh, Nellie, don't make such a fuss! I'm not worth it," murmured Tom, but nevertheless, he looked greatly pleased....[14]

Ellis was equally unadept. As though roaming in woods among Indians and enemy troops were not an exciting enough situation for his naive scouts, he attempted a similar plan of mixed company, but gave to Rosa, sister of one of the scouts, a role of prominence. Ned Clinton nurtured romantic thoughts of Rosa, and when the Mohawk announced her capture, both brother and admirer fell into a state of paralysis, and Lena-Wingo had to rouse them.

"Two of them—three of us," he called out; "come 'long—soon catch—take her away again."

The ringing words roused the others from the stunning shock of the tidings that Rosa was a captive in the hands of the Iroquois, and while the Mohawk moved off they followed him as before. Neither spoke, but their lips were compressed, and there was an iron resolve in the heart of each. If Rosa was a prisoner, she should not remain so! She should be rescued; the foul hands of Colonel Butler should never be laid upon that pure, spotless maiden; no, never![15]

It was Burroughs who could out-romance any of them. Episodes in any volume, if the setting be the African jungle, are extravaganzas with beasts and Tarzan interacting, natives and Tarzan, foreigners and Tarzan. The whole concept of the boy brought up by and among apes is luxuriantly romantic and harks back to legend. The battles between good and evil, between civilized and primitive, go on and on. Surely those three "f" adjectives applied to the noun "romance"—fanciful, fictitious and fabulous—are relevant here on almost any page. The marvel lies not in the described relationship of the mutually-worshipping lovers but in background and setting, circumstances and bold action. Yet the intrepid narrator brings in tones of sexuality that in their own way rival Elinor Glyn of *Three Weeks* and *It* fame.

Note Tarzan's amazement in the long watch at the window of his old cabin. Within, Jane writes a letter by lamplight and then prepares for the night. His yearning to communicate must go unfulfilled, but her beauty enchants him.

> Then she loosened the soft mass of golden hair which crowned her head. Like a shimmering waterfall turned to burnished metal by a dying sun it fell about her oval face; in waving lines, below her waist it tumbled.
>
> Tarzan was spellbound. Then she extinguished the lamp and all within the cabin was wrapped in Cimmerian darkness.[16]

Pages later no cabin wall stood between them. His courting he had accomplished with secret gifts of food and continuing protection. When came the need to rescue Jane again, this time by battling old Terkoz, the girl rushed into Tarzan's arms, and Tarzan dared to respond to the embrace. In humiliation at her own emotion, she then resisted, but a turning point had arrived, and Tarzan followed his instinct.

> Since then Tarzan of the Apes had felt a warm, lithe form close pressed to his. Hot, sweet breath against his cheek and mouth had fanned a new flame to life within his breast, and perfect lips had clung to his in burning kisses that had seared a deep brand into his soul—a brand which marked a new Tarzan.
>
> Again he laid his hand upon her arm. Again she repulsed him. And then Tarzan of the Apes did just what his first ancestor would have done.
>
> He took his woman in his arms and carried her into the jungle.[17]

This is a long way from the occasional touch of another kind of romance with which the resolute writers of the late 19th century might deck their series. More realistic, more in the manner of the steadfast women writers, they looked to day-dreams or insights and nature for fleeting moments of illusion. Kellogg had brought Indians into his New England based fiction but as storied creatures in tales related by the old to the young. And the young so idealized these previous inhabitants of their land that when the Elm Island boys rated a vacation after hard work, they chose to go off and camp Indian fashion in the woods.

> They sewed the sheets of bark together, lapping them over each other like shingles; and as they wanted the fire inside when it stormed, they made a cap of bark to fit the top, with a space under it, to let the smoke go out, but so fixed that the rain could not beat in to any great extent. Never were any creatures more happy, as they sat chatting and sewing.
>
> "I wish we had been Indians," said Charlie.

"So do I," said John. "What a good time they had, the bays full of geese and ducks, and the woods of deer, bears, wolves, beavers, and Indian devils!" It was night when they got their camp done and fire built. In the morning there was a gale of wind and a rain storm, but not a drop of water came through. Proud of their skill, they thought themselves veritable Indians [18]

Nor was romance in distant places always so fervent as in Burroughs' Africa. It proved rather an inactive ingredient in books written according to the adult mode of the day when travel for youth seemed equated with concentrated education rather than plain enjoyment or stimulation. The encyclopedic pages of Knox's Boy Travellers do furnish some appeals to the senses, even though they be second-hand, to tickle the imagination. Street-cries in Cairo offer sound and color to one of the solemn books of the series.

...the water-carrier has a goat-skin on his back filled with water, and as he goes along he rattles a couple of brass cups together, and cries out, "Oh ye thirsty! Oh ye thirsty!" A moment after that he repeats the call, and says,"God will reward me!" And sometimes he says, "Blessed is the water of the Nile!"...The orange peddler says, "Sweet as honey, oh oranges!" And the seller of roasted melon-seeds says, "Comforter of those in distress, oh melon-seeds!" Behind him comes a man selling flowers of the henna-plant, and his cry is "Odors of Paradise, oh flowers of henna!" The rose-merchant says, "The rose is a thorn—it bloomed from the sweat of the Prophet!"[19]

Coming to authorship later, Altsheler nurtured perceptions and imagination that stemmed from verbal recountings absorbed during childhood. His interest in Francis Parkman and his careful research lifted one series to a plane sometimes poetic as well as romantic in a remarkably pure way. Characters allying themselves with nature, Indians, wild animals and communication with and understanding of these components, became mythical, but the union is not only believable but also enthralling.

Consider Henry Ware moving through primeval country alone and reaching a confluence of man and his universe.

He sped down the stream with long, silent strokes, keeping always in the dusk of the overhanging foliage. The stars came out, and with them a full, bright moon, which he worshiped as a sign and an emblem of the Supreme Will that had saved him. He fell into an intense mood of exaltation. The powers of earth and air and water had worked together in a singular manner. Never was his fancy more vivid. The flowing of the stream sang to him, and the willows over his head sang to him also. The light from the moon and stars grew. The dusk was shot with a silver glow. Apprehension, weariness went from him, and he shot down the river, mile after mile, apparently the only figure in the ancient wilderness.[20]

Placed beside romantic elements in series for girls, the Altsheler visions crest beyond the peaks of even the most imaginative reality. However, it is the spiritual plane that invites viewing, a plane scarcely approached by

Foreign settings were not alien among the series.

any other of either sex. Yet this was the realm envisioned by the more serious of the women. That they did not achieve it rested upon what? The restraint they were forced to observe? Fancy's inability at uncurbed flight? Plain domesticity?

Their spirits flew to idealization of components near at hand, and this idealization remained within the confines of possibility for their kind. With the mind's magical eye they looked ahead or into the clouds, picturing what *might* come to pass at some time or other. Grandiose dreams could build up, but they remained more dream than not; they became reason for hoping, reason for affection, for enduring, for virtue, and reason for being. Women writers exercised a regulation of the imagination's wanderings, resigning themselves to settle for a cautiously enhanced reality. That was proper for their sex and for approved comportment. There were never wild oats for sowing and opportunity for unrestricted roving for this segment of society with limited public image and prescribed borders.

Even young Rebecca Randall and some of her peers understood this.

"...Boys always do the nice splendid things, and girls can only do the nasty dull ones that get left over. They can't climb so high, or go so far, or stay out so late, or run so fast, or anything."[21]

So it was that girls found their creative world close to home and security of family. It built itself on personal relationships, innocently idyllic feeling between friends, sometimes even with male friends, and with special adults who might be kin, teachers, ministers' wives or happenchance acquaintances. For instance, Gypsy Breynton had a satisfying relationship with her older brother, and a comforting one with her mother. At times she was self-sufficient, being well-adjusted. In her way she was unique among fictional compatriots for she was not wistful, not without friends, and yet was no goody-goody; probably she committed at least one gross error per chapter. But that was Gypsy.

Gypsy's real name was an uncouth one—Jemima. It was partly for this reason, partly for its singular appropriateness, that her nickname had entirely transplanted the lawful and ugly one....But Gypsy's name had undoubtedly been foreordained, so perfectly was it suited to Gypsy. For never a wild rover led a more untamed and happy life.[22]

Gypsy was by far more vigorous than the Little Colonel who, outgrowing her rather imperious nickname and outbursts, found the one-time boy playmates referring to her as "Princess." Special friendships with both the young and adults marked that whole series and many others as well.

Pollyanna, almost totally involved with adults, instantly won the hearts of domestic help in her aunt's home and charmed the bad-humored recluse, Mr. Pendleton; the invalid, querulous Mrs. Snow, Dr. Chilton and, finally, her own aunt. In the end, Pollyanna brought people together. Mr. Pendleton and the orphaned Jimmy, Aunt Polly and Dr. Chilton, Aunt Polly and herself. It needs remembering that Pollyanna's habits are a bit unexpected, for she coos, gurgles with laughter or delight, purrs, and claps her hands as well as playing the Glad Game; after all, she is eleven years old.

This sort of sunny heroine appeared a bit earlier when Emma C. Dowd began a Polly series. Because of her masterly storytelling and cheering ways, orphan Polly May, after long treatment in a hospital's children's ward, joined the staff by invitation rather than return to the ex-officio aunt's crowded and unattractive home. At close of volume one, when Dr. Dudley and the nurse Miss Lucy married, Polly became their legal daughter. This Polly went into print in March of 1912 and soon found reason to express the quality that made her a favorite with both optimists and pessimists.

"Oh, I'm so glad, glad, glad!" breathed Polly, clasping the note in both her small hands.[23]

Yet sunbeam that she was, Polly did not gain the publicity of Porter's Pollyanna. Perhaps it was because as the story opened she already occupied a royal position with the children and most of the staff. This Miss Sunbeam did too much as she skipped her way in and out of the hospital and people's lives. Within the initial two books she restored one aging lady to life, psychologically, as it were, helped others retreat from the very edge of death, and linked together an overabundance of twosomes, children and adults, adults and their peers. Romance surged floodlike, and three different sets of householders begged her to leave her adoptive parents and come to live with them. Can you believe it?

Of the other young misses, Anne Shirley of Green Gables found quick rapport only with old Matthew Cuthbert and best-friend Diana; she might otherwise have perished or been sent back to the orphan asylum. Fortunately the shy Matthew from the beginning realized the vulnerability of "this stray woman-child."

> Matthew had taken the scrawny little hand awkwardly in his; then and there he decided what to do. He could not tell this child with the glowing eyes that there had been a mistake; he would take her home and let Marilla do that. She couldn't be left at Bright River anyhow, no matter what mistake had been made, so all questions and explanations might as well be deferred until he was safely back at Green Gables.[24]

Gradually Anne found other "kindred" souls, including Mrs. Allan, the minister's wife, and in ensuing volumes there appeared regularly children and adults with whom she felt empathy. She made of the Green Gables community a totally romantic place, perhaps because of being so starved for ordinary affection, family and friends, and a niche in the world, and sight of any dale, woods or path suggested poetic titles.

Sunnybrook's Rebecca was less a dreamer, but her very appearance suggested romance. Naturally her aunt saw nothing of the kind, but the stage-coach driver, Jeremiah Cobb, did.

> ...a small plain face illuminated by a pair of eyes carrying such suggestions, such hints of sleeping power and insight, that one never tired of looking into their shining depths, nor of fancying that what one saw there was the reflection of one's own thought.[25]

Rebecca and Mr. Cobb wasted not a moment in reaching a state of mutual admiration and friendship which Mrs. Cobb, too, came to share. They became Rebecca's protectors and confidants.

Possession of a hyperactive imagination makes for fancies of all kinds and aids in enduring tribulations. With friends, both Anne and Rebecca instigated home-drama, as did the Little Colonel and her companions, and the March daughters of *Little Women* plus the following generations of that family. Young girls, particularly the lone and unattached, needed that, along with devoted friends of several generations, diary-keeping, poem-writing and secret pacts and societies. These pastimes numbered among the "adventures" possible to their sex.

Alcott's romantic streaks were always under control and she found place for everything among the struggling family with adored parents, the bevy of girls well delineated as individuals, the wealthy old grandfather next door and his wistful grandson. True, the sentiment between Laurie and Jo verged on the uncomfortable when moving beyond the easy brother sister relationship, but numerous other instances attest to romanticizing: association of shy Beth with old Mr. Laurence and comradeship between Jo and Mr. Laurence, the separate triumphs of the sisters, the introduction of Professor Bhaer, who became Father Bhaer of *Little Men* and *Jo's Boys*.

The rosy scenes of the latter presented the new generation preparing for professions or studying the arts, so that Daisy's housewifery seemed tame if safe and necessary. There was as well the handsome young wanderer returning with pockets gold-filled and adding mystery and speculation. And all the while the characters from the first volume of the series re-appeared as adults acting as friends and mentors and confidants in an idyllic background: the endowed college setting with Professor Bhaer as president and Jo herself as famous novelist toward whom visitors thronged almost daily.

One might choose as more endearing from this strong series, a homely example as characteristic of Alcott's talent suggesting mystery. With younger players she devoted herself more to storytelling and its intricacies and less to preaching. Her romantic spirit evinces itself immediately in a rather over-shadowed volume.

The elm-tree avenue was all overgrown, the great gate was never unlocked, and the old house had been shut up for several years. Yet voices were heard about the place, the lilacs nodded over the high wall as if they said, "We could tell fine secrets if we chose," and the mullein outside the gate made haste to reach the keyhole, that it might peep in and see what was going on.[26]

If the most forceful of the series are those volumes in which the author herself figured, fictionally speaking, who would cry "Unfair!" The mainstay of the family, Louisa, needed some nourishment, some romance herself, and she accorded the best parts to Jo. A girl could find tears in her eyes regularly through *Little Women*; yes, it *was* a "pathetic family."

There is this to note, that romance in later volumes of any girls' series could not match the drama of the first. That was customarily the failure of a succession of books, and yet when a reader yearned for more, she rarely complained. So long as there was great need of improved situation of the heroine, the book-lover found herself enslaved. Stories such as the fortunes and misfortunes of the cluster of children and their father in the Katydid series seemed not to penetrate as deeply as some other groups. Such recountings are pleasant to follow but if children are already endowed with a good deal, sympathy toward them does not expand. This is true, too, of other series.

By the time that the Alcott life and career ended, Laura E. Richards was beginning a fanciful plotting not yet much seen. Hers was, of course, a more sophisticated world than Louisa's, both in reality and in fiction, and she herself confessed to being "cradled...in poetry, romance and philanthropy." There were governesses and tutors in this home of Dr. Samuel and Julia Ward Howe, and the Hildegarde of the Richards series simply cannot summon compassion of the reader, for it is not needed. However, the first book, with its pastoral setting, presents formally-educated characters balanced off by country people of great kindness and perception, the old nurse of Hildegarde's mother and the farmer-husband.

Queen Hildegarde concerns not only an adolescent girl but a treasure brought back by an old sea captain two generations removed, and buried in the wheel-pit of the unused mill. It is a story of the robbing of Farmer Hartley and of Hildegarde's accidental discovery of the old treasure box when she climbs down to rescue the small dog which a young thief had thrown into the abandoned place. The complications of plotting have increased here and foreshadow later use and popularity of mystery novels. However, here the characters claim attention for their individuality.

"Oh, Hilda, dear!" cried Dame Hartley, "we have been terribly frightened about you. Jacob has been searching—..."

...The girl's dress was torn and draggled, and covered with great spots and splashes of black. Her face was streaked with dirt, her fair hair hanging loose upon her shoulders....But her eyes shone like stars, and her face, though very pale, wore a look of triumphant delight.[27]

After the three rejoice at the miraculous turn of fortune allowing financial rescue of Hartley Glen farm, the farmer again gives contrast to the city-bred girl who grew from snob to appreciative and sympathetic young person trying to take the place, temporarily, of the daughter lost to the household.

But the farmer, to his own great amazement, was crying. He sobbed quietly once or twice, then cleared his throat, and wiped his eyes with the old silk handkerchief. "Poor ol' father," he said simply. "It seems kind o' hard that nobody ever believed him, an' we let him die thinkin' he was crazy. That takes holt on me;...Seems like's as I'd been punished for not havin' faith, and now I git the reward without havin' deserved it."[28]

That all ends happily for Dame Lucy and Farmer Hartley, for Hildegarde and Pink and Bubble Chirk, the neighbor children, is something expected in a romance like this. Formerly governed by a supercilious trait, Hildegarde provided a tender example for the girls coming to the series world later and helping work sinuous ways to the clearing of less poignant enigmas.

Lacking such mystery, but related in sense of background and frequent dream-like impressions, the Little Colonel, growing tamer along with her domineering grandfather, also figured in another era and in comfortable and kind circumstances. Johnston's soft, overall film of romance never faltered as she carried Lloyd Sherman into an exploration of adolescence. The quality sustained the series, supplying the poetic atmosphere that an unsophisticated reader could find so entrancing.

> One is a mariner at sixteen, sailing toward an undiscovered country, with seaweed and driftwood on the crest of every wave beginning to whisper "Land ahead." Toward the dim outline of that untried shore, Lloyd drifted now in her reverie.[29]

That gentle veiling dissolved with the passing of time, not to reappear. Day-dreaming became briefer and writers were more down-to-earth. One who followed, and who turned out a set of classics read and used for decades in special school editions, was Lucy Fitch Perkins, who at times made use of intrigue. The initial romantic element in her Twins series was, naturally, the foreign setting. In the case of the Scotch twins she compiled situation, country setting and speech, easy-to-like children and an easy-to hate scoundrel for a lively conspiracy. Bound together as the Rob Roy Clan, the twins and two friends investigated the poaching and other activity of Angus Niel, the game-keeper.

> "I've been thinking about this," Alan began, "and I'm sure of two things Angus must have a place where he puts the game he kills, and he must have somebody to help him. The other man comes along and carries it down the mountain to some point where he can ship it to the city. I say, let's find out where that hiding place is."
> "What will we do with it when we find it?" asked Jean.
> "That's where the blue chalk comes in," said Alan, "We'll let him know we've been there!"
> "You'll never be writing your name there?" asked Sandy anxiously. "He'd be shooting us next!"
> "Oh, Sandy, you're a daft body" said Jean, and Jock added: "Mind the Chief, you dunderhead, and keep your tongue behind your teeth. He's none so addled as you think!"[30]

Thus did romance touch, linger, enfold character and setting, happening and outcome. In one way or another, it set a reader to dreaming, colored his behavior, and sent him on to more books as well as back to those already read. Whatever its form, romance satisfied a need and a hunger.

It was not only the child, orphan or not, or the uneasy adolescent caught in the in-between transitional land, who found romance an ally. There was also Mrs. Wiggs; it fed her spiritual appetite as well. First off it was a geographical gesture. She had named her daughters after continents, Asia, Australia, Europena and, at son Billy's request, supplied the name of Cuby for the old horse they nursed back to health. The whole family learned to expand its limited sphere in such ways, and the philosophy spread to Cabbage Patch neighbors and newcomers. Out of a will to survive she *thought* romantically at times. When Lovey Mary came on the scene and needed encouragement, Mrs. Wiggs helped her to improve her appearance, praised the white teeth that showed when a smile appeared, and to Lovey Mary's complaint of ugliness, cautioned her not to feed on self-pity. To achieve this she used a reverse sort of romanticism, her own kind of Glad Game.

"Ain't you proud you ain't got a harelip? Why, that one thought is enough to keep me from ever gittin' sorry fer myself."[31]

Chapter XII
Dispensation of Moral Philosophies

Good Children muft

Fear God all Day,	Love Chrift alway,
Parents obey,	In fecret pray,
No falfe Thing fay,	Mind little play,
By no fin ftray,	Make no delay,

In doing Good.[1]

Cultivation of morality was a fact. To begin with, it was an adult duty to practice and to show by example, to set up standards as visible as wooden hurdles, and to inculcate in the minds of infants and children the goal of Christian living, which itself embodied the morality preached. With it walked fear. And even when books of decent fiction found approval with the aim of entertainment as well as instruction (which with most writers and teachers meant moral instruction), and, later, entertainment itself as intention, morality seldom fell entirely away.

There is nothing bad about this. Tiresome, perhaps, but not bad. So long as the writer was a bit subtle the reader could feel a bit righteous. He would by osmosis absorb something of the virtue of the characters, particularly if he admired them. And he could easily skip over "preachy" passages; long practice at selective Sunday-School-paper reading simplified this. Who would not rather wander through a world where some morality and order exist than in one where no criteria at all influence human behavior? Even a young child, despite what he may say in a fit of rebellion, is more comfortable in a daily world of control.

In spite of ironic remarks and ironic criticism of any art or attempt at art which is over-sweetened, there has been a turning back to a sort of Christian brotherhood, to a caring for others as well as for oneself and one's own small coterie of intimates, to a humanism, an acknowledgement of other people and other countries. Whether we like the relativity or not, this concern is the basis of Christianity and of other great religions.

Perhaps it is partly the old fear associated with morality that is bad, fear that God might be displeased, fear that not heaven but a dreadful inferno awaited one. Yet a feeling of, let us call it respect, respect for the unknown, may not be other than sage. Witness the perceptive observer expressing the opinion that there is greater indication of intelligence in young children who display a reluctance at or fear of rushing into something not yet experienced than in those who throw themselves without hesitation into whatever tempts them and then emerge from the experience howling, unhappy or insulted.

In the old series, morality gradually became seasoned and reasonable. There is nothing offensive in, say, the brief pronouncements of the parents and the reactions of the daughters in the Little House books which, although begun in the 1930's, have settings of a much earlier epoch. Indeed, the firm indications of morality strengthen the stories and the characters. One cannot ignore this part of the American heritage, this necessary under-structure of honor and Christian doctrine. The formal education of most writers included religious training to some extent and, sometimes, study for theological degrees. Obviously their home instruction would have done the same, and their basic professions often expected the knowledge and demanded the practice.

It would appear from the supply of old books directed toward women and the treatment of the subject of behavior that society assigned the guardianship of morals to that sex. Could this be a reason why morals expounded by such as Optic and Alger seemed to be tacked on, rather than embodied in development of character and plot?

The Ladies' Guide to Perfect Gentility, first entered in the 1850's, devoted its pages primarily to well-being, to manners and dress at home, abroad, and in "gentlemen's society," and instructed in subjects of beauty aids, physical care, and needlework of all kinds. It also touched upon wife and husband relationships and modest conduct that implied indirectly the application of The Golden Rule.

However, the American Tract Society published *The Young Lady's Guide*, which was of far more sober content, being a compilation of "papers" and letters from writers including Dinah Maria Mulock Craik (author of *John Halifax, Gentleman*), Henry Rogers (who termed most novels "trash"), British reformer Hannah More, and several clergymen. References to godliness are liberal in use, and more than one writer spoke to young women with obvious intent.

...where truth is reverenced at home, where charity is the prevailing spirit shown in the simple affairs of every day, and especially when it forms a prominent and lovely feature in the mother's own character, her children, habitually living in and breathing in an atmosphere of truth and charity, will grow up with characters formed upon this basis, and to them it will become principle.[2]

Hannah More, who stated that it was "...the character of the gospel to exhibit a scheme of principles...," described Christianity in the following manner.

...a new principle infused into the heart by the word and the Spirit of God; out of which principle will inevitably grow right opinions, renewed affections, correct morals, pure desires, heavenly tempers, and holy habits, with an invariable desire of pleasing God, and a constant fear of offending him.[3]

The clergyman who brought the book to a close, as though offering the prayer at the end of an elongated church service, gave a spectacular verbal performance.

Woman is the mother of the human race; our companion, counsellor, and comforter in the pilgrimage of life, or our tempter, our scourge, and our destroyer. Our sweetest cup of earthly happiness, or our bitterest draught of sorrow, is mixed and administered by her hand. She not only renders smooth or rough our path to the grave, but helps or hinders our progress to immortality. In heaven we shall bless God for her aid in assisting us to reach that blissful state, or amid the torments of unutterable woe in another region we shall deplore the fatality of her influence.[1]

Some years after that solemn handbook appeared, a volume subtitled "A Book for Girls and Women," but penned by a man playful enough to be named only as The Author of "How to Be Happy Though Married," "Manners Makyth Man," etc., came from the press of Charles Scribner's Sons. Titled *The Five Talents of Women*, dedicated to Ruskin and to the author's wife, it is a rambling chatty tome. The thesis appears within the first paragraph in large calligraphic type, and numbers four and five of that thesis put the burden directly upon the feminine sex.

The five talents of women are those that enable them:
1. To please people.
2. To feed them in dainty ways.
3. To clothe them.
4. To keep them orderly.
5. To teach them.[5]

This unknown may have been truly admiring of woman or he may have been using her in order to find excuses for the faults of man, or for "buttering up" his own spouse. Certainly he does pay tribute with such pronouncements as "Woman may be the weaker vessel, but she isn't broken up and doesn't go to pieces as soon as a man." And "We believe that the greatest help a wife can give to her husband is to induce him to do what is right."[6]

The book *Good Manners* is truly an advisor on the subject of etiquette, which overlapped morality. Opposite the first page of the introduction appear three maxims, one of which poses earlier judgment: "Manners are the lesser morals of life," ascribed to Aristotle. An unidentified person's warning is: "Guard the manners if you would protect the morals."[7] Still another such volume give space to George Washington's "Rules of Civility and Decent Behavior in Company."[8] A scan of books on manners brought out from the beginning of the 20th century reveals emphasis upon proper etiquette for all occasions, with photographic illustrations, and implication, at least, of consideration for others.

Moral philosophies appearing in print, along with Sunday worship and schoolroom lessons, crossed over into the content of children's series. As decades succeeded each other the concentration upon ethics diminished. Its teaching took on some disguise, thus becoming less direct, but it was there. Textbooks shared in this. Their authors set out Christian principles as such, and did not veil them as fiction writers learned to do. Consequently such teaching had a greater part in classroom instruction than in fiction. Examination of 19th century readers shows pages overflowing with moral declarations.

Reluctant recognition did come that sin did not lie in reading for pleasure as well as for learning. Even if youths ignored the piety running through a story they would absorb the pedagogy to some extent. And fiction writers would not put piety entirely aside. The verbal pointing would never quite vanish, but found reward for many a year, while mean conduct resulted in contrition and/or chastisement. If the philosophy holds true that a child must like himself in order to be comfortable, then likely his instinctive conscience will bid him mind his manners and his morals. Disapproval from some direction can be a strong guiding force, and it is natural to desire approval. It is also natural to conduct oneself sometimes with grace, sometimes without it, and of this children are quite conscious. To behave only with piety is non-human, and they perceive this as well. A small person's impulsive avowal of "I *like* to do bad things" is not shocking, and even as the "bad" child or animal in a story elicits excitement in a young heart, the drama may carry away with it the urge of reader or listener for defiance. Once that is taken care of, he will be right in there applauding the fate of, say, the wicked performance in the tale of the three little pigs. To a three-year-old who begins that story himself with "Once upon a time there was a big, bad wolf," the drooling beast is both hero and villain and takes care of the unacknowledged desire to disrupt the occasionally too virtuous world around him.

Finally the pages of run-of-the-mill series became pale in moral-dispensing and often in realistic liveliness, too. One presumed by the action and speech that fictional boys and girls were aware of good and evil, right

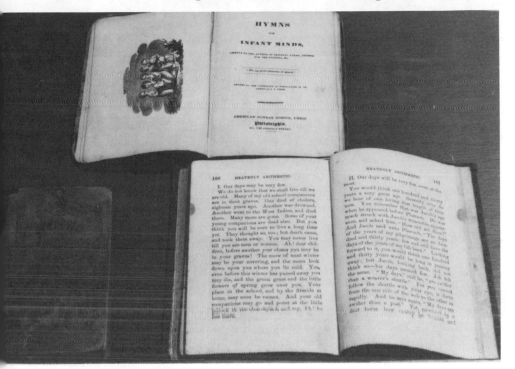

After such spiritual fare as above, the Rollo Books could seem deliriously escapist.

and wrong. Yet conditions became too easy; too few obstacles to personal success and triumph existed. Living lacked challenges, for existence was a long vacation from any demand or notable expectation. There was no particular progression, and that is more irritating than subjection to too many trials. Reality is more threatening than that; one still had to do some measuring up or succumb. And how quickly a reader sides with a character who must pit himself against other characters, situations or threats!

Jacob Abbott did not make morality a frightening element. Although preoccupied with presenting information, he still never omitted the precepts of honorable behavior leading to a disciplined life. About this he was never unpleasant or intimidating. It was just that a child should learn to fulfill the anticipations of preceptors and parents and accept a wisdom that made for a reasonably assured relationship with himself.

Abbott's adults were invariably kind if firm in their guidance of the young. When a London pickpocket helped himself to Rollo's purse, the boy wished aloud that he had, after all, spent the money for the watch chain that had tempted him.

"How unlucky it was," said he, "that I did not buy that chain, instead of saving the money to have it stolen away from me!..."

"No," replied Mr. George, "you ought not to be sorry at all. You decided to postpone buying it for good and sufficient reasons of a prudential character. It was very wise for you to decide as you did; and now you ought not to regret it. To wish that you had been guilty of an act of folly, in order to have saved a sovereign by it, is to put gold before wisdom...."[9]

Some stories lacked the little congratulations that Rollo's uncle tendered him. The praise must have acted as at least a thin salve on Rollo's feelings. Responsibility, like a Christmas pudding, weighed heavily, but it was not very plummy. Yet all of the early writers considered it vital. All such burdensome traits as humility, forbearance and fulfilling of obligation were necessary to personal structure, and sometimes a child rebelled and needed setting right by a patient adult.

Susy Carroll, a child of fiction, was not uncommon, and author "Cousin Mary," pausing in her story to give instruction, turned the session into a catechism of sorts.

"I hate *duty*, mother; it is always disagreeable. Everybody has to do what they don't want to. Does everybody have duties?"

"Yes, my child; every one, young and old."

"*Little children*, mother?"

"Yes; it is the duty of children to love each other; be kind when playing together; to be obedient to their parents and teachers; respectful, attentive and courteous to older people, and do all they can to make others happy around them..."

"O mother, are all these things you teach us *duties*?"

"Yes, my daughter; and it is one of my many duties to teach you these things. Little children are given to parents that they may love them, and teach them to be unselfish, and all that is good and holy..."[10]

Now that is a massive and indigestible lump to serve up in what passes as fiction. A decade later Sophie May was putting out incomparably more palatable stories. Her series never lack a few moralistic turns and phrases, and yet a reader of distinct empathy with young children remembers not the solemn concerns of duty and God but the traits and ways of those refreshing scraps of humanity bearing such names as Prudy and Susy, Percy and Dotty, Horace and Flaxie and Grace and all the others. Although several of the names came by reason of sound and diminishment to suggest false virtues, it is not true that these children were all sweetness and light. They were not, and there was no resemblance to Elsie Dinsmore.

The Sophie May moppets were full of joy, oftimes, and always believable; they were naughty with human regularity; it was hard for them not to behave like unpredictable human beings. They became jealous, selfish, angry, rude and thoughtless. Yet they were alternately kind and sympathetic and certainly loving and endearing. Their tongues ran away with them, as the phrase goes, and they could be headstrong. As every child knows, they had to *learn* some sort of goodness, and moral training was a part of the scene of their day.

When Prudy fell on the stairs as Susy verbally "hurried" her on Christmas morning, and sustained an injury that showed up only after time passed, it was the Quaker Grandma Read who could best comfort Susy, who felt guilt.

"But, Susan, thee must think how innocent thee was of any wrong motive. Thee did not get angry, and push thy little sister, thee knows thee didn't, Susan. Thee was only in a hurry, and rather thoughtless. The best of us often do very foolish things, and cause much mischief; but thee'll find it isn't best to grieve over these mistakes. Why, my dear little Susan, I have lived eight years to thy one, and if I should sit down now and drop a tear for every blunder I have made, I don't know but I could almost make a fountain of myself, like that woman thee tells about in the fairy story."[11]

The young Bradfords of the Bessie books seemed to avoid many pitfalls by means of household prayer sessions and discussions with their father. Bessie and Maggie needed further clarification on a subject, in one instance, and Papa was glad to oblige.

"...You mean if Bessie and I were to put all our money into that box...and just count it and count it, and never take any out, or spend it for the library or anything else, we would be little misers even if we are not old men?"

"Papa," said Bessie, "yesterday morning at prayers, you read about the lord who went away and gave his servants money to take care of, and how one of them put his money in a napkin, and dug a hole in the ground and hid it there; and when his lord came home, he was angry with him, and punished him. Was that man a miser?"

"Yes, dear, I think we may call him a miser...We may be miserly with other things than money. If we do not use any of the gifts which God has given us as he intended we should do, for our own good and that of others, we are misers..."[12]

For all their grave discussions, Maggie and Bessie and their brothers were somewhat human at moments. As for the little heiress Elsie Dinsmore, described as "so meek and patient," she can speak for herself.

"No, Lucy,... I cannot disobey papa, even if he should never know it, because that would be disobeying God, and He would know it."[13]

So intense was her piety that she could quote long Bible passages at will without eye-reference to the source of goodness and humility from which she preached. This was one reason that kinfolk among whom she lived found her tiresome and took advantage of her saintliness to make life miserable for her. Even if today's reader disapproves of Elsie's kin, he is still irritated beyond measure with behavior so maddeningly unreal. Several volumes later she began the morning with her own Elsie, Eddie and Baby Violet.

"...'God is love!' Never forget it, my darlings; never forget to thank Him for His love and goodness to you; never fear to trust His love and care. Can you tell me, dear, of some of His good gifts to you?"

"Our dear, kind mamma and papa," answered Eddie quickly, leaning affectionately against her, his dark eyes lifted to her face, full of almost passionate affection.

"Mammy, too," added Violet.

"And dear, dear grandpa and grandma; and oh, so many more," continued Elsie....

"But Jesus the best gift of all, mamma,..."

"Yes, my precious ones," returned the mother, in moved tones...[14]

Isabella Alden's characters, also directly concerned with Christian living and teaching, moved against harsher backgrounds than the wealthy one of Finley. Julia Ried had problems all along the way, and Dr. Douglas counseled her.

"Do you find rest and peace in your religion nowadays, Julia? Do you find comfort in prayer?"

"No, I do not," I answered with quivering lip. "I try to pray, and it seems to me that I can't. I am not at rest at all. I don't know anything about peace. My heart is all wrong, and I can't get it right."...

"Why, my dear child, don't you see you have reached the very center of all the trouble?...Why not take it all to Jesus and tell him: 'Here, Lord, is my heart; it is all wrong. *I* can't do anything with it. Create in me a *clean* heart, and renew a right spirit within me.' "[15]

The preface to Optic's *The Boat Club* expresses the author's intent "...to combine healthy moral lessons with a sufficient amount of exciting interest to render the story attractive to the young." Like others, this author provided contrasts with extremes of behavior, opposites of characters and with diversified displays of emotion. One Optic hero, Paul Duncan, had deliberately disobeyed his mother in taking out the boat during a "blow" for the purpose of making fifty cents as well as accepting the dare of his friend. The result was not the swamping of the boat or the failure of Paul to prove his courage. Whatever victory he felt was more than cancelled out that very day, for his father fell from the ship on which he was working, sustaining fatal injury. Capt. Littleton gave Paul the news.

"...I am afraid he is very badly hurt....He is conscious, and asked for you...."

Paul burst into tears at these words, for he realized the nature and depth of his mother's feelings...and how bitterly did he regret his act of disobedience! The dreadful event had come to intensify the anguish of his penitence, and he felt that, if he had not done wrong, he could have met the calamity with patience and resolution. When children do wrong, they know not what event may occur to increase a thousand fold the bitterness of their remorse.[16]

Forthright Horatio Alger habitually stated moral precepts early, late and in between. There was nothing subtle about the introduction of uprighteousness and unrighteousness, nor was there meant to be. As did Optic, he delivered a statement to fortify the point.

The author trusts that John Oakley, his young hero, will find many friends, and that his career will not only be followed with interest, but teach a lesson of patient fortitude and resolute endeavor, and a determination to conquer fortune, and compel its smiles....[17]

Others were kinder to their readers. After all, youths could associate cause and effect and try to live up to standards without didactic preaching. Better series incorporated a more subtle treatment. Trowbridge made his occasional messages more personal and thought-provoking, as when his boys, after a good deal of country drama, became friends once more.

"But it was foolish in me to stick to it as I did," said Worth. "I never like to be put down, you know. Though I ought to be willing to be put down by you, especially when you're in the right."
"Pshaw!" Chase replied, with a modest laugh and blush. "I had no idea of putting you down. I wouldn't do such a thing for the world; and you know it, Worth."
"Of course I do," cried Worth warmly. "You are a most generous fellow! But it was your duty to set me right, when you knew I was wrong."[18]

Nor were Kellogg's young people shy about expressing their feeling for each other. One of them, Walter, away from home, was reminiscing about a conversation with Charlie Bell on an evening when the two were sitting under an oak tree at Pleasant Cove.

"...he said there would be nights at sea when the moon would be shining on the ocean, just as it was then upon the waters of that cove; that he should look at it and think of me; hoped I would look at it and think of him and his words; and that as the same planets were above us, so the same God was around our daily paths..."[19]

Charles Stephens was of the same school. The "war-waif" circle of six cousins figuring in some of his stories measured up to the standards of the Old Squire, their grandfather, or endured the consequences. But he was a fair and kind man. When Addison, the leader, proposed a new contract for a work project in the maple grove, the Old Squire stated his position.

Gramp glanced at him and divined his motive instantly; for he was very quick to appreciate a touch of sentiment. But he only laughed. "No, no," he said, "we will stick to our agreement. You couldn't make a young man of me again, if you were all to try ever so kindly," he added. "I have had my time. Others must soon take my place. It is the law of nature. The main thing is for each one to do his part well, during his allotted time." With that he abruptly dismissed the subject and began to speak of the fire-wood for boiling the sap....[20]

In that era Sunday meant church attendance, possibly twice. The children prayed at bedtime and might take part in family prayers, too. In New England Sunday began at Saturday's sundown. The small Kendall offspring felt the burden of obligation when Saturday's sun began to lower. One had to cease playing, study the Sunday lesson and submit to bathing.

...Sunday wasn't so bad after you were actually in it; some parts of it were rather pleasant than otherwise....The children all felt that it was Sunday, partly from the deep stillness, partly because they were oppressed by the solemn consciousness of having on their best clothes....[21]

The procedure of self-improvement through Sunday service and teaching usually met with snags. No one, least of all that rebel Mark Twain, could take Tom Sawyer's efforts at reformation very seriously. Tom's occasional resolutions fell away from him at almost the slightest touch; observance of the moral code existing in the village was terribly dull and led nowhere. However, even though he was wretched with fear thereafter, his inner unease sent him finally to reveal that it was Injun Joe, not Muff Potter, who killed young Dr. Robinson there in the graveyard. It would seem that young boyhood ought to be a golden period not much hampered by restrictions of any kind. So went the dream of Samuel Clemens.

James Otis' Toby Tyler certainly did not find it roseate. Only too soon he discovered that existence was harsh, demanding payment for transgressions and for any kind of spiritual well-being, too. There was no struggle with young Toby at coming to terms, and he expressed this himself.

He ran down the gangplank before it was ready, and clasped every boy he saw there round the neck, and would have kissed them if they had shown an inclination to let him do so....

Some of the boys ventured to predict that Toby would get a jolly good whipping for running away....

"I hope I will, an' then I'll feel as if I had kinder paid for runnin' away. If Uncle Dan'l will only let me stay with him again he may whip me every mornin', an' I won't open my mouth to holler."[22]

It was not to follow custom that Elizabeth Stuart Phelps introduced a controlled amount of moral instruction into Gypsy Breynton's life. After all, the writer was daughter to a clergyman, herself studied theology and used religious motifs in adult fiction. Yet for her time her touch was light. No one knew what Gypsy would do next, and everyone wondered. Even Gypsy wondered. As a younger child she had identified her primary fault, that of ginger-beer's being one ingredient of her make-up and of the cork's popping at the wrong moment. After her most frightening escapade, Gypsy ended up with "golden mottoes" to help her remember. Mrs. Breynton supplied them.

"It is all the old trouble, Gypsy,—you 'didn't think.' A little self-control, a moment's quiet thought, would have saved all this."

"Oh, I know it!" sobbed Gypsy. "That's what always ails me. I'm always doing things, and always sorry for them. I mean to do right, and I cannot remember...."

"Gypsy," said her mother, very soberly; "this will never do. You *can* think...You must learn to think..."[23]

In the literary world of this era a girl usually discussed her shortcomings with her mother in this way. Such talks seem the low points of a story, and a reader finds it easy enough to forgive Gypsy her transgressions; she is that personable.

The March sisters were more often plagued by duty and virtue than by outright misdeeds. For one thing, both parents appear rather saintly; one can guess that saintly people have no trouble in being good and that they expect their progeny to live up to parental standards. Good Mr. March, conveniently gone from home as a chaplain for several hundred pages, did his counseling by letter to his wife, who in turn read the letters aloud to the assembled family.

"...I know they will remember all I said to them, that they will be loving children to you, will do their duty faithfully, fight their bosom enemies bravely, and conquer themselves so beautifully, that when I come back to them I may be fonder and prouder than ever of my little women"[24]

It was simple, during the get-togethers at evening in front of the fireplace, for Mrs. March to instruct her girls. The same evening that saw the reading of the above letter she reminded them of earlier days when they played Pilgrim's Progress and ascended from the City of Destruction to the top of the house to build a Celestial City. Mrs. March told the girls that they were never too old for such journeying.

"...because it is a play we are playing all the time in one way or another. Our burdens are here, our road is before us, and the longing for goodness and happiness is the guide that leads us through many troubles and mistakes to the peace which is a true Celestial City. Now, my little pilgrims, suppose you begin again, not in play, but in earnest..."[25]

One must admit that Alcott sermonized regularly. *Eight Cousins*, a novel of the same series, however unrelated, seems at times a virtual compendium of moral reminders having to do with healthful ways of living, with comportment, slang, personal habits, and nourishment of the spirit. Is "refinement" the key word, perhaps, in the effort expended toward a cleaner, neater, purer way of thinking and living?

Here the speaker is "Mrs. Jessie," mother of the three most attractive boy cousins of Rose. It was by no means the first time she had railed against lack of quality in fiction which her sons were reading, stories of "scapegraces and ragamuffins." However, this time young Archie and Charlie had made a pact with Rose to give up their cigars if she would give up wearing earrings, and Mrs. Jessie was wishing that another such agreement might do away with rubbishy reading matter.

"But my sons are neither boot-blacks nor newsboys, and I object to hearing them use such words as 'screamer,' 'bully,' and 'buster.' In fact, I fail to see the advantage of writing books about such people unless it is done in a very different way. I cannot think they will help to refine the ragamuffins, if they read them, and I'm sure they can do no good to the better class of boys, who through these books are introduced to police courts, counterfeiters' dens, gambling houses, drinking saloons, and all sorts of low life."[26]

There is little doubt but that Louisa Alcott was thinking in terms of dime novels and of writers like Alger. Passage after passage concerns just such protagonists used again and again by series authors writing for cheap magazines. She believed that vulgarity, wickedness and false ideals were set forth, and wished that stories might be "...lively, natural, and helpful,—tales in which the English should be good, the morals pure, and the characters such as we can love in spite of the faults that all may have...."[27]

It did seem, indeed, to be women's role to put forth week-day sermonettes whether they had training in theology or not since they had the upbringing of children and were by their place in the world supposed to occupy pedestals of a sort.

Margaret Sidney's morality was observable, too, but it was of homely kind associated with family sentiment and individual behavior. Duty impelled Polly Pepper to do what she believed right and thus deprive herself, but carry out her concept of the only way she could live with herself. Polly went through painful hours chastising herself for not remembering her mother's counseling that insult could not harm if nothing were said or done in return. As a result, she subjected herself to active penance. She had a prime example in her mother.

"Mother's rich enough," ejaculated Mrs. Pepper; her bright, black eyes glistening with delight, as the noisy troop filed back to their bread and potatoes; "if we can only keep together, dears, and grow up good, so that the little brown house won't be ashamed of us, that's all I ask."[28]

While the Oz books incorporate ethical principles in abundance, those principles often go unexpressed. Like Mark Twain, Baum had a mischievous turn of mind and often phrased beliefs, as he did humor, in a backward or roundabout manner. The story was the thing. Yet he did put into the mouth of Ozma a very plain declaration when news came of invasion of the Land of Oz by tunnel.

> "But I do not wish to fight," declared Ozma, firmly. "No one has the right to destroy any living creatures, however evil they may be, or to hurt them or make them unhappy. I will not fight—even to save my kingdom."[29]

In orphan-heroine series the virtues received equally candid treatment. There was little chance to stray from the path of righteousness when the combined eyes of the community were on the watch. Volatile Anne Shirley wished for a flowery name, a romantic, dreamy name, and asked Marilla to call her "Cordelia." Marilla refused, of course. She saw not in terms of imaginings but in terms of bare truths.

> "I guess it doesn't matter what a person's name is as long as he behaves himself," said Marilla...[30]

Rebecca, trying to add small adornments to her unembellished life, was forever transgressing. Her Aunt Miranda knew how to bring her down to earth.

> "...An ounce of good behavior is worth a pound of repentance. Instead of tryin' to see how little trouble you can make in a house that ain't your own home, it seems as if you tried to see how much you could put us out...."[31]

Pollyanna's strong point was a philosophy supported by that copyrighted Glad Game; yet duty and the eight hundred Biblical texts formed the underpinnings. She pointed out to her maiden aunt that according to the schedule of instruction no time had been allotted for "just living."

> "...Just breathing isn't living!"
> Miss Polly lifted her head irritably.
> "Pollyanna, you *are* the most extraordinary child! You will be allowed a proper amount of playtime, of course. But surely, it seems to me if I am willing to do my duty in seeing that you have proper care and instruction, *you* ought to be willing to do yours by seeing that that care and instruction are not ungratefully wasted."[32]

In the Little Colonel books there was no cause for harsh counseling; guardians discussed need for correction in a calm and firm way, and characters worked at improvement. The standard of behavior was sweetly dreamy and considerate wherever it appeared. It embraced a cheerful, inspiring, a pure and perfect code of honor. Bearing the misfortunes of life was easier when one had not only the beautiful people of that world but also a noble goal to fix the eyes upon.

When Phil Tremont hopefully and romantically offered Lloyd a bit of turquoise he had carried as talisman, he suggested having it set in a ring for her.

> "No," she answered hastily. "I couldn't do that. Papa Jack wouldn't like it. He wouldn't allow me to accept anything from a man in the way of jewelry, you know. I couldn't take it as a ring. Now just this little unset stone"—she hesitated. "Just this bit of turquoise that you say cost only a trifle, I'm [sic] suah he wouldn't mind that. I'll tell him it's just my friendship stone."
> "What a particular little maid of honor you are!" he exclaimed....[33]

Mrs. Wiggs was of quite another world, but her spunk and determination could nearly always discover a way out of any dilemma. She had organized an afternoon Sunday-School class and found it difficult to retain control there in her house with the mischievous children of the Cabbage Patch.

> "What I think you childern need is a talk about fussin' an' fightin'. There ain't no use in me teachin' what they done a thousand years ago, when you ain't got manners 'nough to listen at what I am sayin'... First an' fo'most, I am goin' to learn you all manners...."[34]

Once the assortment of children had sung "Pull for the Shore," she prayed over them briefly. It was a matter of fitting the lesson to the time, to the background and to the variety of persons involved, and some writers managed this with a certain finesse. Witness Lucy Fitch Perkins when dealing with her twins in beleaguered Rheims.

> The Verger nodded. "That is true," he said, "yet it is hard to smile in the face of sorrow."
> "But we must smile—though our hearts break—for France, and for our children, lest they forget joy!" cried Mother Meraut. She smiled as she spoke, though her lip trembled. "I tell you the truth, Henri, sometimes when I think of what the Germans have already done in Belgium, and may yet do in France, I feel my heart breaking in my bosom. And then I say to myself, 'Courage, Antoinette! It is our business to live bravely for the France that is to be when this madness is over....' "[35]

When men and women wrote for themselves and were not for hire, feelings ran deeper, principles were more clear-cut, characters more firmly drawn. By the time that the common series took over the market, the stark realism had vanished. No longer did protagonists face painful decisions and contemplate or discuss ethical matters. Less weighty subjects replaced bald morals just as books on etiquette alone supplanted those dealing at least in part with comportment. As consequence, series were less colorful, less definitive, and readily forgotten.

With interest primarily in adventure, characters as well suffered loss of distinction. They might appear mischievous at times but one expected them to be good-natured and reasonably thoughtful of siblings. Occasionally a player might introduce the possibility of reform to an evil-doer. Stratemeyer had already set an example with his Rover brothers. Dick had just managed to free himself and get out and away from the cottage in which the blackhearted Mr. Baxter had imprisoned him, when lightning struck the house and set it a-flame. (Was this the hand of heaven intervening?) The thought of even a villain in danger sent Dick back to find Mr. Baxter caught under brick and stone fallen from the fireplace. Forcing entry and dragging the man to safety made a hero of Dick. In due time Mr. Baxter was contrite, and requested that Dick come to see him.

"I—I want to thank you for what you did, Rover," said the criminal in a low voice. "It—it was noble, very noble. I shan't forget it."

"Mr. Baxter, why don't you try to turn over a new leaf?" questioned Dick. "Haven't you found out that it doesn't pay to be bad?"[36]

Of course Stratemeyer did have cultivation of moral character in mind. In the introduction to *The Rover Boys in Alaska*, he implied intention of some sort of instruction through the series. After exclaiming over the total of sales of the Rover books, he mentioned his gratitude to readers and their parents and ended with "I trust with all my heart that the reading of the books will do the young folks good."

With those not yet ready for adventure of the Rover kind, the hints at immoral behavior were relatively impersonal, and sometimes so slight as to involve careless language which adults deemed "not nice." The little broods loved their parents and numerous aunties and grandparents, and the kinfolk in turn cared for the children and were ready to take them to the country or the sea-shore or just a-picnicking in the woods in order to widen their experience and give them pleasure. The small Bunkers, once voyaging by steam-ship, heard a lesson expounded with the crew's rescue of a wounded sea-eagle

...The quartermaster declared that, without much doubt, the bird had been shot at from a small boat and by some idle and thoughtless "sportsman."

"It is wrong," Daddy Bunker said, "to call such people 'sportsmen.' There is no real sport in shooting at and laming an inoffensive creature, one that cannot be made use of for food. That excuse does not hold in this case."

"True word, sir," said the quartermaster. "It was a wicked trick, I'll say..."[37]

In the Little House books, everyday life with strict but loving parents demanded observance of philosophy of a bygone day. Its tenets were as clear as prairie sunlight and applied to minor moments as well as large issues.

After the crisis of the Indians' visit, Pa repeated a condensed rule for the girls: "Do as you are told...and no harm will come to you."[38]

He might have added that the Ingalls children should behave in the way expected of them. They knew very well what that meant, and they had always known. It was not always simple, however. When Mary, for whom it was so, so easy to be good, gave up her share of the beads found around an old Indian encampment, Ma expected Laura to give up hers, too. For Laura it was terribly painful to follow Mary in sacrificing the beads for a necklace for Baby Carrie. Even while the sisters sat threading the beads Laura did not want to look at Mary because of the impulse to slap her. Yet there were no two ways about it; there was no choice.

Life following World War I, however, did not require heart-rending decisions in the expanded nation. It was more comfortable; the outlook was one of prosperity; the moral code was fading; Sunday was a day for diversion, too, and church attendance could give way to recreation. The population generally believed that it was better to observe conventional precepts, and that right would win and villainy would bring punishment. And a show of virtue in children could be a sop to adults, including those who expected meritorious conduct from children even while, secretly or not, disregarding ethics in their own worlds and justifying that disregard.

Chapter **XIII**
Caprice and Comicality

One of the pleasures of reading lies in actual and immediate expression of emotion as eyes move from page to page, chapter to chapter. Such is not possible with all emotions because some of them are secret and to be guarded, for their revelation might bring embarrassment. The quickening sense of romance, or of expectation may make the heart pound unseen; tears might need hasty rubbing of the eyes; private joy might add boisterousness to behavior. But one could always chuckle, allow his sense of amusement to bubble, and read aloud to anyone within hearing a phrase or paragraph, because it is hard not to share witticism or humor.

Another characteristic of the series was to incorporate some humor if at all possible; this custom was not one confined only to series. Everyone, almost, likes the vivacity of the capricious. An unexpected touch of whimsy, if harmonious, alleviates sober plotting, eases a critical situation or supplies a tender element to an earnest characterization. There were times that such humor was labored as well as times that it was quite in accord, depending upon the writer's ability, his philosophy and his imagination.

Contemplating accumulated series, a woman may wonder if the feminine sex lacks a substantial sense of this effervescent quality or whether her serious attitude toward the world (and perhaps her treatment by it, as well) has made her seem to be lacking this attribute. Observation shows that it is the male who is wont to play practical jokes, devise incredible tales based on little or nothing, laugh at accident or error, maintain and relate a repertory of "jokes," and express mirth both in the telling and the listening to others reciting their own. Inhibited by tradition, woman perhaps confines herself to the narrower space allowed her. For all her yen for romance and dreaming, she has had to be plain practical as house-keeper, wife, instructor, mother-to-the-world. Yet her perception of humor, such as it has been along the way in children's stories, appears more natural if controlled than that of the male. She has almost never played the clown, the jester, the buffoon, the rustic, the wag. Not equipped with a like temperament, she has dealt with her close realm. Her humor has been circumspect, often ironic as if she is quite aware of her shortcoming. She has not soared to exorbitant altitudes in her attempts to amuse. Does all this mark her as less imaginative than man? Or is it that her imagination differs in composition and seeks outlet in other directions? Certainly she does not number among humorists remembered for frivolity in the series.

Almost everyone has some measure of talent for turning phrases in such a manner as to achieve comic idea or aspect and uses it unintentionally or with purpose. Some writers toiled at this with heavy hand, while with others success seemed spontaneous. To mention three altogether varied authors whose gifts included drollery, there were Howard Garis with his nonsense, Tarkington who wrote tongue in cheek, and Mark Twain, illustrious humorist-satirist. The inner eyes differed; Garis reached for absurdities which vanished like the light of fire-flies; Tarkington's seemingly innocent images did not stray far from reality and, dateless, continue to cling to memory; as for Twain, neither time nor space limited his ingenuity. He aimed at the utmost and reached wondrous effects with human frailties. Tarkington turned his eyes upon the astigmatism of humankind. Garis struck fanciful fuses for abrupt flares.

Means used by men in general to incite amusement were "tall tales," semiprivate jests, impudent manners of recital, a boy's yen for exaggeration in speech or act, the use or misuse of uncommon words. Regional speech patterns supplied levity if not overdone. Those who strained at the manufacture of humor resorted to hackneyed methods: employment of the absent-minded old professor, mockery in the form of behavior and parlance of black people in minstrel-show fashion, or of ethnic group such as the German. Sometimes casts of characters came equipped with ludicrous names, or nicknames related to physical traits or even the opposites of those traits. Other factors were mannerisms, idiomatic slang, boasts and brags, doggerel, infrequent vulgarities.

Sardonic comment by one person putting down another was a practice shared by women writers. However, the general endeavor in girls' series was less dominant. Women worked into the scheme a more refined brand of humor associated with a child's misconception of words or ideas, with imaginative and absurd proposals, with uncommon phrases employed in small flights of fancy, with mimicking of adults, romantic revelations and fictional names suggesting individual peculiarities.

In series written for the younger set, humor turned up in easy and odd fantasy, simple foolishness, teasing and quaint phraseology typical of those who have not yet mastered the language.

Humor was something that Abbott was too occupied to consider as an element in itself. It was enough that he combined learning and entertainment, relationships between children of varying ages and between youths and adults. Yet the door was but opening upon the library of recreational reading for children, and no one would expect it to open fully at first touch.

In the early, serious years, writers did not meaningly display much original wit. After more than a century some of them are amusing in ways not at all intended; reason finds explanation in today's perspectives and styles of writing, and in the conversion of standards, customs and manners. Those with the most earnest motives did not aim at amusing readers; it was not their purpose to do other than sermonize and promote reform.

Optic was engrossed in setting forth virtuous and contrasting characters; humor bore little relationship to a righteous world. One bent on inculcating "...none but the best sentiments" gave little public thought to laughter. Occasionally in confrontation he allowed a protagonist to toss out a flippant remark. Levi Fairfield of *The Starry Flag* once told his enemy, "I don't care how much you talk, though I'd just as lief hear it thunder." A scoundrel in one Optic novel accused a poor boy of "hooking" eggs in someone's barn.

> "I am not a thief."
> "I bet you ain't," drawled Tim, placing his thumb against his nose, and wagging his four fingers back and forth.[1]

Alger's stories now and then exhibit some spice, usually in accord with the low stations in which the boys began life. Among those quick at repartee was Sam Barker, ex-bootblack and newsboy. Having returned a lost child to his parents, Sam, now in possession of a five-dollar reward and promise of a job, went out to replace his ragged garments. When he entered a second-hand store, the owner, doubting Sam's ability to buy, participated in a verbal sparring that began as follows:

> "Look here, old man, have you got any tip-top clo'es to sell today?"
> "Yes, my son," answered the old man with an air of alacrity.
> "Who are you a-takin' to? I ain't your son, and I wouldn't be. My father's a member of Congress."[2]

Nor was Alger, whose books seldom seem to reflect his formal education, above a grossness of humor. An adult character of doubtful integrity indulged himself at the breakfast table by making a remark at the point of "...leaning back in his chair, and picking his teeth with a fork."

Comic characters provided rather weighty humor among Stratemeyer's accounts of the roaming Rovers. The despised assistant to the school's headmaster was one Josiah Crabtree. Pigley, Flapp and Tubbs were opponents in competitive sports. Peleg Snuggers, called by the boys "Mr. Peleg Snugsomebody," was odd-job man at school, while black Alexander Pop of ludicrous speech was man-of-all-work at the Rover home. Butt of continued fun-making was student Hans Mueller. Having heard of the Rovers' experience as castaways on a Pacific island, thick-tongued Hans was impressed.

> "You vos regular Robinson Roosters," he said.
> "Great Scott! Robinson Roosters!" yelled Tom, bursting out into a fit of laughter "Boys, we are discovered at last."
> "Well, if you are, you needn't crow over it," came from Larry.
> "Roosters and crowing! Oh, Larry, I didn't think you'd begin to pun so early," put in Sam.
> "He just hatched it out," said Tom.
> I suppose you think that sounds *chic*," joined in Dick....[3]

The tactics of Victor Appleton (Stratemeyer collective pseudonym used for early Tom Swift series written by Garis) were similar but carried out in airier manner at times. The "odd gentleman," Mr. Wakefield Damon, close friend to Tom, constantly blessed everything from his shoe-laces to his eye-lashes. Black handyman in the Swift household was Eradicate Sampson. In one story Tom suspected that "Rad" had somehow suffered injury and began questioning him.

> "Boomerang, your mule, didn't kick you; did he?"
> "No, sah, Massa Tom, no sah. 'Twern't nuffin laik dat....I'se had a shock!"
> "A shock?"
> "Yas, sah, A shock. A lickrish shock."
> "Oh, you mean an electrical shock. That's too bad. I suppose you must have touched a live wire."...
> "Well, yo' see, Massa Tom, I were playin' a joke on Koku....Dat giant man he were in de telefoam boof in de pattern shop—you know—de one where yo' all been tryin' to make pishures."
> "Yes, I know. Go on!" exclaimed Tom, impatiently.
> "Well, he were in dere, Massa Tom, an' I slipped into de boof in de next shop....I called out on de telefoam, loud laik de Angel Gabriel gwine t' holler at de last trump: 'Look out, yo' ole sinnah!' I yell it jest t' scare Koku....When I put down de telefoam I got a terrible shock..."[4]

Edgar Rice Burroughs inserted this kind of entertainment in between episodes of heavier drama. When not concerned with Jane's huge and excitable maid, Esmeralda, the humor involved the heroine's father, Professor Archimedes Q. Porter and his secretary, Samuel T. Philander. Pursued by a lion, the strange pair wandered naively about beach and jungle, carrying on unbelievable, erudite conversations until rescued and re-rescued by Tarzan.

Among other writers foolishness sometimes abounded, as with a comic-strip collection of names. Percy Keyes Fitzhugh put together a story peopled with: Pee-wee, Ebenezer Quig, Simeon Drowser, Aunt Jamsiah, Pepsy (alias Penelope Pepperall), Deadwood Gamely, Doctor Killem, Licorice Stick, Constable Beriah Bungel, Darius Dragg and others in a locale named

Everdoze, through which "Crackerjack" touring cars infrequently traveled. In the Twenties this may have been comic, indeed, to a half-grown boy.

The out-and-out "humorist" in the days of declamatory readings for the public was George Peck. "Humorists" were blatant, earthy and outrageous, and Peck's "bad boy," Hennery, was scandalous both in tongue and action. All that he needed, to set him off verbally, was a foil. In this case it was the grocery man.

> "Well, great Julius Caesar's bald-headed ghost, what's the matter with you?" said the grocery man to the bad boy, as he came into the grocery on crutches, with one arm in a sling, one eye blackened, and a strip of court plaster across his face. "Where was the explosion, or have you been in a fight, or has your Pa been giving you what you deserve, with a club? Here, let me help you; there, sit down on that keg of apple-jack. Well, by the great guns, you look as though you had called somebody a liar. What's the matter?"...
>
> "O, there's not much the matter with me," said the boy, in a voice that sounded all broke up, as he took a big apple off a basket, and began peeling it with his upper, front teeth. "If you think I am a wreck, you ought to see the minister. They had to carry him home in installments, the way they buy sewing machines...."[5]

Peck (who would fit in easily with some television "show") was alone in lavish use of crudity and quite at an opposite pole from serious writers who were too engrossed with travel or other adventuring to consider that much manufactured humor need be an integral part of a book. Castlemon judged his action-crammed stories sufficient unto themselves without ludicrous sparring.

Journalist Thomas Knox, friend and correspondent of explorer Henry M. Stanley, and surely the most traveled of series authors, packed his books solidly with facts, leading a reader on a hunt for non-pedestrian passages. With female family members at hand, Knox gave two youths leave to have modest fun, a relief to the reader. In Wiesbaden, Mrs. Bassett, caught up in "taking the waters," followed a regime for a week. Then, feeling refreshed, she cancelled the remainder of the treatment whereat the doctor quickly suggested one of the various "cures." Mrs. Bassett decided to discuss the idea with her son.

> "What is the grape-cure, for example?" she asked.
>
> "It consists of living upon grapes and very little else. You have a pound of grapes for breakfast, another pound for dinner, and a third pound for supper...."
>
> "Very little variety in that bill of fare," said Mrs. Bassett.
>
> "Pardon me, mother," replied Frank, "but there you are mistaken. Think of the many kinds of grapes that are produced, and you can have a different kind for each meal."
>
> "Yes, I see. And what is the milk-cure?"
>
> "In that you live on milk," was the reply. "Milk for breakfast, for dinner, and for supper, and milk between meals and at bedtime..."

"I wonder if you can find any variety in *that*? Milk all the time would be very monotonous."

"You can get plenty of variety," said Frank, with a laugh, "by arranging for milk from different cows."[6]

Travel-writer Charles A. Stephens was not putting down the intelligence of women when he inserted a bit of dark humor. An exaggeration of comic sorrow brightens the too informative chapters as the Knockabout Club examined Spain. This was a story within a story.

Anent these bull-fights, an acquaintance told us the following story: A Spanish friend of his came to his door one night, late, and...threw himself upon the bed, with sobs and cries. For a long time he lay there overpowered by some bitter grief. At last he said in broken tones: "My sister—dead. I must go to the funeral....She is dead—and that is not all. I must go to the funeral; and if I go to the funeral I can't go to the bull-fight! Oh, my sister! my sister! Oh, why did you die at this time! My sister—the bull-fight. To think,—eight bulls, four *espadas*! Oh, my sister—the bull-fight! Alas! Why did you die at this time! I am most miserable—my sister—the *toros*! Never shall I see them again!"[7]

For finesse in humor, one tends to measure talents, not always a wise exercise but still a requisite in appraisal. Raconteur Twain with an imagination extending to any horizon and beyond, could create the perfect pictorial impression. Aunt Polly's eye-glasses were a source of reader-wonder.

The old lady pulled her spectacles down and looked over them about the room; then she put them up and looked out under them. She seldom or never looked *through* them for so small a thing as a boy; they were her state pair...and were built for "style," not service—she could have seen through a pair of stove-lids just as well....[8]

Aunt Polly could have used proper spectacles for the detailed picture of Huck Finn, had she really cared to note the general effect.

Huckleberry was always dressed in the cast-off clothes of full-grown men, and they were in perennial bloom and fluttered with rags. His hat was a vast ruin with a wide crescent lopped out of its brim; his coat, when he wore one, hung nearly to his knees and had the rearward buttons far down the back; but one suspender supported his trousers; the seat of the trousers bagged low and contained nothing...[9]

Tarkington, too, could be deceivingly transparent. Always delightful with child characters in any kind of fiction, he began his little saga of a boy with a description of that boy's dog, grandly named Duke.

He wore a grizzled moustache and indefinite whiskers; he was small and shabby, and looked like an old postman.[10]

There is really little finer in the story than the suave near-finish to the volume. This is a visit, upon Penrod's twelfth birthday, with Great-aunt Sarah Crim, who was as remarkable in her way as Penrod was in his. For the occasion she had prepared, for her niece and grandnephew, refreshments of lemonade and a plate "freighted" with ginger cookies of a secret recipe.

Then, having set this collation before her guests, she presented Penrod with a superb, intricate, and very modern machine of destructive capacities almost limitless. She called it a pocket-knife.

"I suppose you'll do something horrible with it," she said, composedly. "I hear you do that with everything, anyhow, so you might as well do it with this, and have more fun out of it. They tell me you're the Worst Boy in Town."

"Oh, Aunt Sarah!" Mrs. Schofield lifted a protesting hand.

"Nonsense!" said Mrs. Crim.

"But, on his birthday!"

"That's the time to say it. Penrod, aren't you the Worst Boy in Town?"

Penrod, gazing fondly upon his knife and eating cookies rapidly, answered as a matter of course, and absently, "Yes'm."

"Certainly!" said Mrs. Crim. "Once you accept a thing about yourself as established and settled, it's all right. Nobody minds. Boys are just like people, really."[11]

Growing boys were not very high on anyone's list for virtuous behavior and yet authors and readers alike cherished images of these mischievous creatures. The youthful hero concocted by Clarence Budington Kelland, Marcus Aurelius Fortunatus Tidd, could not match the ingratiating quality of Tom Sawyer and Penrod. His exaggerated adventures, while less coarse, are mindful of those accorded Hennery Peck, but Mark's intentions were good, at least. An absurd fat boy, he kept close company with Tallow Martin, Plunk Smalley and Binney Jenks. Narrator Tallow described the leader in mercilessly frank manner.

Yes, sir, he's fat, and he stutters. His cheeks puff out like apple dumplings and his eyes are almost shut in by them, and his nose is just a kind of blob, but it doesn't interfere with his head....He's about as sharp as they come, and nobody wants to go poking fun at him on short acquaintance....[12]

Country bumpkins they were, these four, but in possession of natures shrewd enough to warrant carrying concealed weapons, slingshots, which served well during investigation of mysteries and foiling of con men.

L. Frank Baum could bring a smile with a slash of his pen, as when a soldier at Emerald City, first sighting that strange mortal called the Patchwork Girl, asked impulsively: "My dear child—what are you, a rummage sale or a guess-me-quick?"[13] The Baum humor was of homely, realistic variety, and not an open, vital ingredient of fantasy in which wonder and amazement provided primary effects. Sometimes playful, sometimes labored, it was also ironic. At the close of book one, Dorothy is describing the state of affairs to Glinda.

> "My greatest wish now," she added. "is to get back to Kansas, for Aunt Em will surely think something dreadful has happened to me, and that will make her put on mourning; and unless the crops are better this year than they were last I am sure Uncle Henry cannot afford it."[14]

Being feminine, Dorothy was practical. Louisa Alcott was the same, but managed light-heartedness now and then, as when the March sisters Meg and Jo compared notes on their way home from a rare party. Here Jo speaks first.

> "I saw you dancing with that red-headed man I ran away from. Was he nice?"
> "Oh, very! His hair is auburn, not red; and he was very polite, and I had a delicious redowa[15] with him."
> "He looked like a grasshopper in a fit, when he did the new step. Laurie and I couldn't help laughing...."[16]

This was a merry moment for Louisa; she was perhaps grimmer in the first of the series than later when much less worried about income, and yet in retrospect she seems more vivacious in *Little Women* than ever again. She gained humorous effects in delineating the youngest March, Amy, whose lot was hand-me-downs not much in favor when one has social ambitions and precise taste.

> "My only comfort," she said to Meg, with tears in her eyes, "is, that mother don't take tucks in my dresses whenever I'm naughty, as Maria Parks' mother does. My dear, it's really dreadful; for sometimes she is so bad, her frock is up to her knees, and she can't come to school. When I think of this *deggerredation*, I feel that I can bear even my flat nose and purple gown, with yellow sky-rockets on it."[17]

Green Gables Anne was getting into scrapes more often than lady-like Amy March. Some were funny, some serious, some too dramatic even for Anne, but L.M. Montgomery had a way of lightening household tragedies with comedy. Naturally Marilla was scandalized when she scrutinized Anne's hair and found it green, and naturally she demanded an immediate explanation.

> "I dyed it."
> "Dyed it! Dyed your hair! Anne Shirley, didn't you know it was a wicked thing to do?"

"Yes, I knew it was a little wicked," admitted Anne. "But I thought it was worth while to be a little wicked to get rid of red hair. I counted the cost, Marilla. Besides, I meant to be extra good in other ways to make up for it."[18]

Mrs Phelps' charm in portrayal of character extended to all members of a family. Although Gypsy was obviously heroine, her creator included a small brother in the Breynton family as well as the older Tom. Young Winnie was almost irrepressible and could be a trial to the other two. When Tom turned down a request to accompany them to the pond for a boat-ride by saying that they did not care about the company of "little boys" that afternoon Winnie was insulted.

"*Little boys!*" said Winnie with a terrible look; "I'm five years old, sir. I can button my own jacket, and I've got a snowshovel!"[19]

It is an interesting point that Laura Richards, in recounting the story of Hildegarde, awarded her snatches of humor, except in fanciful names, to male characters. Hildegarde's father possessed, fittingly, a more elegant sense of the comic than did Farmer Hartley.

"It is a sad thing," Mr. Graham would say when his wife fluttered in to lunch, breathless and exhausted and half an hour late (she, the most punctual of women!), —"it is a sad thing to have married a comet by mistake, thinking it was a woman. How did you find the other planets this morning, my dear? Is it true that Saturn has lost one of his rings? and has the Sun recovered from his last attack of spots?...."[20]

Alice Hegan Rice was obliged to place her humor with women, for male characters were rather scanty in number, and less memorable, too. When Lovey Mary had the offer of a part in a Cabbage Patch play, and needed to make answer to a query of whether she could learn lines, she was no more at a loss for words than Mrs. Wiggs herself.

"I can learn anything!" cried Lovey Mary, recklessly. "Already know the alphabet and the Lord's Prayer backward...."[21]

Yet she could not best Mrs. Wiggs, who was self-appointed public information official in the neighborhood and who cannily edited the news spread by word of mouth. Protecting Lovey from gossip, she became a Mrs. Malaprop in giving explanation for the presence of a strange young woman in the community.

"This here lady has been at the hospittal. She got knocked over by a wagon out there near the factory, an' it run into celebrated concussion. The nurse told Lovey Mary this mornin' it was somethin' like information of the brain...."[22]

Except for the kingdom of animal tales (almost a strictly male province), the series for the youngest readers were written by women. Howard Garis lingers on library shelves in the form of Uncle Wiggily, while the dozens of other series he turned out are mostly forgotten. The word play in which small children delight is the key to Garis and that famous Uncle Wiggily and friends. Nonsense and the sound of it, perhaps in rhyme, and foolish phrases without relationship to anything else, bubble out from nowhere and ascend to shimmer for an instant before flickering out. "Oh, trolley cars! Oh, horse-radish!" Or "My goodness me sakes alive and some popcorn pancakes!"

He used fanciful ideas for the same purpose, as when Uncle Wiggily, Sammie, the rabbit boy, and a fish-hawk went out for a walk.

Up out of the lake came a bad old tiddlewink, looking for trouble. A tiddlewink is something like a flump, only worse. A tiddlewink is like an alligator, with hands, and it always looks sad and unhappy. It can crawl on the land or swim. It is always growling and grumbling, is a tiddlewink, and is never satisfied....[23]

Gentle was the humor of the women writing of little people in a good many series, some of them not widely known. Once past that first reading stage, a child is not likely to return for re-reading, as with the more advanced series. There was that Southern drama of young William Green Hill arriving at Miss Minerva's home to set the household into a spin from which it could never return to the old, staid stance. The imps, William Green Hill and playmates, were discussing the arrival of twins in someone's home, and curiosity brought them to sharing what knowledge they had of infant source. One thought that the doctor's bag had held the surprise, while backwoods Billy, whose way of speaking cannot be swallowed easily today, was positive that doctors found babies in hollow stumps and that *only* doctors could find them.

"I certainly do think he might have given them to us," declared Lina, "and I'm going to tell him so, too. As much money as father has paid him for doctor's bills and as much old, mean medicine as I have taken just to 'commodate him; then he gives babies to everybody but us."

"I'm awfully glad he never give 'em to my mama," said Jimmy, " 'cause I never could have no more fun; they'd be stuck right under my nose all time, and all time put their mouth in everything you want to do, and all time meddling....But I wish I could see 'em. They so weakly they got to be hatched in a nincubator."[24]

Unfortunately Mrs. Calhoun, who termed herself "a Southerner of Southerners," never knew of the success of the one and only book she wrote. Only a few months after its publication she died, and eventually Emma

Speed Sampson took over the story of William Green Hill, his kin and his friends.

Series written by the sturdier Mary P. Wells Smith cover a long span of time and are set against an historical New England countryside with opportunities for the older generations to relate small tales about their forebears. In the farm home even small children had tasks to perform, and as Millie led the way on the path from barn to house, they were speculating about the eggs Millie carried.

> "It don't seem as if these eggs would make chickens, does it?" asked Millie. "I suppose the yolks make the bodies, and the whites the feathers."
> "I should think they'd all be white chickens, then." said matter-of-fact Teddy. "And where do their legs come from?"
> "Oh, they just grow, you know."[25]

It was Sophie May who expressed most captivatingly the viewpoints of the young. A spinster, auntie to many nieces and nephews, she drew on these relationships for her many series. The devotion-to-Christian-duty of her era she always tempered with frequent references to human sensibilities. When the father of the Clifford children decided to "go to the war" (and this was a story of the 1860's), the mother and children packed and left Indiana for Maine, Mrs. Clifford's family home. Vigorous Horace, once in his grandparents' house, renewed summertime acquaintances readily, but had to defend the Indiana manner of speaking.

> "I never knew before," laughed little Dan Rideout, "that my name was Dan-yell!"
> "He calls a pail a bucket, and a dipper a *tin-kup*," said Gilbert Brown.
> "Yes," chimed in Willy Snow, "and he asks, 'Is school *took up*?' just as if it was knitting-work that was on needles."
> "How he rolls his r's!" said Peter Grant. "You can't say hor-r-se the way he does! I'll bet *the ain't* a boy can do it, unless it's a Cahoojack." Peter meant *Hoosier*.
> "Well, I wouldn't be seen saying *hoss*," returned Horace, with some spirit; "that's *Yankee*."[26]

Thus it was in those unsophisticated days that the series writers worked at bringing a breath of airiness to stories for children who had for so long awaited not only fiction devised especially for them, but as well for that yeasty ingredient, drollery, to offset the gravity of their lives.

Chapter XIV
Stylistically Speaking...

When all is read and done, assuming that a tale is engrossing, a bookworm gradually re-enters the everyday world. Often the transference is a reluctant one. The reader has figuratively immersed himself and literally given himself over to an author's creation, stepping into the guise of primary character and living out the adventure. He may have smiled or laughed aloud during this absence from reality, let out some ejaculation of admiration or envy, perhaps even brushed a dewiness from his eyes with a sleeve or the back of the hand. Although he rushed into the story as rapidly as possible only to sigh involuntarily when reaching the final page, he does not really know what has happened to him or why.

What has taken place is that the writer has drawn together and combined a set of ingredients: characters, plot, some kind of romance, perhaps some humor and perhaps not, and, in other days, some "lesson," a moral truth or set of principles. The way that he has interwoven these ingredients, be that way labored or deft, comes under the heading of "style." With the written word, style is a manner of expression, a way with words, a choosing of phrases and a fitting of them together in the accomplishment of something not readily visible. Generally, concepts and perceptions, imagination and originality see first involvement, because good style needs a basis. At its best it is a distinctive and original enough means of expression to identify or at least suggest its creator.

The manipulation of words might well depend upon the aims of the writers as well as the abilities. Some of them wanted to be mentors, to teach or to impart messages having to do with moral behavior. Certain of them felt the importance of their positions as more or less learned adults who ought to be influencing youths at the same moment as entertaining them, earning a livelihood and becoming known through magazine and book pages. Others had expectations primarily of providing income, and a number became entranced with storytelling itself. The shared desire of all was to draw readers close, to lure them into some magic circle or secret garden or whatever special realm one cares to imagine for total involvement in fictional happenings.

The reaction of the young reader, however, was not likely one of appraising the style of a story just finished. Probably he never considered the word. His completion of the book was itself recommendation. Had he found it tiresome, he would have abandoned it with a "That's no good" remark unless required to make a report. He might even boldly write a terse opinion on a page or upon a school-library card. "In case of fire throw this in!" Or, "This is the funnyest book." Despite his total unconcern with and non-recognition of style as such, it was this handling of story components which held him page after page to the final one.

An author of first-rate stature, selecting his elements and searching for best means of joining and presenting them, used, knowingly or not, a certain amount of intuition. Perception and imagination, best handled only half consciously, advanced the skill at narration, but deliberate choice and arrangement of words might be part of the whole process, just as would playing it by ear, so to speak.

Naturally not all the series writers, despite education, experience and empathy for the young, were first-rate. For those awkward at the art of expression, there were alternatives: conjuring up an excess of adventures, dreaming up endearing or curious characters, dressing scenes generously with manners and morals, and employing tricks of various kinds to embellish the stories and distract from meanness of verbal ability. Some used dialects, buffoons, bucolic humor, slang, or added verbal ruffles and lace and ribbons to a degree of embarrassment, or juggled phrases, ornamenting them with uncommon words in an effort to display cleverness. Some wrote with what appears in this era as a naivety suggesting arrested mentality. Others never went beyond the homeliest ways of expression because they wrote as a business and saw no reason, or had no talent, to do otherwise. Showing off with bouquets of flowery terms seems more noticeable among women writers, but the inclination toward lofty phraseology is frequent among male authors.

There are even times that manner of writing causes embarrassment to the eye as well as to the mind, either for ineptness or for too large a measure of sentimentalism. One must concede that in some cases an improved style would make no difference in the impression brought about by foolish plotting or humdrum players or a hopelessly limited world.

It was Harry Castlemon who declared that boys wanted adventure and not "fine writing," which might or might not have referred to the truly literary style that a numbered few possess during any one age. Yet a fact is that style, if one thinks of it as *quality* in expression, is not necessary at all provided that an author puts forth something to feed the young. Witness the work of such authors as Horatio Alger, Oliver Optic and Martha Finley. Yet these were highly popular novelists.

With the demand exceeding the supply and the public of several minds as to what they were ready to read, there was space in the publishing world for both able and clumsy writers and eventually for ghost-writing. Thus the old series exhibit gradations from the preposterous to common, to at-moments commendable, to superior and to distinguished. This is one of the fascinations of the period. One can only conclude that tastes were as varied as they are today, for clearly many readers were quite satisfied with superficial writing as well as questionable plots and characters. Individuals like Louisa Alcott raised voices in condemnation of "trash." Now, strangely, critics, official or self-appointed, sneer at yesterday's trash and tolerate today's.

Whatever category writers fell into, by reason of individual nature and inborn and acquired abilities, they presumably worked with whatever they had in order to attain their aims. Naturally they reflected their environment both as to time and place, employing terms that sound quaint today or which paradoxically appear surprisingly current. It is not by accident that fragments from bygone books hang in the mind as do some of those appearing in these pages.

Pattern-setter that he was, Abbott wrote in plain, correct manner as an exemplary teacher is wont to do. He could and did unbend a bit as he proceeded in quiet, steady way without introducing verbal histrionics but from time to time making explanation or inserting a tale, a practice that many who followed him adopted. At his best, he provided tidy examples of insight in a graphic way. It is no surprise that the adults in his stories seemed to inherit Abbott's fondness for children even while aware of duty to guide them. Thus it was with Miss Mary.

"Tell me the whole of your name," said Miss Mary, laying down at the same time a penknife, with which she had been sharpening a pen.

"Dovey Brome," replied the new scholar, taking up the knife, at the same time beginning to cut the table with it.

"You must not touch the knife, Dovey," said Miss Mary, and she gently took it out of her hand, and laid it down again. "How old are you, Dovey?" . . .

"I shall be eleven next June."

"It is June now," said Miss Mary; "do you mean June of this year or of next year?"

"The next year."

"Then you are *ten* now?"

"Yes," said Dovey, "a few days ago."

Miss Mary smiled a little, but Dovey did not know what for. She leaned her elbows upon the table, and put her cheeks in her hands, and then, a moment after, she took a pen out of the inkstand before her, and began to mark upon the back of her hand.[1]

That small confrontation is effective both as to content and style. Others showed their particular strengths according to their own powers.

Elijah Kellogg, whose boys might make frank statement of affection, had a sturdy style descriptive of his lifetime and of the geographical region he knew best, New England. A sample illustrates his handling of men and boys gathered for a barn-raising that would end with a celebration to include friendly wrestling.

> ...He was a splendid specimen of physical strength combined with activity; upwards of six feet, weighing, apparently, about two hundred,—evidently accustomed to severe labor, and without superfluous flesh. The assembly, so well accustomed to judge of men by their thews and sinews, gazed upon him with admiration.
>
> "By Heavens," said Barney Weaver, "there goes a game-cock for you; see how light he steps; look at his legs."
>
> "And his arms," said Captain Rhines.
>
> "See how he's timbered about the breast and shoulders," said Smullen; "he's hard-meated, too; that man has been brought up to hard work; none of your brash, white-livered fellows. I shouldn't wonder if he might be a match for Ben."[2]

Unusual terms smack of a man's world of sea and coastal farm with Kellogg, while a sprinkling of familiar phrases among old-fashioned ones with Trowbridge startle the eye. In a sober story of broken friendship, a father counseling his son on the matter of personal relationships, advised, "Don't be such a satellite to him...; he ain't the centre of the universe..."[3] And one of the boys tells the other, "I had no idea of putting you down." Complex effects brought about by the pocket-rifle school prize ensnared innumerable people of the community as well as the Damon and Pythias friends and illiterate but shrewd Mr. Pavode himself.

> "Them's the two boys I had my eye on when I offered the prize to the school," said Mr. Pavode, standing in the boat, which he kept in place with an oar. "Bright fellers, both on 'em; an' great friends they was then, till the consarned pocket-rifle played the mischief atween 'em."[4]

Not all imaginations plunged deep or found verbal shading. While "hack-writing" ordinarily applies to persons hired for routine and transient work, one feels inclined to expand that category. At times volumes of published material appeared to be the goal, for "fine writing" was certainly not. Accord them a kind of ambition, but not sensitivity. That the mode of expression of some lacked quality does not mean that such writers did not have "style" per se, since the term also indicates characteristic manner. Optic's diction was not refined although there is the surmise that he likely considered it elegant at times. Usually he wrote of older boys who lived in shabby circumstances but aspired to cultivate the niceties of polite society. Tirelessly formal and moral, he is almost more believable when introducing his young villains. Like Alger, he wrote of "high spirit, and of high aims and correct principles," as someone expressed it in an old review.

Paul was overwhelmed with astonishment and delight at this unexpected declaration. His eyes filled with tears, and he could not utter a word to express the gratitude that filled his heart.

"Yes, Paul, you shall hereafter be the skipper of the Fawn," repeated Captain Littleton.

"And I shall be first mate!" exclaimed John, jumping up and clapping his hands with rapture.

"Yes, and you shall be first mate, John; for I have not forgotten that a part of my debt of gratitude for the rescue of my daughter is in your favor, my fine fellow. The Fawn shall be owned between you."

"Thank you, sir," replied John; "but it was Paul that saved Carrie."

"If you had not handled the old boat well, Paul could not have saved her. You are fairly entitled to a share of the honor of that noble exploit."[5]

Inclined to be overly ceremonious in like way, Alger wrote straightforward narrative often employing clichés and old-time melodrama. Contrasting with primness are instances of gross taste which apparently Alger considered fitting to characters of lower dimensions. Have a look at the scheming Mr. Huxter, brother of the equally corrupt stepmother of John Oakley. John was about to become victim of an evil turn that would rid the stepmother of him and give her brother a chance to benefit from a forced apprenticeship of the unfortunate hero. Need it be said that the chivalrous boy managed to outwit the forces of darkness?

When he became a prisoner in Mr. Huxter's home, the ineffectual wife tried to be kind.

"...I am afraid we can't accommodate you very well, Mr. Oakley, but we'll do our best."

"What's good enough for us is good enough for him," said Mr. Huxter, fiercely. "He's as poor as we are. Sister Jane's got all the money. She's a deep one, is sister Jane."

"I hope you won't be offended at what he says, Mr. Oakley," said Mrs. Huxter, in an apologetic tone. "He don't mean what he says."

"Shut up, Mrs. Huxter!" said her husband, who was disposed to be quarrelsome. "Don't make a fool of yourself, but get supper as soon as you can."[6]

Pedestrian style by no means ruled out popularity so long as the author served up adventure in continuing streams or ranged from one side of the continent and sometimes one side of the world to the other. In between exploits, happenings might be as mundane and conversation as flat as the uninspired recountings of everyday doings written for very small people.

Yet for their time the heroes were dashing and envied individuals to some of the reading world, the boy, half-poet, half-swaggerer, edging into manhood and intoxicated with the illusion that ahead lay romantic action without end, years and years of moving hero-ward from dream to shining dream. Somehow the common fictional protagonist was a Lancelot in common clothing.

Edward Ellis had rather ineffectual young men almost ceaselessly roaming the woods without very clear purpose and naively but with brave speech creeping from one danger to another. As usual, Ned Clinton was not sure just what to do next when the friendly Mohawk scout appeared, and after Ned's greeting, put on "his usual broad grin."

When Ned had told Lena-Wingo all...he attempted to draw from the Indian an idea of what he had been doing since he left them. But the youth did not gain much satisfactory information....On the way to where the brother and sister had been left, the Mohawk turned off to the right, and drew from beneath a fallen tree two goodly loaves of bread and fully ten pounds of well-cooked meat.

"Where in the name of the seven wonders did you get that?" asked Ned.

"Lena-Wingo make bread and cook meat," grinned the redskin.

"Come, now, that won't do," laughed his young friend. "You might have cooked a piece of meat, but you never baked a loaf of bread in your life. You have been making a call upon some of the folks in the valley."

"No—not that—Tory call on settler—Tory make bread—then go to sleep—then Lena-Wingo call on Tory—go 'way—take bread."[7]

Everett Tomlinson, in fictionalizing the Revolutionary era, built complex intrigue. However, young John Shotwell and compatriots asked endless questions so that detailed historical explanations load the chapters to heaviness. It is eye-opening that a hanging which Mr. Shotwell took the boys to witness was that of an Irish member of Washington's "life guard" and the person acting under someone's plan to try poisoning Washington by means of green peas, for which the general had particular fondness. This is not so distracting as other background information.

By dint of inquiry, curious John learned of British Ministry plans to form a "strong line of military posts" through New England and on into Canada, and of the colonial plan to counteract that through a northward mission by a group of men for the purpose of establishing invincible ties with Canada.

"When was it they went?" asked John.

"It was on the second of last April. They started out here in a frightful storm, but they finally arrived at Albany and General Schuyler took care of them. I saw a letter that Charles Carroll wrote, in which he said of the general: 'He lives in pretty style; has two daughters (a Betsy and a Peggy), lively agreeable, black-eyed gals.' But they didn't stay long there, but pushed on through the snow and ice, and finally arrived at Montreal. They had to make all their way from St. John in calèches."

"What are they?" asked John.[8]

For series under his own name, Stratemeyer used historical backgrounds, too, colonial settings, the Far East, South and Central America, Mexico. A Stratemeyer protagonist is an all-American boy whatever his name, and endures whatever comes, and receives the same kind of treatment wherever he may be battling evil elements.

Here friends Ralph and Oliver are part of the command moving over the plain toward Monterey to the distant sound of cannons rumbling and rifles fracturing the air.

Presently, Ralph and Oliver found themselves moving over a rough road leading to a hillside upon which was located one of the Mexican forts. Here the cannon were blazing away madly, and in a twinkle several members of the company were cut down.

"Oh, this is terrible!" panted Oliver. His face was covered with perspiration and gun-smoke, and he was dirt and dust from head to foot.

"Don't lag!" shouted Ralph, "Come on!" And away they went, with thirty or forty others, up the hill. They fired as they ran and reloaded with all possible rapidity....[9]

One of the Stratemeyer Syndicate's busiest writers, Howard Garis, was of the same order stylistically, but he offered more variety and leavened his stories with a light, humorous tone. This skill emerged regularly in the Motor Boys' adventures, which Garis wrote under the name of Clarence Young. In one volume the boys were discussing the "balloon and aeroplane carnival" to be held in a nearby town and the news that the town bully, Noddy Nixon, was one of the competitors.

"Queer," murmured Jerry. "I wonder what sort of a machine Noddy has?"

"I can tell you," exclaimed a voice behind the motor boys. "It's great—regular fly—tin wings—flop up and down—faster than you can count—whoop! there they go— up goes the machine—down again—round in a circle—flip-flap-flop! Start the motor—twist the rudder—look out—here she comes—that's the way!"...

"Oh, it's Andy Rush. No need to turn around to tell that, boys," remarked Jerry, stretching out in the grass again. "Well, Andy, aren't some of your cylinders hot after that spring?"

"I guess so—I don't know—heard you talking about Noddy Nixon—his airship—I thought you wouldn't mind—I came up closer—I heard about it—I've seen it—it's great—say—"....

"...let him tell us about it," suggested Jerry. "Now just shut off a little of your gasolene, retard your spark a bit, and you'll do better...."[10]

Despite his opinion of what boys wanted, Harry Castlemon exhibited a style that was a sort of liaison between the unadorned narrative method and that in which an author paused to sketch in a setting or atmosphere indicating attitude and mood and providing little verbal niceties that cause one to linger and re-read.

...The train took up its line of march at daylight, halted at noon..., and shortly after sunset encamped for the night. The fight with the Indians had not driven all thoughts of the antelopes out of the boys' minds. And while the train journeyed along the road, they scoured the prairie, in search of the wished-for game. The appearance of the "sea of grass," which stretched away on all sides, as far as their eyes could reach, not a little surprised them. Instead of the perfectly level plain they had expected to see, the surface of the prairie was broken by gentle swells, like immense waves of the ocean, and here and there—sometimes two or three days' journey apart—were small patches of woods, called "oak openings."[11]

Authors talented at description may receive low ratings because many readers consider only action and conversation worthy of attention. A few dared to create descriptive passages of some length, but there is a difference between description as such and descriptive action. Child-eyes fly over the former but linger on the latter. After all, serious writers bent on doing more than sketching, writers talented at fiction-building, are for serious readers, who expect and want more than bare bones and bodiless voices droning out lifeless repartee. Charles A. Stephens could and did bring spirit into a narrative with literary ease so that it was neither over-embellished nor too sparse.

Again I seem to smell the early morning odors from the swaths of grass, fresh-reeking from the scythes, or catch the noontide fragrance of the hot windrows of hay as we "tumbled" it up for the rack-cart, which came rattling out into the field. Again I hear the merry whit to whit of the whetstones, the low rip of the severed grass-stalks, the wearying note of the grindstone, and at last—after forenoons of infinite length—the welcome toot of the old dinner-horn.
Once more I see Theodora, or Ellen, or Halstead, coming afield in the blazing sunshine, bringing that longed-for jug of cold water, tempered with a dash of molasses and ginger to keep the inordinate quantities which we drank from hurting us. Yet again the loud black thunder-shower rises in drear gloom over the mountain, bent on drenching the whole day's batch of hay. And then what hurry and scurry there would be to pile a big load on the cart and rush it to the barn before the sheeted rain struck![12]

Horace Scudder employed whimsy and a good many touches of imagination to come up with a curiously endearing style. His series—narrative broken up with long poems by known authors, with prose stories, with fairy tales in verse—also include some outright fancy. Perceptive seems the word for one introductory passage.

The sun was shining brightly one morning in April, and in such good-natured fashion that he was warming both rogues and honest men, and not only spreading his light and warmth over the fields...but hunting through the narrow, high-walled streets of the city, in search of cold and damp places, and traveling just as far from one side of the street to the other as the houses would let him. It was pleasant to see what he was doing in Asylum Street, for he had sought out the Orphan-house, and now its whole red front was glowing; and it seemed as if the sun were trying its best to work through the thick walls and get at the children with his gigantic smile. The windows let him in,....[13]

And of course there was Joseph Altsheler. A few writers fearlessly challenged the imagination with romantically descriptive passages. Altsheler did, and his books still hold place on library shelves. His talent was rather special for he threaded description with action in an able way. Like some others he felt the necessity of building up an atmosphere to produce a complete drama. He knew that the invisible portion of an individual, the spirit, was vital to effective storytelling. Otherwise the figures might be mere phantoms with only names to differentiate them.

The Altsheler style can be strangely exalting to the mind's ear. At times it becomes like music emanating from the silence, from a still earth, from a jeweled night sky, or like phrases springing from watching eyes and frozen stance of a wild beast, or yet from the mind of man perceiving the significance of surroundings.

An Altsheler hero, captured by the Indians, living with them and becoming an admired warrior, learned well to hunt, to interpret behavior and expressions of animals, especially the wolves, so that he seemed to hear the voices of such beasts speaking in the Indian tongue. To his ears a wolf leader chanted in the following manner.

"They are there, O, my comrades, the creatures that stand upright and walk on two legs, ...the beings that, larger than we are, are nevertheless helpless against us with their own bare paws! But they carry with them the strange shapes that send through the air the long twigs with sharp ends that burn like fire, when they strike us! These creatures are men, and I have counted the men...They are ten, and they are strong and skillful!...If we rushed at them they would pierce our sides...and at last kill us! That is why, O, my comrades, I cry my grief to the heavens, and you cry your grief with me. The savory odor of them fills our nostrils, but our teeth must remain clean, at least tonight.!"[14]

Earlier, Hezekiah Butterworth was writing poetically if less dramatically of Indian lore. In one historical series he created a memorable heroine, Faithful Heart, in the image of "forest sibyls, or wise women," who as a young girl constantly challenged her elders.

"I found a partridge nest while picking strawberries," said the girl. "I almost touched the bird in the nest. She was just the color of the dead leaves where the berries were ripe. Why does the partridge build her nest among the leaves that are of her own color?"

"Why does the green snake run among the green grass?" said old Moxas.

"Does the partridge reason that the dead leaves will hide her from the hawk? The partridge that I saw spread her wings on the brown leaves and slid away, so that I might not see her. Who taught her to do that? She did it to draw me from her nest. The partridge will die for her young. She will flutter at your feet while her little ones are hiding. How does she know? Who taught her first? I love the partridge because she knows; I love her because she will die for her young. Who made her heart?"

"The Spirit that made the partridge's heart made yours, my girl. It is a good sign that you and the partridge are friends. You have the same heart together."[15]

While Kellogg and Castlemon, too, were definitely masculine in style, the envisioning Altsheler and Butterworth, among others, had more in common with the proficient women authors, for it is more than possible that style and its differences concerned perspective and intention. Thus arises that inevitable subject of sexes. Fictional girls and those best at creating them focused on emotions and imagination and dreams, with the well-being of the spirit very much a concern along with the realm of the mind and the subconscious and superconscious. With the boys so popular in fiction, life was action and reality and the primary senses. With the boys it was often a matter of see and touch, set out and conquer. Living was more upon the surface, and when there came a pitting of wits, the jousting was not profound.

If the more apt women, who could swiftly carry a reader away to that wondrous land of storytelling, used some sweetening along with other ingredients, what matter? It is quite human to be susceptible to emotions and human relationships, particularly in ages when the regulation of manners and morals subjected the feminine contingent to a confined and confining world. It does seem that readers were perfectly willing to accept some sentimentality when a story in all its detail offered so much to affect them. Perhaps during their middle growing years girls do not really recognize an over-supply of emotion, so absorbed are they in situations and happenings and their own reactions, so deep are they in disguise of an entrancing heroine. It may be only in adult re-reading aloud to a child that a parent finds herself startled at some embarrassment of feeling.

Louisa Alcott's well-known manner was to apply romantic touches to her procession of scenes as the saga of the March sisters unfolded.

...A low hedge parted the two estates. On one side was an old, brown house, looking rather bare and shabby, robbed of the vines that in summer covered its walls, and the flowers which then surrounded it. On the other side was a stately stone mansion, plainly betokening every sort of comfort and luxury, from the big coach-house and well-kept grounds to the conservatory and the glimpses of lovely things one caught between the rich curtains. Yet it seemed a lonely, lifeless sort of house...

To Jo's lively fancy, this fine house seemed a kind of enchanted palace, full of splendors and delights, which no one enjoyed. She had long wanted to behold these hidden glories, and to know the "Laurence boy," who looked as if he would like to be known, if he only knew how to begin; and then...and Jo began to think he had gone away, when she one day spied a brown face at an upper window, looking wistfully down into their garden, where Beth and Amy were snowballing one another.[16]

Elizabeth Stuart Phelps, less verbose, used a style similarly romantic. Her Gypsy Breynton had a startling habit for a time of sleep-walking and one night awakened to find herself out on the pond in an oarless boat which she had herself forgotten to "lock." Once panic subsided, she spent the hours first in adjustment to the situation and then, making herself as comfortable as possible, allowed the splendor of the setting to absorb her.

All around and underneath her lay the black, still water,—so black that the maple-branches cast no shadow on it. About and above her rose the mountains, grim and mute, and watching as they had watched for ages, and would watch for ages still, all the long night through. Overhead, the stars glittered and throbbed, and shot in and out of ragged clouds. Far up in the great forests, that climbed the mountain-sides, the wind was muttering like an angry voice.[17]

On the other hand, the verbal mode of the widely-popular Little Peppers was of another level, relatively commonplace, and mirroring its era, sometimes in an archaically formal manner; yet the narrative always moved easily along and the pace seemed right for this kind of sentimental family story.

In a moment, Phronsie was perched upon old Mr. King's knee, and playing with his watch; while the others, freed from all restraint, were chatting and laughing happily till some of the cheeriness overflowed and warmed the heart of the old gentleman.
"We go tomorrow," he said, rising, and looking at his watch. "Why, is it possible that we have been here an hour! there, my little girl, will you give me a kiss?" and he bent his handsome old head down to the childish face upturned to his confidingly.
"Don't go," said the child, as she put up her little lips in grave confidence. "I do like you—I *do!*"
"Oh, Phronsie," began Mrs. Pepper.
"Don't reprove her, madam," said the old gentleman, who liked it immensely....[18]

In the same general period there was one woman who in no way allied herself with feminine contemporaries but turned instead to the style of Alger and Optic, and used a double title to indicate quick rewards for industry and grit. Unfortunately she could not fulfill the promise of a single, first-rate delineation which deceives the reader into believing that a realistic story might ensue. Here is Mrs. Down.

Fat, lazy, and good-natured—you could see that with a glance; an undecided mouth, and shallow blue eyes; a general shiftlessness pervading her whole arrangement, or rather derangement for her light, fady hair was untidily lumped up with a broken comb, and her soiled dress parted company both at throat and waist; her apron boasted one white string and one black one; her feet were slip-shod; and though she had the frame and build of a man, you could not have been with her half an hour before you discovered her insignificance. An intelligent baby could have got the upperhand of her....[19]

This displays but a momentary skill, for the novel became a farcical melodrama of a woe-begone household comprised of a trio of moronic sons, and one enterprising daughter who literally saved the family by her dogged work during a single year. And although the siblings and even the parent showed improvement in responsibility, the story is full of exaggerated turns and players with some of the supercilious city folk falling from high places and the lowly ascending from the rural soil.

For the most part the competent writing women used an easy, flowing style that went on its way like a usually merry little stream and at a gait just right for keeping up with and for wanting to follow.

Irrepressible Katy Carr of the Katy Did series "...felt as if she were all legs and elbows and angles and joints," but was at the same time full of schemes and fancies for noon play at school. Susan Coolidge handled such qualities with just the right kind of vigor and sense of the dramatic, as is plain in the execution of Katy's Game of Rivers.

It was played in the following manner: Each girl took the name of a river, and laid out for herself an appointed path through the room, winding among the desks and benches, and making a low, roaring sound to imitate the noise of water. Cecy was the Platte; Marianne Brooks, a tall girl, the Mississippi; Alice Blair, the Ohio; Clover, the Penobscot; and so on. They were instructed to run into each other once in a while, because, as Katy said, "rivers do." As for Katy herself, she was "Father Ocean," and, growling horribly, raged up and down the platform....Every now and then,...she would suddenly cry out, "Now for a meeting of the waters!" whereupon all the rivers, bouncing, bounding, scrambling, screaming, would turn and run toward Father Ocean; while he roared louder...and made short rushes up and down, to represent the movement of waves on a beach.[20]

The more famous of the young orphans endeared themselves for just such coltishness and defiance as Katy sometimes displayed. Their originators always understood, and style was attuned to it and carried it along in a way harmonious to communication with spirit and sentiment that characterized the developing child.

Orphans or even half-orphans must compensate for meager personal worlds with some flowery conceptions; a compassionate girl reader never begrudged them that, never criticized an author's style though it seemed occasionally florid. The Anne who lived at Green Gables was the most extravagant of the big three, but her background had been the meanest, and it is true that in all the volumes that followed, the language was tempered, as was Anne. She initiated Mathew Cuthbert on that spring night as they drove from the station to Green Gables and passed under the long arch of blossoming apple trees in the twilight.

"Oh, Mr. Cuthbert," she whispered, "that place we came through—that white place—what was it?"

"Well, now, you must mean the Avenue," said Mathew after a few moments' profound reflection. "It is a kind of pretty place."

"Pretty? Oh, *pretty* doesn't seem the right word to use. Nor beautiful, either. They don't go far enough. Oh, it was wonderful—wonderful. It's the first thing I ever saw that couldn't be improved upon by imagination. It just satisfied me here"—and she put one hand on her breast—"it made a queer funny ache and yet it was a pleasant ache. Did you ever have an ache like that, Mr. Cuthbert?"[21]

Quick-tongued Rebecca had gumption enough to be just about always a match for Aunt Miranda. Of course Rebecca had the invisible backing of a family on the home-farm: a mother and a whole flock of children, and she could be more realistic than Anne.

"How are you gettin' on, Rebecca Rowena?" called a peremptory voice from within.

"Pretty good, Aunt Miranda; only I wish flowers would ever come up as thick as this pigweed and plantain and sorrel. What *makes* weeds be thick and flowers be thin?— I just happened to be stopping to think a minute when you looked out."

"You think considerable more than you weed, I guess, by appearances. How many times have you peeked into that hummingbird's nest? Why don't you work all to once and play all to once, like other folks?"

..."I don't know, Aunt Miranda, but when I'm working outdoors such a Saturday morning as this, the whole creation just screams to me to stop it and come and play."

"Well, you needn't go if it does!" responded her aunt sharply. "It don't scream to me when I'm rollin' out these doughnuts, and it wouldn't to you if your mind was on your duty."

Rebecca's little brown hands flew in and out among the weeds as she thought rebelliously: "Creation *wouldn't* scream to Aunt Miranda; it would know she wouldn't come..."[22]

Pollyanna's Glad-Game gait rather dragged along in the single follow-up book written by Mrs. Porter. (Others took over from there.) Volume one apparently exhausted the heroine as well as the reader and, perhaps, the creator, too. While volume two is not really what one might expect, there were moments when Pollyanna was properly ardent.

And Pollyanna looked; and she saw:

Over by one window, backs carefully turned, Jamie and Sadie Dean; over by another window, backs also carefully turned, Mrs. Carew and John Pendleton.

Pollyanna smiled—so adorably that Jimmy kissed her again.

"Oh, Jimmy, isn't it all beautiful and wonderful?" she murmured softly. "And Aunt Polly—she knows everything now; and it's all right. I think it would have been all right, anyway. She was beginning to feel so bad—for me. Now she's so glad. And I am, too. Why, Jimmy, I'm glad, *glad*, GLAD for—everything, now!"

Jimmy caught his breath with a joy that hurt.

"God grant, little girl, that always it may be so—..."[23]

The Page Company of Boston sometimes encased Pollyanna editions in pink covers, a glossy self-patterned stripe and fleur-de-lis design. They also used that girlish pink, a moire, which traditionally has a wavy, watered pattern, on some of the Little Colonel books. Although Lloyd Sherman was not an orphan she was still an uncommon kind of girl, rating privileges and a special place in the fictional world. Annie Fellows Johnston, who was still writing about Lloyd and/or her friends after three decades had piled up, made all girls princesses, very nearly, while the few who did not measure up were gathered in the figurative arms of royalty and elevated at least to more romantic position.

Exemplifying the dream world which the little ladies of these stories inhabited is a scene from the Tennysonian tableau arranged for a lawn fete.

Mary, standing back in the shadow of a tall lilac bush, clasped her hands in silent admiration.... It was wonderful how the moonlight transformed everything. Here was the living, breathing poem itself before her. She forgot it was Lloyd and Malcolm posing in makeshift costumes on a calico-covered dry goods box. It seemed the barge itself, draped all in blackest samite, going upward with the flood, that day that there was dole in Astolat. While she gazed like one in a dream, Lloyd half-opened her eyes, to peep at the old boatman.

"I wish they'd hurry," she said, in a low tone. "I never felt so foolish in my whole life."

"And never looked more beautiful," Malcolm answered...

"Sh," she whispered back, saucily. "You forget that you are dumb. You mustn't say a word."

"I will," he answered, in a loud whisper. "For even if I were really dumb I think I should find my voice to tell you that with your hair rippling down on that cloth of gold in the moonlight, and all in white, with that lily in your hand, you look like an angel, and I'm in the seventh heaven to be here with you in this boat."[24]

With some writers the degrees of control fell away. Prime example among these would have to be Martha Finley. That she did not confine her festooned descriptions and speeches and founts of tears to the long Elsie series is apparent to anyone dipping into the Mildred books. In this case a sleeping child, Fan, has fallen from a boat; a brother rescued and carried her to the parents.

"Mother's little Fan, mother's darling baby-girl!" she moaned, as she chafed the cold limbs, and pressed her lips to them again and again.

"Do not despair, love," her husband said; "I do not," he added, trying to speak cheerfully, and even to smile, though it was but a poor attempt. So they worked and prayed on for another hour, and at last were rewarded by the opening of the sweet eyes that had seemed to be closed forever, and a faint whisper from the pale lips. "Mother, I'm so tired!"

Then, again the mother's tears fell fast, as she clasped her recovered darling to her heart. And even the father, strong, courageous man that he was, wept and sobbed aloud, but there was no bitterness in those tears, they were but the outpouring of a joy and gratitude that was beyond words.[25]

This is an exaggerated example, of course; although it is typical of Finley, it is not, fortunately, of most. Yet there were times even for younger readers that a writer poured on sweetness and light with lavish hand as if should a little of it be good why shouldn't a lot of it be that much better? Heroines of two series, Princess Polly and Dorothy Dainty, were almost less likeable than the little child-villains of the stories. Saintly characters and their opposites, who committed shocking misdeeds or were vulgar beyond any limits, moved against one-dimensional backdrops complete with butlers and paradisiac gardens. The stories, composed for "the very little folks who can read," sometimes ended with cliff-hangers, with a character of tender age lost or stolen, and woe to the unfortunate child until the next volume should come out. Adults carried the responsibility of behaving nobly to teach virtue and brotherhood by example. For the benefit of these "very little folks," possibly, author Amy Brooks set off, whenever possible, a single sentence as a paragraph in itself.

How they crowded around him. Dorothy and Nancy each took one of his hands.

Vera clapped hers as she cried, "Oh, I've read about heroes, but now here's a *truly* one!"

"Dear friend, dear cheery neighbor," Mrs. Dainty said, "that was a brave act and it proved you to be a noble man, the best kind of nobleman."

Aunt Charlotte bent to look at his downcast eyes.

"If I had had a son, I should have liked him to be such a man," she said.

Uncle Harry was, for a few moments, too deeply moved to speak.

When he did look up, his fine eyes were wet, and his sensitive lips quivered.

"I value your regard," he said, his voice unsteady, "but believe me, I only did my duty to another man. It was no more than *any* man would do."

"Oh, it was, it *was!*" cried Flossie. "Just you think of my Uncle Harry holding a *dirty* man up close to him, when he never can bear a speck of dust on him anywhere!"[26]

It was not always women who iced the cake heavily. Consider Edgar Rice Burroughs. Dr. Frank Luther Mott judged the Tarzan stories as typical of pulp-magazine serials, possessing "extravagant imagination,...good story-telling and...mediocre writing."

Burroughs, seemingly ill at ease when dealing with the "civilized" world, reverted to awkward humor or pomposity. Stilted and pedestrian though he was in some scenes, one must judge him vigorous and exuberant in many others, for he was more at home in imagination than in the factual world. Observe his narrative power in a contest when an enraged bull-ape charged John Clayton, alias Tarzan, who, during a two-year absence from the jungle, had learned ways to enhance his physical strength.

His strong, white teeth sank into the hairy throat of his enemy as he sought the pulsing jugular.

Powerful fingers held the mighty fangs from his own flesh, or clenched and beat with the power of a steam-hammer upon the snarling, foam-flecked face of his adversary.

In a circle about them the balance of the tribe of apes stood watching and enjoying the struggle. They muttered low gutturals of approval as bits of white hide or hairy bloodstained skin were torn from one contestant or the other. But they were silent in amazement and expectation when they saw the mighty white ape wriggle upon the back of their king, and, with steel muscles tensed beneath the arm-pits of his antagonist, bear down mightily with his open palms upon the back of the thick bullneck, so that the king ape could but shriek in agony and flounder helplessly about upon the thick mat of jungle grass.[27]

As absorbed in the combat as the beasts who witnessed it, readers could follow graphic phrase by phrase to a climax replete with sound effects.

The little audience of fierce anthropoids heard the creaking of their king's neck mingling with his agonized shrieks and hideous roaring.

Then there came a sudden crack, like the breaking of a stout limb before the fury of the wind. The bullet-head crumpled forward upon its flaccid neck against the great hairy chest—the roaring and the shrieking ceased.[28]

For adventure the heart must be stalwart since the nucleus of a boy's desire was to step out with figurative sword or lance and accept a challenge dropped, or to seek and find some sort of contest, or to defy the world itself if no other opportunity presented itself. Mark Twain expressed this again and again in the Tom Sawyer books. A hero must be inventive, and his range of vision ought to include comedy as well as drama.

When Huckleberry Finn was posing as Tom Sawyer (accidentally, to begin with,) and Tom himself as his half-brother Sid—this in the southern home of Aunt Sally and Uncle Silas Phelps—Tom made the principle plain. Recovering from a wound received during the elaborately trumped-up attempt to free the runaway slave, Jim, Tom heard Aunt Sally telling that Jim was again chained in a cabin.

Tom rose square up in bed, with his eye hot, and his nostrils opening and shutting like gills, and sings out to me:

"They hain't no *right* to shut him up! *Shove!*—and don't you lose a minute. Turn him loose! he ain't no slave; he's as free as any cretur that walks this earth!"

"What *does* the child mean?"

"I mean every word I *say*, Aunt Sally, and if somebody don't go, *I'll* go. I've knowed him all his life, and so has Tom, there. Old Miss Watson died two months ago, and she was ashamed she ever was going to sell him down the river, and *said* so; and she set him free in her will."

"Then what on earth did *you* want to set him free for, seeing he was already free?"

"Well, that *is* a question, I must say; and *just* like women! Why, I wanted the *adventure* of it; and I'd 'a' waded neck-deep in blood..."[29]

Tarkington's Penrod series had an undercurrent of irony, or call it an invisible underlining, through the pages. His boys' plottings, infantile in conception by comparison to those of Tom and Huck, were nonetheless related to that province of reasonable explanation for exploits of unexpected nature. One of them built itself upon an encounter with Whitey, an aged horse who had been "his own master" for several days.

...He had but one eye, a feeble one, and his legs were not to be depended upon; but he managed to cover a great deal of ground...and to get monstrously hungry and thirsty before he happened to look in upon Penrod and Sam.

When the two boys chased him up the alley they had no intention to cause pain; they had no intention at all. They were no more cruel than Duke, Penrod's little old dog, who followed his own instincts, and making his appearance hastily through a hole in the back fence, joined the pursuit with sound and fury. A boy will nearly always run after anything that is running, and his first impulse is to throw a stone at it. This is a survival of primeval man, who must take every chance to get his dinner. So, when Penrod and Sam drove the hapless Whitey up the alley, they were really responding to an impulse thousands and thousands of years old—an impulse founded upon the primordial observation that whatever runs is likely to prove edible. Penrod and Sam were not "bad"; they were never that. They were something which was not their fault; they were historic.[30]

There was another way, too, a broad and blunt, often vulgar way delivered in slapdash manner as if the speaker, an elocutionist in an era of that profession, were declaiming from a platform. George Peck started a story and went galloping along at a voice-exhausting clip. His twists and turns were sufficient to make one wince, and while likely some readers of other days, particularly the ladies, turned coldly away, not everyone ignored Peck and his shameless "bad boy."

"What is it?" asked the grocery man, as he took a stool and sat out by the front door beside the boy who was trying to eat a box of red raspberries on the sly.

"Well, Uncle Ezra and me bribed the nurse girl to dress the baby up one evening in some old, dirty baby clothes...and we put it in a basket and placed the basket on the front door step, and put a note in the basket and addressed it to Pa....Ma and Pa and Uncle Ezra and me were in the back parlor when the bell rung, and Ma told me to go to the door, and I brought in the basket...and told Pa there was a note in it for him....Pa read part of the note and stopped and turned pale, and sat down then Ma read some of it, and she didn't feel very well, and she leaned against the piano and grated her teeth. The note was in a girl's hand writing, and was like this:

'OLD BALD HEADED PET:—

You will have to take care of your child, because I cannot. Bring it up tenderly, and don't, for heaven's sake, send it to the Foundling Asylum. I shall go drown myself. Your loving, ALMIRA.'

"What did your Ma say?" said the grocery man, becoming interested.

"O, Ma played her part well. Uncle Ezra had told her the joke, and she said 'retch,' to Pa...and put her handkerchief to her eyes. Pa said it was 'false,' and Uncle Ezra said, 'O brother, that I should live to see this day,'..."[31]

Occasionally Frank Baum worked into his style some dead-pan humor, but one must do a bit of searching for this characteristic in the Oz books. Acknowledged as clumsy with words, Baum had no trouble in luring and holding a reading audience. This he managed with ideas and fancy and astounding happenings that capture child-attention for decade after decade. His is a plain, everyday style of writing, a style apparently perfectly satisfactory to and understandable by a child whose interest is deep in the fantasy. The impossible appears perfectly reasonable; the action amazes the listener; the characters belong to a never-never land and are capable of great kindness or of inconsistencies and wicked deeds. The young reader accepts all elements as the adventures unroll.

"Come in," called Oz, and the Woodman entered and said,

"I have come for my heart."

"Very well," answered the little man. "But I shall have to cut a hole in your breast, so I can put your heart in the right place. I hope it won't hurt you."

"Oh, no," answered the Woodman. "I shall not feel it at all."

So Oz brought a pair of tinners' shears and cut a small, square hole in the left side of the Tin Woodman's breast. Then, going to a chest of drawers, he took out a pretty heart, made entirely of silk and stuffed with sawdust.

"Isn't it a beauty," he asked.[32]

To the adult, excerpts appear not so pedestrian; it is while reading through an entire volume that style sometimes grows tiresome. Perhaps an economical method of expression has the merit of being stripped of extraneous terms; perhaps with the skeleton of a story more nearly visible, tedious construction shows up and can more easily undergo improvement.

Following some of the travel series is a chore because the style employed by the serious writer was dutiful and based upon presentation of detailed information as though one must ingest endless facts and figures in order to appreciate other cultures. In this field, the authors followed those who had gone before, the early travelers, including the missionaries; however, the writers for young people did attempt to lighten guide-book accounts with small stories and infrequent bits of humor. Thomas Knox was responsible for a tremendous set of heavily illustrated tomes. Impressive for bulk and sheer weight, they range from the Far East in both directions to cover the world in an encyclopedic manner.

"What is the jin-riki-sha?" the reader naturally asks.

Its name comes from three words, "jin," meaning man; "riki," power; and "sha," carriage: altogether it amounts to "man-power-carriage." It is a little vehicle like an exaggerated baby-cart or diminutive one-horse chaise, and has comfortable seating capacity for only one person, though it will hold two if they are not too large. It was introduced into Japan in 1870, and is said to have been the invention of an American. At all events, the first of them came from San Francisco; but the Japanese soon set about making them, and now there are none imported....For a short distance, or where it is not required to keep up a high speed, one man is sufficient; but otherwise two, or even three, men are needed. They go at a good trot, except when ascending a hill or where the roads are bad....[33]

Those who tried to introduce the rest of the world to the small Americans fortunately settled for simpler aim: they concentrated upon a central character and his small universe and built up a simple story. The comprehensive Little Cousin series had a number of authors, but first and best among them was Mary Hazelton Wade, who managed more adroitly than some others.

And Etu was like the rest of his people. He was always finding some new source of fun and pleasure. When he was still a tiny baby, left to amuse himself on the platform inside the house, he would watch for the dogs to appear in the passageway, and throw his ivory toys at them. Then he would laugh and shake his sides as they dodged the playthings and scampered away.

Sometimes one of the older children would bring him a ball of snow or ice and teach him to kick it into the air again and again, without touching it with his hands...

When he grew older and braver he allowed himself to be tossed up in the air in a blanket of walrus hide. He must keep on his feet all the time, and not tumble about in the blanket.[34]

Lucy Fitch Perkins did even better, sturdy, practical woman that she was, and submitted her stories to a neighborhood "gang" for judgment. Had she bedecked her mysteries and day-to-day adventures with gingerbread trim, it is probable that her face-to-face critics would have expressed uninhibited disapproval. This focus upon plausibility extended to her illustrations for the Twins books, which opened up the world at large to young American citizens. Sometimes Mrs. Perkins diminished her own physical stature by getting down on her knees to join the child-view and catch true perspectives for her sketches.

When the new little brother of twins Take and Taro was one month old, the entire family went for a priestly blessing of the baby.

When they reached the great door of the Temple itself, the Father said: "Now we must take off our shoes." So they all slipped their toes out of their clogs, and went into

the Temple just as the bell in the courtyard rang out with a great—*boom*— BOOM—
BOOM! that made the air shiver and shake all about them.

The Temple was one big, shadowy room with tall red columns all about.

"It's just like a great forest full of trees, isn't it?" Taro whispered to Take, as they
went in.[35]

This was more effective than conscientious endeavors to introduce other
cultures by carrying American children off to foreign lands. Gadabout Mary
Jane, sister Alice, their mother and "Dahdah" tripped about Europe, seeing
the sights, running upon American friends and making new acquaintances
among other tourists, eating tremendous meals duly detailed and spending
time at shopping. Sight-seeing did wear one down, Mary Jane concluded.

"But I've decided on one thing I'm going to buy. I'm going to get a pair of gloves
for my doll and a pair for Betty's doll, too," she added.…."You should see how cute
they are."[36]

The strength of a style moving steadily on its way, dressing the framework
of a story adequately but not lingering over an abundance of verbal
gymnastics, needs extra praise. It is easy to find quotable examples in Sophie
May, who combined reality and simplicity in admirable combination. Here
is Dotty Dimple, about to make a trip westward with her father and
consequently "…happy up to my throat."

Just as her patience was wearing to a thread the hack arrived, looking as black and
glossy as if some one had been all this time polishing it for the occasion. Dotty disdained
the help of the driver, and stepped into the carriage as eagerly as Jack climbed the beanstalk.
She flirted her clean dress against the wheel, but did not observe it. She was as happy
as Jack when he reached the giant's house; happier, too, for she had mounted to a castle
in the air; and everybody knows a castle in the air is gayer than all the gold houses
that ever grew on the top of a stalk.[37]

The way in which Laura Ingalls Wilder portrayed Midwestern pioneer
days was equally honest. So remarkably even is her style that one can quote
from almost any chapter of any volume in the Little House series as
illustration. Possibly credit belongs to the thoughtfulness of maturity during
which stage there may come the shucking off of pretense as well as even
an increase in clarity of vision and memory. Publishing date of *The Little
House in the Big Woods*, first of the series "reborn" in the 1950's, was 1932,
and Mrs. Wilder's birth year was 1867.

In these family recountings calamity and near-calamity are part of life
and accepted as such, but the joyous moments stand like sign-posts in prairie
country.

"No fair!" Lena yelled. The other pony was galloping in a circle, held by its picket rope. Lena grabbed its mane, unsnapped the rope, and sailed right up from the ground onto the back of the running pony.

Laura stood watching Lena and Jean race in circles, yelling like Indians. They rode crouching, their hair streaming back, their hands clutched in the flying black manes and their brown legs clasping the ponies' sides. The ponies curved and swerved, chasing each other on the prairie like birds in the sky. Laura would never have tired of watching them.[38]

Obviously that long century ending during the depression years shows an amazing array of styles ranging from the didactic to the foolishly formal, from the flowery to an easy flow of rhythmic phrasing. It was a free-for-all time, with magazine and book editors wanting, requesting, sometimes coaxing and waiting for manuscripts, sometimes writing desired stories themselves, and of a young public in as eager a state of mind to receive and consume all that the presses turned out. It is no wonder that a good many competent and a good deal more than competent writers supplied the pages on which to build flesh-and-blood as well as ephemeral dreams. This was a rainbow era for girl and boy readers, for youth magazines, and for writers. At its close there ended as well the time of really classic series. Was it that the first avid appetite was gone? Was it that competition in entertainment moved in too fully with the gross flowering of moving pictures and development of radio? Sophistication was spreading and the horizons of the world were diminishing in distance. At the same time the economy was falling apart.

More often than not, any new series concerned straight mystery (some of which had regularly invaded syndicate and other light series for perhaps twenty years) or scientific adventure and had as sole aim entertainment and commercial success. Often the characters were really but names, not three-dimensional. The stories satisfied a desire for reading minus intellectual or emotional demand upon the consumer. True, some series by able authors did evolve but not so often as series to be read and re-read and carried along through ensuing decades. Probably the change was inevitable. The old comfortable sense of permanency was vanishing as the world whirled on in great forward movement in science and invention, in wild multiplication of knowledge itself, and in ever and ever more scheduled hours and seasons for the young who, it seemed, no longer developed powers of invention and imagination for self-occupation.

However, and after all, the old series, a few of them, did weave themselves into the literary background for the youthful portion of the population. Children still wanted a continuity, symbolizing security, in fiction, while also liking a process of visualization in keeping with the age, thus to accomplish the kind of indelible impression common to the lost era of simpler dimensions and magnetism of the written word.

Chapter XV

Little People and Small Animals (Mostly)

In a used-book store that seemed to serve well the ordinary citizens of a somewhat isolated foothill town, a coltish child past the easy age of simpler stories appealed for help.

"I'm looking for animal stories."

"What kind?" the clerk asked.

"Horses and dogs," the girl answered, and received directions for finding a special shelf.

"*You* don't have a horse," her father put in brutally more than once. "What do you want a horse story for? You don't want a horse story."

What he had forgotten, or perhaps never knew, was that animal stories have a lure for the young. They dote not only on domesticated animals and friendly little beasts of field and woods but also on grizzly bears, proud and wild horses, lions and tigers and elephants and prehistoric creatures.

Even the timid have empathy for small varieties and for other life in lesser forms than themselves. They construct resting places for birds found dead after a summer storm, for squirrel victims of vehicular traffic. They seek help for injured fowl, and get down to watch insects engaged in transportation or more mysterious activities. Eyes of wonder look upon so miniature a universe. Perhaps this is because in imagination children identify more easily with still smaller beings or because in such cases they feel themselves giants in comparison and can give tender aid.

The world of animals is the natural world of children and of anticipated rapport, thus the fascination of circus, zoo, wild animal preserve, and agricultural countryside of old-time farm, which today may be one assembled for the pleasure of visiting children. Who cannot remember a child "woofing" at a dog or "meowing" in a cat's presence to draw its attention, or crowing, bawling in calf or lamb fashion, neighing or whinnying? Or the sight of grazing cattle on a dewy summer morning as the prairie goes flying by and a child, announcing, "I have to practice my mooing," leans out of a car window and repeats a long and doleful call?

Animals have had eternal attraction for children. When was there *not* inclusion of birds and beasts in literature? Well before children had any kind of library designed especially for them, they were reading and listening to fables, legends, myths, old folk and fairy tales. Ancient literature handed down by verbal recounting or by printed page would not disappear so long as animals played parts in it.

An infant finds himself in a fresh, compact realm, innocent and unsoiled of spirit. In this basic kingdom he links himself with other newly-arrived beings who may be equally guileless. This attraction when translated into pictures has always provided pleasure for adults. In the 19th century postal cards carried imprints of children and young animals, while colored cards presented by merchants show children and animals along with flowers and insects on one side and extol products or services on the other. Readers of the second half of that century had access to stories of "dumb creatures" which became classics: Brer Fox and Brer Rabbit, Miss Cow and all the others of Joel Chandler Harris' *Uncle Remus* (1880), Britisher Anna Sewell's horse called Black Beauty (1877), and Canadian Marshall (a woman, incidentally) Saunder's dog named Beautiful Joe (1894).

It was a series author, Hezekiah Butterworth, editor of *Youth's Companion* at the time, who composed an introduction for Beautiful Joe's autobiography. He wrote of "...the influence that shall *teach* the reader *how* to live in sympathy with the animal world; how to understand the languages of the creatures that we have been accustomed to call 'dumb' and the sign language of the lower order of these dependent beings."[1]

It is not to be wondered that a ready-made world already supplied with birds, beasts, insects and water-life should become setting for education and for entertainment. Graced with a certain freedom by reason of tolerance for the infantile and dependent, this "proving ground" became launching place for many a classroom reader. This was quite in keeping with small, imaginative individuals fascinated by other life, and inclined to make inanimate objects animate, invisible creatures companions and to represent their second-selves as the wrongdoers. And it seemed perfectly normal that animals should speak in voices like their own.

About thirty old textbooks, from a few primers and first through third readers, published between 1860 and 1930, have illustrations of almost every variety of animal. Primary books exhibit brief rhymes and folk tales featuring animals as often as children. First readers follow the same pattern, adding such information as identification of birds and how to care for them, as well as subjects of insects, flowers and fairies. Second readers expand to include re-told legends, fables and folk tales from American Indians and several foreign lands. How or why things happened is a prime element of narration: why the eagle is the king of the birds and why the wren's tail extends upward, how the squirrel got a curly tail and how the frog lost

"'Lord save us!' cried the duck. 'How does it make up its mind?'"

The rare pushmi-pullyu (now extinct, finally agreed to accompany Doctor Dolittle back to England. (from *The Story of Doctor Dolittle*, courtesy of Christopher Lofting)

After 1900, little readers could flee from an enclosed world into a realm of meadows, woods and fantasy.

his. Bees, bats, reptiles, ants, fowls, camels, tortoises enter scenes as well as human beings. As a *New Franklin Second Reader* of 1886 phrases it in the preface, "While the stories are full of interest to our young readers, they are also fitted to inculcate right views of conduct—truthfulness, honesty, kindness and other virtues."

In its second volume, the *Wheeler Graded Reader* of 1903 terms the second-reader pupil as "still a beginner." Opining that the child will like best the stories of children like himself, the preface-writer goes on immediately to state, "He will like the stories about heroic dogs, wonderful parrots, intelligent cats, naughty kittens, busy bees and idle butterflies. One animal that talks is worth all scientific observations about animals."

Two third readers of 1860 are solemn and frankly moralistic and lack even simplified stories. One of them dwells with dreadful solemnity upon evils of alcohol, tobacco and crime. Yet the *New Education Third Reader* of 1901 carries a prefatory message that, with the purpose of helping the child to develop a taste for choice reading and to feel interest in what he is reading, "...the larger part of the stories have been drawn from the fruitful field of myth, legend, fable, biography, and fairy tale, and various selections having an ethical value." Needless to say, the first three categories are rife with animal characters.

The *Holton-Curry* 1914 third reader uses animal folk tales, the legend of "How Fire Came to the Indians," with animals as vital characters, and a version of Louise de la Ramée's *Dog of Flanders*. A *Pennell* and *Cusack* is bright with dog show and twin bear stories, recountings of animals of various lands, an adaptation of Charles D. Roberts' cat story and the English account of Dick Whittington and his cat. It has as well a version of how the turkey acquired his "war whoop" and why the bear has a short tail.[2]

The scene was set for every kind of animal adventure. The background encouraged such creation. The air echoed with pertinent phrases and descriptions: "A man's best friend is his dog," "wise as an owl," "sly as a fox," "strong as a lion." There were also symbolic uses. The bluebird signified happiness, the owl denoted sagacity, the American eagle, power.

What was more natural than that series should become, among many other things, vehicles for bringing to the tell-me-a-story population the lore and life of beasts and birds? Produced in number, they appeared like so many adjuncts to children's museums or like so many beckoning petting zoos with stock line-ups of rabbits, raccoons, ravens and owls, 'possums and woodchucks and cubs of various kinds.

In time young people of some maturity found series and collections of animal stories for satisfying their common appetite. Edgar Rice Burroughs wrote of savage jungle animals, Charles D. Roberts favored creatures in cold lands, and Elliot Whitney (pseudonym) covered the world with his The Boys' Big Game series. And there were the popular dog stories of Albert Payson Terhune, collie specialist, who said that he did not write for children and was surprised to learn that a sizable segment of his readers consisted of older children.

Although constructed usually upon simple lines, the tales for the very young nonetheless exhibited some of the same qualities known to the more complex series. Characters, however, were more subject to "lessons." Why? Because they were often young. Or mischievous. Or downright naughty. Because morality needed early teaching and learning, and presenting it in a roundabout way through animal behavior made it less personal and thus more acceptable.

Somehow or somewhere, someone (and one feels with these nicely vague terms a kinship to Thornton Burgess with his stories answering the cryptic journalistic questions), someone concluded that children slept blissfully after a short animal tale or two of an evening. There was also the assumption that young of all species have much in common so far as natural traits are concerned, and who is to say that they do not? A third reasoning seemed to be that it was natural for animals and birds to communicate with the familiar human voice.

Hugh Lofting's Doctor Dolittle, however, learned the truth about animal communication. It was Polynesia, his parrot, who informed him of dual languages: people's language and bird language. Polynesia illustrated with "Ka-ka, oi-ee, fee-fee?" meaning "Is the porridge hot yet?"[3] Doctor Dolittle spent the afternoon learning, taking down the birds' ABC's and their words. Then Polynesia, when dog Jip entered, pointed out how an animal also spoke with ears, feet, nose and tail, and proceeded to assist the doctor with all animal languages.

Can anyone wonder that these bilingual beasts and birds (body language of human beings was a term of the future at that time) posed powerful rivals to the small bland beings who came out so often and everywhere by families and in pairs and alone: Mary Jane and Honey Bunch, the Bobbseys, Dorothy Dainty and Princess Polly and all the others?

During the early decades of this century the read-aloud animal stories took over children's "corners" in daily newspapers. Thornton Burgess, whose boyhood dream had been that of becoming a naturalist, began syndicating Bedtime Stories in the United States and the Canadian papers. The year was 1912, the rule was a story a day, and more than seven thousand carried his name.

Journalist Howard Garis began earlier than that. Fulfilling the publisher's request, he introduced Uncle Wiggily Longears to the public in January of 1910 in the *Newark News*, according to his son Roger. The adventures of that wily rabbit, a central figure with divers characters revolving about him, appeared six times weekly for more than fifty years. Garis maintained a three-month stockpile and wrote until his death at eighty-nine.

There was also Albert Bigelow Paine, who spent a year as children's editor for the *New York Herald* and from 1899 to 1908 as League editor with *St. Nicholas*. It was during this period that he wrote the Hollow Tree and Arkansaw Bear stories. Having supplied children's stories for various publications he gathered them, as did Burgess and Garis, for hardback books and had the good fortune to rate J.M. Condé as illustrator.

Additional experiences and "doings" of woods and field friends found a plenitude of space on shelves in shops and libraries and homes. Arthur Scott Bailey (1877-1949), a Vermonter and graduate of Harvard, became literary adviser to a press, did special work as a newsman and composed stories for the young in years. His Tuck-Me-In Tales, Sleepy-Time Tales and Slumber-Town Tales added up to a total of forty-three volumes. New Yorker George E. Walsh (1865-1941) joined the staff of the *New York Tribune*, served as special correspondent for other papers, free-lanced and contributed voluminously with serials and short stories. He followed his Twilight Animal books with the Twilight Bird stories. The impression continued to be that parents or older siblings read to the small people only as inducement to get them into bed.

Naturally the syndicate entered the field, this time under the pseudonym of Richard Barnum. Here there was no restriction to evening hours for reading. The Kneetime Animal books display on their duplicate covers a self-confident, white-collared father with open book and, on his knee, a curly-haired daughter in her Sunday best. Flanking her is an older brother, replica of the pictured parent, and leaning against him with a hand placed on that parent's free knee. Illustrations are inferior, and book titles range from *Mappo, the Merry Monkey* to *Lightfoot, the Leaping Goat.*

On what rested the popularity of such stories? On simple style and subject, on definitive characterization and on action—something surprising nearly always happened—and upon reasonably gratifying settlement with ethical principle. Considered wholesome and informative entertainment, they satisfied parental desire to instill tenets of exemplary behavior.

Not unnaturally, familiarity with small animals extended in the direction of both real and fictional parents, the readers, as well as to small people, the listeners. And Uncle Wiggily's name, at least, was of wide repute if not always sanctioned. Here a British novelist allowed his entry.

> ...Feeling utterly wasted, she went to say good night to Michael and Marigold.
> "Oh, Mummy, Mummy, my darlingest Mummy! Read us a story!"
> "Read us Uncle Wiggily in the paper!"
> "Uncle *Wiggily!* Darlings! You know Mummy never reads you anything like that."
> "Daddy does."
> "You know Mummy only reads you things that are beautiful or true."[4]

"Mummy" might well have approved of Burgess, the author acknowledged to be a master at such narration. Elizabeth Nesbitt, who prepared one section of *The Critical History of Children's Literature*, said this: "Thornton Burgess' *Old Mother West Wind* stories are told simply and with charm. The personification of animals and the tales of their lives in the meadows are successful because they are convincing and interesting. The imitations are maudlin, artificial, and monotonous."[5]

A more recent critic spoke of Burgess' "pastoral landscape" as reflecting the "author's longing for a simpler time out of time, an edenic rural past." That the Burgess "plots lack complexity" is understandable in light of the age group for whom he was writing as well as the era during which he wrote. That his stories are somewhere in the middle of "...a genre which includes, at one extreme, stories featuring animals which are actually humans masquerading in feathers or fur, and, at the other, stories presenting the cycle of animal life with strict and often brutal realism" is an esoteric means of seeking a category for stories which accomplished exactly what Burgess meant them to accomplish. The same critic called the Burgess animals "hybrids," concluding that "they operate in a realm at once natural and yet infused with a human moral code."[6]

"I do preach," Burgess himself once wrote when referring to his dream of becoming a naturalist and that of his mother of his becoming a preacher, "—the gospel of the oneness of all nature and love for the humane treatment of the lesser folk in fur and feathers...."[7]

As always, he used clear phraseology just as he fashioned his small fieldfolk in primary strokes. The critic did not. He used the terms "formulaic and didactic" and declaimed that Burgess' "...supra-zoological animal characters are often one-dimensional, embodying a single emblematic characteristic." His concession was that the characters are "charming, cuddly and gently whimsical," and that despite the "dated" impression, "their concern for conservation is certainly current."[8]

It hardly seems necessary to rebut the accusations. Mother West Wind, who could be firm, might carry the matter to the realm of meadow and stream where probably Grandfather Frog would "open his big mouth," emit a "Chug-a-rum!" and thereafter begin a once-upon-a-time story. It would hark back to the days when the world was young and the ancestors of critics, fifty or one hundred times removed, blew hard and often.

Styles of writing in this division were in all cases straightforward. Paine, the earliest born of the group, was in demand at home as a teller of tales. Calling himself "The Story Teller," he wrote in an old-fashioned rambling way somewhat in the tradition of the Uncle Remus stories but without their vernacular although he slurred or dropped syllables at times. It was a mode less primary than that used later. His characters spent their days trying ingeniously to trick each other. "Little Lady" was the one who did the initial questioning and the spurring on to more tales, while it was "the little boy" who kept Uncle Remus in a recounting humor.

This is the story that Mr. Jack Rabbit told to Mr. 'Coon and Mr. 'Possum when they sat together on the edge of the world and hung their feet over and looked at the moon. After Mr. 'Possum had finished his story, the Rabbit leaned back and swung his feet over the Big Nowhere awhile, thinking. Then he began.

"Well," he said, "my folks used to live in the moon."

"Humph!" said the 'Coon.

"Nonsense!" said the 'Possum.

"Yes," said Jack Rabbit, "they did. The moon is a world, away over on the other side of the Big Nowhere, and it doesn't stand still and stay top side up like this world, but keeps moving about and turning over, so that you have to look sharp and hang on tight to keep from falling off...."[9]

An aura of agelessness hangs over such stories, whether they concern Jack Rabbit, Burgess' Old Man Coyote or Mr. Mocker, Bailey's Chirpy Cricket or Solomon Owl, Washer the Raccoon of Walsh, or Garis' Uncle Wiggily.

Any one of them is, in reality, the folk tale, the story handed down verbally and meant to be read aloud once someone had set it down on paper. "The little boy" and "Little Lady" and any of their ilk could listen and several decades later tell the self-same story with small variations to their own progeny, who would be equally at ease eavesdropping on Little Joe Otter or Mrs. Ladybug.

The question-answering stories which Burgess related remain legend-like, espousing animal behavior and reasons for peculiarities. Sometimes those peculiarities resulted from nature's disciplining. Burgess invariably aimed at demonstrating the "gospel" he confessed to preaching; yet he could on occasion go into an entertaining Old South dialect, as with Ol' Mistah Buzzard.

> "Way back in the days when Grandpap Buzzard had his lil falling out with ol' King Eagle and done fly so high he sco'tch the feathers offen his haid, he had a cousin, did Grandpap Buzzard, and this cousin was jes' naturally lazy and no 'count...."[10]

However, it seems only fair to display a more typical example and to show Burgess at one of his most forceful moments. The drama features the bison Thunderfoot, who had become proud and haughty. When he almost collided with Mother Nature she knew that she must set his world in proper perspective again.

> " 'My Lord of the Prairies seems in fine spirits,' said Mother Nature softly. 'Is all well with my Lord?'
>
> "Thunderfoot tossed his head proudly. 'All is well,' said he.
>
> " 'I am sorry that others cannot say as much,' replied Mother Nature, and all the softness was gone from her voice, and it was sharp. 'I seem to hear the sobs of a broken-hearted little Meadow Lark,' she continued. 'Little though she be and humble, she is as much to me as is my Lord of the Prairies who has made her suffer.'
>
> "Stooping swiftly, Mother Nature picked up her staff and with it struck Thunderfoot on the neck, so that his head was brought low, and in fear of another blow he humped his shoulders up. 'Thus shall you be, still big, still strong, but hump-shouldered and carrying your head low in shame, no longer Lord of the Prairies, until such time as you restore to Mrs. Meadow Lark the eggs you destroyed,' said she, and turned her back on him.
>
> "It was so. From that day on, Thunderfoot ceased to rule over the Wide Prairies. He was hump-shouldered and he carried his head low, looking and looking for the eggs he never could find...."[11]

Liking to place his wood-folk in ridiculous situations, Bailey wrote in lighter, sprightlier manner. Consider the case of Solomon Owl, who found himself a bit on the sick side. He went to Aunt Polly Woodchuck, who was an herb doctor, and followed her counseling for some time but found no benefit from eating small chickens rather than mice. When she learned that he swallowed his food whole, she was quite bowled over.

"Gracious me!....It's no wonder you're ill....You have a wishbone inside you. I can feel it!" she told him, as she prodded him in the waist-coat.

"I wish you could get it out for me!" said Solomon with a look of distress.

"All the wishing in the world won't help you," she answered, "unless we can find some way of removing the wishbone so you can wish on that. Then I'm sure you would feel better at once."

"This is strange," Solomon mused. "All my life I've been swallowing my food without chewing it. And it has never given me any trouble before....What shall I do?"

"Don't eat anything for a week," she directed. "And fly against tree-trunks as hard as you can. Then come back after seven days."[12]

Buffoonery, of course, was Garis' trademark despite the little "lessons" to be found here and there. It showed itself in phraseology, in traits, in overall inventiveness. His was a particularly animated world. Although he employed a crowd of young animals, his star was Uncle Wiggily, while lesser performers were such creatures as Sammie and Susie Littletail (and Cora Ann Multiplicationtable, Susie's doll), ducks Lulu, Alice and Jimmie Wibble-wobble, and Arabella, the chicken girl. The seeming senselessness of irrational behavior and the lovely up-and-down-hill sounds of unrelated words thrown together in mad sequence tickle the mythical funny-bone and delight the spirit. Uncle Wiggily was rather omnipotent which quality put him in a classification similar to that of Burgess' Mother Nature.

...His house was in a hollow stump, and he called it a bungalow, to be proper like and stylish...And with Uncle Wiggily lived Nurse Jane Fuzzy Wuzzy, a muskrat lady who kept the hollow stump bungalow nice and tidy for him, getting his meals and dusting the piano.

One day Uncle Wiggily put on his glasses, took his red, white and blue striped rheumatism crutch down off the bird cage and hopped out on the front porch.

"Where are you going?" asked Nurse Jane.

"Oh, just for a little ride in my airship," answered the bunny uncle. For Mr. Longears had an airship...The airship was made of an old clothes-basket, and toy circus balloons were fastened to it with strings to pull it up in the air. There was an umbrella to keep off the hot sun, and an electric fan in the back of the basket, going around whizzie-izzie to push the airship. Uncle Wiggily steered it by turning a baby-carriage wheel.[13]

That is a sedate opening for the old gentleman rabbit whose stories abound with exclamations and end with a certain type of absurdity for which Garis was never at a loss.

And next, if the dogwood tree doesn't bark at the pussy willow and make its tail fluff up, I'll tell you about Uncle Wiggily and Nurse Jane.[14]

It was Garis who introduced female characters, while the others generally awarded all positions to the other sex with the exception of occasional motherly roles. As for titles of address, the usual trend was toward distinctive traits of the various animals: Grumpy Weasel, Sandy Chipmunk, Jolly Robin, Paddy the Beaver, Chatterer the Red Squirrel. An elderly animal might be termed "Old Man" or "Grandfather." With Burgess the young rabbit was always "Peter." Paine called his "Jack," but otherwise it was his custom to add a simple "Mr." to the species, dog, turtle, crow, polecat or other creature.

Except for the Walsh and Barnum beasts and birds, the animal players customarily appeared in one garb or another, perhaps just a waist-coat or hat, depending upon physical make-up and illustrator. J.M. Condé illustrated Paine's work in the tradition of A.B. Frost, illustrator for some 20th century editions of *Uncle Remus*, furnishing both trousers and coat or shirt and sometimes even shoes. Frost garbed characters more completely than did Harrison Cady, who illustrated the Burgess books. Not only the clothing but also the conceptions of the Cady pictures give a simple and comic look to the wearers, while those creatures clothed by Condé appear quite at ease in their garments. The varying and non-memorable Garis illustrations show characters dressed, at least to some extent; the same is true in the Bailey books.

There was also a "bad boy" in the animal universe; this was the bold, comic-strip Billy Whiskers in a series begun by Frances Trego Montgomery, who also wrote dog stories. One cannot but feel that the audacious Billy's appeal directed itself toward boys, particularly, and toward a group an age-step above the Burgess crowd. In a feminine company discussing this young goat, none spoke with any warmth for goat Billy; none spoke of anything but dislike and, indeed, so little did a particular individual respect him, even though she was "a born reader," that she confessed to having "thrown away" the Billy Whiskers book given to her.

As for admirers, it is no doubt a joy to witness a creature doing all the wicked things denied to self, and perhaps supplies a satisfaction, possibly even performing a service in blunting instincts of not so great value.

One of Billy Whiskers' bold habits was to go where he was quite uninvited, and quite unwelcome, unless there were boys present. In company with Betty, who was Señorita Burroetta, he once went to church.

...while the organ was playing and the priests were kneeling, Billy and Betty walked the whole length of the middle aisle, side by side, as if they were a bridal couple. When they arrived at the altar, Billy stopped and commenced to eat some roses that were in a vase on the altar steps.

The congregation sat stupefied with horror...The music made Betty lonesome and she threw up her head and let out such a loud, mule-like bray that it frightened the kneeling priest and he jumped up as if shot for he thought he heard Balaam's ass bray; but when he turned and saw standing behind him a live burro and a goat, his astonishment knew no bounds and he stood gazing at them with open mouth, while the choir boys laughed and giggled and thought it a good joke.[15]

He survived, surprisingly when one considers all the scrapes that he got into, for several dozen volumes. The style is quite as plain and direct as that used for the Bad Boy series, and the guffaws would no doubt be quite as loud—given an appreciative audience.

And, for a satisfying finish to this particular fictional field, there were the relatively gentle water-color animals of Hugh Lofting, whose Doctor Dolittle stories, cast with a mixture of human beings outnumbered by well-spoken creatures of other orders, verge on fantasy. Ruth Hill Viguers, in *The Critical History of Children's Literature*, links the series with the "modern fairy tales" appearing after World War I

Having seen the military employment of animals who lacked the medical care accorded to human beings, Lofting devised the idea of a doctor whose affection for animals would cause him to relinquish conventional practice for concentration upon their welfare. The vision was a happy one with treatment entirely different from that of already established animal-story-authors. No Deep Woods or Green Meadows for the Dolittle characters! They made the world their own, even voyaging to the moon by means of a giant moth, Jamara Bumblelily, and were capable of inspired moves and brilliant reasoning as well as other talents. And it is true that the animals found human beings as peculiar as human beings found them. When the doctor announced through the monkey Chee-Chee that the little company must return home from Africa despite offers of various inducements to remain, the Chief Chimpanzee said to the Oldest Orang-outang, "Cousin, surely these Men be strange creatures!"[16]

Lofting animals form a sometimes superhuman category of their own, and the subtle touches are recognizable by adults if not by children. The author expected wide age appeal, for the initial volume carries this dedication: "TO ALL CHILDREN children in years and children in heart I dedicate this story." That is not all. The detailed title page of the 1920 edition displays impressions of the uncommon doctor and numerous friends and is inscribed thusly: "The Story of DOCTOR DOLITTLE being the history of his peculiar life at home and astonishing adventures in foreign parts. Never before printed. Told by Hugh Lofting. Illustrated by the author."

Home was Puddleby-on-the-Marsh, and the doctor was not without an assortment of pets as the story began. Favored among them were the duck Dab-Dab; the infant pig Gub-Gub; the owl Too-Too; Jip, the dog; Chee-Chee, the monkey; and, of course, Polynesia, the parrot. Clients were farm beasts and other people's pets until Chee-Chee came bearing an African cousin's message, brought by a swallow, of a great sickness causing death by the hundreds among the monkeys, and imploring the aid of Doctor Dolittle. Money matters being what they were, a voyage seemed hopeless until a sailor lent his boat. So, locking up, the doctor and primary pets left on the first long adventure, and the Cat's-meat-Man brought a suet-pudding as farewell gift.

When the indeed astonishing African experiences came to a close, with the monkey population again in good health, the company had to commandeer a pirate ship for the return voyage on which they bore, as gift, a rare pushmi-pullyu, with a head at each end.

Even then the drama by no means ended. At one time they suspected that some one or thing was waiting beyond the locked door of a small room. It was Too-Too who alerted the doctor.

"I hear the noise of some one putting his hand in his pocket." said the owl.

"But that makes hardly any sound at all," said the Doctor. "You couldn't hear that out here."

"Pardon me, but I can," said Too-Too. "I tell you there is some one on the other side of that door putting his hand in his pocket. Almost everything makes *some* noise— if your ears are only sharp enough to catch it. Bats can hear a mole walking in his tunnel under the earth—and they think they're good hearers. But we owls can tell you, using only one ear, the color of a kitten from the way it winks in the dark "[17]

Viguers wrote that "The nonsense is logical nonsense. Mr. Lofting had respect for children's intelligence and for their imagination: within the framework of his fantasy everything that happens is possible, yet it is never dull....."[18]

With the second book of the series, *The Voyages of Doctor Dolittle*, came the Newbery Medal. At one time Lofting, too, had association with newspaper publishing. Record lies in the introduction to the final book, for which Mrs. Lofting's sister wrote an introductory first chapter and the concluding one. Mrs. Lofting herself wrote: "When my husband...wrote and illustrated the story of Pippinella, the green canary, for the Herald Tribune Syndicate his intention was to publish it one day in book form. He used some of the material in *Doctor Dolittle's Caravan* in which the little canary appeared as the prima donna of the Doctor's canary opera and became a well-loved and established member of the Doctor's household....."[19]

In its way the animal world is a delightful one. Delving into the thoughts and dreams and desires of animals extends horizons in all directions. Perhaps it is instinctive to apply human criteria and human speech to the inhabitants of that breezy realm, just as a child finds it natural to dream life into an inanimate object such as a doll or stuffed toy. Surely it must satisfy some urging. Yet for all the limitations real or imagined, the abilities of other forms of life than our own, under testing and measuring, indicate often surprising talents. And sometimes an animal presence makes for more comfort than a human one because so little is demanded of one and, after all, how could an animal, even while driven by instinct, be crueller than man?

Chapter XVI
Among the Souvenirs

The splendor of the great series era, some of it only falsely burnished, had ended. A lavish outpouring had reached a crest and taken the only route possible, a downward one. Long gone was the day when a new Alcott title should be announced. Well gone the day when a Little Colonel or Pollyanna volume should come out in rosy pink or spring green covers with gilt lettering. Some of the last series about nobody in particular written by who knew whom went into storage until the day should come that collectors were ready to buy series of any kind at all provided that related books were available in impressive number.

The heyday of children's periodicals was history, too, and prosperity of even the long-lived ones had waned. *Youth's Companion* bowed out in 1929, while *St. Nicholas*, which had published many writers of standing, was in its last years. The foreword for a *St. Nicholas* anthology mentions the slow demise. "After Mrs. Dodge's death, in 1905, the magazine she had created and made great enjoyed a long twilight and then slowly declined, though it was not until 1939 that it finally stopped."[1]

The world had changed in other ways as well. Now a great backlog of children's literature had built up and classics were there for the reading. Public libraries had increased in number and school libraries were in existence in some communities. A child could read widely without ever owning any kind of private library. Additional means of entertainment had arrived with the advent of the radio and "talking pictures." What was more, hard times, in this case called "The Great Depression," had shocked the population and meant, among many other things, a reduction of publishing and of book-buying.

Only echoes rose from the frenzied, dare-devil days of the Twenties. Minds, sobered as well as hearts, surely wondered how a bourgeoning young nation upheld by the invincible American pioneer vision could collapse. That the country which any citizen's forebears had helped flourish should culminate in failure was frightening. A Biblical judgment seemed to hang in the air: years of plenty, then a falling from grace and years of drought and destruction that extended to the spirit and sent self-respect tumbling as though punishment were due for vague sins committed. Men, and at times entire families, sold what they could, packed up and started out afoot, hitched rides or crowded into battered vehicles to get away and seek elsewhere what they had lost at home. They became transients in a sad and disturbed land.

It was a time for and of looking back, not only at a near yesterday but at yesteryears. Certain of the writers did just that, turning their eyes in reverse direction and contemplating historical materials, just as did Mrs. Wilder, who began bare-bone accounts of a very young child progressing methodically toward young womanhood and examining widening perceptions and emotions with the passing of years. Family and heritage rather than status became important again, and the old ethics of work and responsibility as well. Life was once more real and earnest.

Series themselves never came to a halt; it was that the pace slackened. The pattern of grouping related books was firmly set. Young readers *liked* series, liked the sequence of a set of players, and for several reasons: to gain the secure sense of continuity running along in the lives of fictional people even as it proceeded in their own, and to read of further adventures of make-believe boys and girls they had come to admire. While the very young demand hearing favorite stories repeated endlessly, those who read well for themselves enjoy progression and daring flights away from the known environment. The still older child wants not only to part from anchorage but to get into the wide, wide world.

Classics were still available; Oz books still appeared although L. Frank Baum was not writing them. Tarzan carried on with his marvelous encounters, and Doctor Dolittle went forward with exploratory voyages. The Stratemeyer Syndicate, dropping titles, kept Nancy Drew and the Hardy Boys on the list; mysteries had already found distinct popularity. The Dana sisters, also facing enigmas, joined them, and the syndicate added a "Jr." to the name of the boy wonder of the scientific world, Tom Swift.

Able writers other than Mrs. Wilder were turning to series now and then, often stretching out less lengthy groups over intervals of time rather than rushing them out year after year in the consecutive and feverish fashion of ghost-writers. Frequently they were thoughtful women, librarians or teachers, intent on providing superior fiction.

Eleanor F. Lattimore's *Little Pear*, featuring a Chinese boy, saw introduction early in the Thirties; forty years passed between the first and the fourth volumes. Using as basis stories related by her grandmother, Carol Ryrie Brink brought pioneer-and-Indian days in Wisconsin to life again with a family of mostly red-haired adventuresome children. This book, *Caddie Woodlawn*, won the 1935 Newbery Medal awarded annually since 1922 by the Children's Librarians Section of the American Library Association. Like Mrs. Wiggin with her Rebecca, Mrs. Brink added, several years later, additional stories of Caddie, *Magical Melons*. Much later in her career she wrote *Louly* and then a novel focused on a pair of Louly's friends.

Prolific Elizabeth Coatsworth, whose *The Cat Who Went to Heaven*, had taken the 1931 Newbery Medal, authored a small group of Sally books. Illustrator-author Elizabeth Enright wrote much adult fiction but also concentrated upon junior novels for a period of time. The Newbery award came her way in 1939 for *Thimble Summer*, and soon thereafter she produced a short series about the Melendy family, linking two boys and two girls, a favored combination. At the same time Eleanor Estes was writing about another foursome, the Moffats, and in 1952 was the Newbery prize-winner for *Ginger Pye*, which eventually had a companion story, *Pinky Pye*. During that same decade E.C. (Elizabeth) Spykman began relating the chuckle-provoking ordeals and pleasures of the well-delineated four young Cares (aptly named!) against a picturesque background of the early 1900's.

Often honored by Junior Literary selections from her more than thirty books, Marguerite Henry was the 1949 Newbery winner for *King of the Wind*. *Misty of Chincoteague*, one of her three stories dramatized for the movies, brought into prominence the Virginia coastal islands of Chincoteague and Assateague, and was the first of three related volumes. *Sea Star*, Orphan of Chincoteague, followed in 1949, while *Stormy, Misty's Foal*, appeared in 1963.

The Orphelines by Natalie Savage Carlson first came out in 1959 with subsequent happenings spread as far as 1980. The creator of *A Wrinkle in Time*, a Newbery choice in 1963, Madeleine L'Engle, had already begun a perceptive series with *Meet the Austins*, the fourth of which appeared in 1980.

Beverly Cleary was writing, over a long period of time, less sophisticated stories for young readers, featuring Henry Huggins in one series and small Ramona in another, while Carolyn Haywood provided Betsy books and Eddie books during an overlapping cycle of time. Mary Calhoun wrote a few Katie John stories, and Patricia Coombs, self-illustrator, the Dorrie books.

Among those looking back were two who chronicled in threesomes their own family heritages. Jennie Lindquist dealt with her Swedish background while Anne Pellowski recounted and illustrated with family tree the lives of generations of Polish-American children on a Wisconsin farm.

Men of talent were not entirely lacking. Robert Lawson, illustrator and author, brought out *Rabbit Hill*, which rated the Newbery Medal in 1944; in the Fifties he provided a sequel, *The Tough Winter*. And there was Walter Farley who first wrote about that famous stallion in high school and again during college years. The year of his first published book was 1941. Nineteen Black Stallion volumes followed that first, and after World War II Farley managed to become owner of a farm whereon to breed and raise horses.

All of these books stand, sometimes side by side on public library shelves, with the classics and semi-classics from other days, the works of Louisa Alcott, Horatio Alger and Joseph Altsheler, L. Frank Baum, of course, Thornton Burgess and Edgar Rice Burroughs, Susan Coolidge, Howard Garis, Hugh Lofting, L.M. Montgomery, James Otis, Lucy Fitch Perkins, Eleanor II. Porter, Margaret Sidney, Booth Tarkington, Mark Twain, Kate Douglas Wiggin and Laura Ingalls Wilder. Old and middle-aged and relatively new, they often possess shabby bindings and weak spines. Not all children's libraries give space to detective-type series; some boards frown at this kind of reading matter.

There exist some historical collections of lesser known old series but because of fragility and value as artifacts they are not always available for inter-library lending. Certain publishing houses issue good paperback reprints of old books such as *Billy Whiskers*, but these are for catalog-ordering. Book shops themselves offer a representation of junior classics including Oz and Alger, Burgess and Burroughs as well as Montgomery and Alcott, the Little House books, some of Doctor Dolittle and the little Peppers, Mark Twain, naturally, Tarkington, Wiggin and a selection of Uncle Wiggily. Add to this scattering special cardboard racks exclusively for Nancy Drew and Hardy Boys mysteries.

Another outcome, and certainly a positive one, to the vast blossoming of fictional series was their aid in building up a library of children's literature and opening up that field of publishing concerned with appeal to the young. Even the fictional children, as mouth-pieces for authors, noted reading and acquiring of Rollo and Sophie May books. And with all the editions put out from time to time, there was opportunity for the flourishing of talented illustrators. One must concede that related volumes also assisted in the development of formal education with the introduction of series such as Mrs. Perkins' Twins and the multi-authored Our Little Cousins into the schoolroom, and with the inclusion of excerpts from various writers in some school readers. Influence seemed to extend even beyond that to the writing of texts in somewhat story-telling style for increasing interest. In these ways education and child-life were brought into greater prominence.

In a myriad of ways modern life testifies to reflections of that great age of series. Television and motion pictures are among them.

While non-commercial institutions have been selective, television hucksters have had no qualms about feeding the common taste to satisfy that intermediate mystery-loving age with girl and boy detectives. However, fictional puzzles and perplexities find devotees in all age-groups for excitement and the enjoyment of wit-teasing as recreational pastime, and who is to criticize youth for joining in such a choice?

A California journalist writing in 1977 of the Hardy brothers and Nancy Drew alternating TV showings called these sleuths "indestructible" and "the world's oldest teen-agers." The death in 1982 of Harriet Stratemeyer Adams, who was responsible for their adventuring, stimulated nostalgia among some who had at age nine or ten been Nancy Drew fans. During her fifty years this assured young lady changed only her manner of dress and her coiffure. Admiration seemed based on her self-confidence as she went on her way in an adult world clearing up mysteries and, in that occupation, being accorded respectful treatment as an expert and an equal. That itself is a telling sentiment, the yearning for such treatment.

For some TV series—and note that compelling power of sound and sight presentations and relationship to the *printed* series for which readers had to wait a good deal longer than do TV watchers—there was the long run of Little House stories. They started in simpler fashion but with small girls wearing white pinafores in a one-room cabin set out in the pioneer land of Nowhere, and then broke away with increasing sentimentality into more and more civilized settings and situations and with gross departures from Mrs. Wilder's recountings.

Such serialization not unnaturally brings to mind the enormous drawing-power of TV segment-showing for adults on both educational and commercial stations. While the former ordinarily break up lengthy dramas into weekly showings, and go into much greater depth, the latter, sensing impatience of viewers, perhaps, sometimes schedule long segments with brief intervals between, except for those revolting melodramas which continue week after week through death, disaster and the machinations of one-dimensional men and women. This illustrates the less commendable aspect of television but has a shallow relationship to that old lure of early published series and of people hungry for more and more about characters and plots. Surely the desire for continuity never submerged entirely, and the practice of using serialized stories, as did *St. Nicholas* as well as adult magazines, is, according to predictors, on the return.

Classics have often re-appeared via television, it is true. At one time educational TV scheduled a six-part showing of Susan Coolidge's Katy Carr. *Katy Did* stories were lumped together, opening when the heroine was fifteen, rather than twelve, and the dramatization seemed to generate more liveliness than the old story itself in reading. That at least one *Peck's Bad Boy* movie was made, this in 1938, revealed itself with a television re-showing of *Peck's Bad Boy with the Circus.* One may even happen upon a rather dreadful updated version of an Alger novel "based upon" *Frank and Fearless* and aimed at a youthful audience.

Old favorites have come in for more than a re-showing. Some of them, filmed more than once, return irregularly, as with *Tom Sawyer* and *Little Women,* or regularly, as with the 1939 filming of *The Wizard of Oz.* Children have grown up with annual renewal of the Oz fantasy and, through that means, of young childhood, at which time they may have skipped their way around a garden border singing of the intention to visit the wizard. Now a new Oz film has come out, not as sequel to the 1939 production but as an adaptation of several books from the series, with new allies for Dorothy, with spectacular camera tricks, but without the endearing human ingredient of the first movie.

Those of feminine sex also clutch the teary memory of the spirited British lass playing Pollyanna in the bigger-than-life color film which took frank liberties with the story. There have been revivals of any number of classics of series and non-series, which underwent distortion in a process of becoming song-and-dance shows for the curly-haired American screen darling of earlier years. Tarzan narratives, filmed and re-filmed, have come in for frequent re-showings. A musical Doctor Dolittle seemed aimed as much at adults as at children, but Dolittle-subtleties are beyond young children, anyhow.

So much for such immortalization of the series. The American vocabulary has benefited. Terms or phrases have entered the language to symbolize behavior, character and characteristics, and morals. "The Rover Boys" as a name denotes all-American youths who move victoriously from one adventure into another. "Tom Swift" signifies scientific ingenuity and science-fiction adventures. "Tarzan" is a famous title implying miraculous strength and courage, and brings to mind chest-beating and the drawn-out Tarzan halloo of supremacy. The Scarecrow and Wicked Witch of the West along with other Oz figures stand as representations of virtues and ideals— or lack of them. "Horatio Alger" applies to one who makes it on his own by means of virtue, honest labor, pluck and a little luck, "Pollyanna" is a signpost for the sweetness and light of her Glad Game, and "Dotty Dimple" and "Little Prudy" for a prissiness that they really did not possess at all. "A regular Tom Sawyer" indicates a scamp who outwits people part of the time and gets neck-deep in trouble the rest of the time. So it goes, this verbalization, this bringing-into-the-language of ideas, either as amplification or as irony. The words "girls" and "boys" saw so much use in common titles—Meadowbrook Girls, Moving-Picture Girls, Motor Girls, or the Saddle Boys, Baseball Boys, Army Boys, etc.—that those familiar with some of the old series tend to improvise, thus calling exuberant garbage collectors "The Bang-Bang Boys of Webster Street."

Meanwhile, more and more feverishly, collectors (dealers among them) rove across the land. And it is by no means merely classics that they hunt at rummage and estate sales, in thrift shops and old-book stores and antique show-and-sale halls, and in classified ads. Almost any aged book is considered collectible now, even nondescript series be they of great number. Knowing hands snatch reprints of those harder to find, although naturally early editions possess more monetary value and give more pride and pleasure.

Memory hallows more than the obvious classics in the realm of nostalgia. A garden-variety scout hunting in the interest of library collections as well, and questioning adults about childhood reading, hears reactions of sentiment associated with all manner of series and receives enquiries concerning identities of old authors and possibilities of locating certain series.

"*I* read Elsie Dinsmore and found so much pleasure in the Elsie books," offers the ancient dame in a retirement home; "I had them from the Sunday School library." "A teacher asked for our favorite authors, and I said, 'Harry Castlemon,' " reported one professional librarian, female in gender. "And I read the Rover Boys and Tom Swift, too." A mother speaking proudly of her young daughter said, "Julie never really got into reading—until she discovered the Nancy Drew books." "I just *loved* Honey Bunch," a grandmother pronounced fervently. And a question came about the Dorothy Dainty series. "Do you happen to know who the author is? I don't know her name, and I'd love to find some of that series because she was my favorite heroine."

Collecting is a fashionable hobby among the American public with its increased free time and fatter purse, and possession is sometimes a matter of well-being although one is inclined to suspect that some collectors feel secretly that somewhere over the rainbow waits a potential customer possessed of real yearning for a dozen volumes of the Automobile Girls or of Don Sturdy. Finally some libraries are getting the message that substantial old series, well put together and typifying certain lost decades, are worth nurturing as examples of antique or semi-antique literature. And the gathering of memorabilia does not stop with books themselves. For individuals there are related objects, outgrowths of some series: games, dolls, cups, toys, calendars, records, maps, pins and posters.

Interestingly enough, there were also strictly official trade-marks. "Glad" and "Pollyanna" belonged to the publishers of the series begun by Eleanor H. Porter and finished by other writers. Even earlier, the "Little Cousin" trade-mark appeared, stamped on the backs of those editions, and this not too long after the series appeared when the century began; by 1934 a copy of *Our Little Vatican Cousin* listed seventy-nine titles to form two long columns. The name "Uncle Wiggily" carried a patent, and the Burgess books boasted the "Quaddies" trade-mark. Edgar Rice Burroughs designed his own "personal mark," which later came into use as colophon on spines of the books his company began publishing in 1930. And illustrators sometimes gained fame because of their associations with series as well as their abilities to depict: W.W. Denslow for Oz, and then John R. Neill, Harrison Cady for Thornton Burgess, J. Allen St. John for Burroughs. Garth Williams followed the covered-wagon route of the Little House family in order to furnish illustrations related in spirit as well as in time and place. And new, fresh editions of old classics whose often smudged pictures went unsigned, advertised illustrations by acknowledged artists.

Some legends, series-connected, have never fallen away. In 1973, a "new" Alger story appeared on the market. Once serialized in *Argosy* magazine (1889) under a pseudonym, the story had never seen reprinting in book form, a fact discovered by "an Alger scholar." Out came *Silas Snobden's Office Boy*, an astonishing event, seventy-four years after Alger's death. Yet in 1974 there was still another, called "the last" of the Alger books. Ralph D. Garner, one of the directors of the Horatio Alger Society and said to possess the most comprehensive collection of Algeriana, again wrote the foreword.

That society's creed has been "To further the philosophy of Horatio Alger, Jr., and to encourage the spirit of Strive & Succeed that for half a century guided Alger's undaunted heroes—lads whose struggles epitomized the Great American Dream and flamed hero ideals in countless millions of young Americans." The society's publication is "...a magazine devoted to the study of Horatio Alger, Jr., his life, works and influence on the culture of America."

That influence does not confine itself to so specialized an organization. For years The American Schools and Colleges Association has presented annual Horatio Alger Awards to "...persons who rose to success from humble beginnings."

Nor does the Alger society exist alone. There is also The International Wizard of Oz Club, Inc., which for membership purposes maintains geographical divisions, rendering Californians "Winkies" and New Yorkers "Munchkins." *The Baum Bugle*, published three times yearly, is a respectable magazine with cover in color. Founder of the organization, Justin Schiller, a thirteen-year-old at the time, originated the *Bugle* in 1957 with five mimeographed pages for a circulation of sixteen. Interestingly enough, Baum himself, at age twelve, wrote and printed a monthly publication at his New York state home. The *Bugle* has served as "primary source of information about bibliographical history" of the Oz books. It keeps club members current with the Oz influence on today's world. Articles, reminiscences and research on both the life and writing of Baum, who disguised himself under numerous pseudonyms, too, quizzes and puzzles round out magazine contents. "Trading Post" sheets list Baum books, toys, games and records for sale or trade, or request certain books. Conventions, national and regional, are outgrowths of the club.

A record commemorates the 1939 soundtrack of the famous Oz film while another carries a version of the Oz story read by Ray Bolger, who played the Scarecrow. A commercial celebration of Oz country and characters undertook the issuance of a limited series of china plates described as the first "ever to honor a classic of motion picture artistry." The initial piece, not unnaturally, was titled "Over the Rainbow," and featured Judy Garland as Dorothy, basket on one arm and Toto under the other, walking the yellow brick road in an idealized setting of hills, fruit and flowers and, of course, a rainbow arch.

A Thornton Burgess dream achieved reality: that Laughing Brook, the home where he lived and worked for thirty-seven years, should have some lasting part in children's lives. In 1966, a year after Burgess' death, the Massachusetts Audubon Society purchased the property located at Hampden, not far from Springfield, with the plan to establish "a major educational center and memorial to Thornton W. Burgess." Referred to by Burgess as "the home of Peter Rabbit," the original eighteen acres with its ancient Cape Cod dwelling and barn-studio, expanded to two hundred and sixty acres of fields and woodlands. Laughing Brook Education Center and Wildlife Sanctuary offers natural history tours, workshops, story hours and programs, and trails, one of which is "touch and see" for those visually handicapped.

Tarzan comes in for immortality in other ways. All over the country young boys and men, early aware of the symbolism of jungle and forest inhabitants, know the superman titles, and indicate the adoption of Tarzan's identity by crying out strength and victory and dream with that triumphal call. Likely they are more in earnest than they realize. James D. Hart called the first of the Tarzan series a "new extreme" in "the novel of masculine escape." Who can doubt that "Promethean sense of power"[2] while listening to boy or man hallooing and celebrating or pretending to celebrate jubilation with that jungle yodel and literal chest-beating?

Edgar Rice Burroughs never visited Africa. Yet at one time, leafing through a magazine, a reader could find invitation to "See where Tarzan met Jane," this in a European airline's ad suggesting that one visit Africa and join a safari there. "Drive up to a black-maned lion or watch the rhinos water themselves from the comfort of your own water-hole—a wide, glass-enclosed bar. ...And swing where Tarzan swung."

After all, there is an alternative. The less adventurous can remain on this continent and go to Tarzana, California, or Tarzan, Texas.

Literary shrines, one-time homes of series-connected authors, have long existed. Orchard House in Massachusetts' Concord was not the Alcott residence while the sisters were growing up, and because of its association with family misfortune, Louisa was not happy in that place; yet she wrote *Little Women* there. The Green Gables of L.M. Montgomery and Anne Shirley stands on Prince Edward Island, nicknamed PEI, and reached easily from Nova Scotia or New Brunswick; it is a serene place, except in tourist season, of farms and fishing villages. And there are numerous homes special to the memory of that man from Missouri. The now-enclosed birthplace at tiny Florida is less known than the famous Hannibal house. In New York state the Quarry Farm octagonal study was, alas, carried down to the Elmira

College campus. In Connecticut the strange, gabled Hartford house, so happy a place while it nurtured the young Clemens family, is now a museum.

Today there is a steady surge of young girls with parent or entire family, and adults alone as well, making pilgrimage to Midwestern locales commemorating the Little House girls and especially the one among them who grew up to re-create the family and pioneering times. Near Mansfield, Missouri, is Rocky Ridge Farm, which became home to the adult Laura, her husband Almanzo and small daughter Rose; now it bears the title of the Laura Ingalls Wilder Home and Museum. It was here that she wrote her books.

In De Smet, South Dakota, the Laura Ingalls Wilder Memorial Society maintains the restored surveyor's shanty where the Ingalls family spent the first winter in that state; its small neighbor is a replica of the twelve by fifteen foot claim shanty in which Laura first taught school. Elsewhere in this prairie town stands the later Ingalls house which the society restored. Some visitors remain in De Smet for the summer eve open-air production of *The Long Winter*. Some visit the public library, which possesses translations of the series, and puzzle over thought of children in India and other far places reading about pioneer American life. Also in the library are several paintings intimately related, but unintentionally so, to Little House books. They are the work of painter-illustrator Harvey Dunn, born in that area in 1884, and presented to the community after a 1950 exhibition there; the remainder of the collection hangs at a nearby branch of the state university system.

The several dozen paintings carry a viewer back to Little House beginnings with unexpected force, because the Dunn brush and palette knife stroked the Ingalls era into a revival of the old life and times which Mrs. Wilder had re-created verbally. The airy prairie, in both kind and cruel seasons, demands attention with its hard-bitten figures against sweeping seas of grass and clumps of spring flowers, with homesteads huddled in a harsh land, with drovers and ploughmen, oxen and schooner, storms and snow, heat and drought, buffalo bones, proud warrior astride a pony. Beyond and above, the infinity of space and the great bowl of heaven imply the diminution of man. It is all there, just as Laura told it.

Souvenirs should by rights include an acknowledged appreciation of the period by those with any ties to the old books and those concerned with literary history. A wholesome sentiment upon reflection reduces itself to a tribute due the legion of writers responsible for the series output. In a way the summation by one journalist a long while ago pointed toward this.

He was Allan Eric, writing for the *Journalist* in the year 1889, and his particular subject was someone known to him, Hezekiah Butterworth, associate of *Youth's Companion* magazine and author of travel and historical series and other books. Focused on the life and abilities of Butterworth, Eric's feature appeared as introduction to *Zigzag Journeys Around the World* and had something to say about "...the army of literary and journalistic workers."

> The people, the readers, the intelligent of humanity, assign every literary worker to some place, some position, in the galaxy of crowned and uncrowned kings. But it is not to this fact alone that such successful writers owe their position. It is owing to their own exertions. It is for what they have done to educate and elevate mankind, for what they have given to the world, that they have the gratitude of nations; and just in proportion to what they have done, will their positions be.[3]

And so do all the authors have their places in the century which they filled out between Jacob Abbott's first Rollo and Laura Ingalls Wilder's Laura. It is just possible that some time during their trekking, the Ingalls' acquaintanceship included Rollo—if not within the Rollo books themselves, then from excerpts borrowed for elementary readers. In her series Mrs. Wilder, too, paused to explain calmly the "how" of processes and the "why." While she developed stronger story lines, a reader can recognize the mature purpose that prompted her books and the fact that primarily she was acting as storyteller, while Abbott had the dual role of instructor and entertainer. The Wilder world was also a disciplined world, but there were no secrets and there was no wall between children and adults. The sharing made a comfortable if serious universe. The re-awakening of attention to the series has been due, in part, to the return of public interest in simple basics of living and to "beginnings," so that adults, too, at least in the prairie and plains country, have been reading Little House books for information and finding pleasure in effective recounting.

In a certain way it was a circular route, because Mrs. Wilder found ability to return to that fundamental simplicity in labor, in gratification and in fulfillment. Thus ended a period with an aim as thoughtful and as lasting as that with which Abbott began it.

Chapter XVII
In Defense of Reading Matter

In the old *New England Primer*, that "Guide to the Art of Reading," one finds seven words linking the human being and the printed word.

My Book and Heart
Shall never part.

An additional four lines entitled "Good Boys at their Books" reveal more.

He who ne'er learns his A, B, C,
Forever will a Blockhead be;
But he who to his Book's inclin'd,
Will soon a golden Treasure find.[1]

Even with the choice reading and the required reading, which was the Holy Writ, the importance of this "art" was plain in black and white, implying that the world cannot really open up to the beholder until he is able to read. To the non-reader is even half a world visible?

Kate Douglas Wiggin in her volume of reminiscences spoke of books as being "the dearest of all our friends." She understood well the barren qualities of a universe without the printed word. "Oh! the unconscious misery, the dullness, the loneliness of the child who does not care for reading!" she wrote. The "joy of joys," and this seemed a lifetime belief even as she turned back in later years, was "To write a book that two successive generations of children might love, read twice, and put under their pillows at night..."[2]

So there is joy twice-over, that of writing and that of reading. But the second is the more common. It is expected that everyone should learn to read, with joy or without it. Possibly only the "born reader," who learned the art easily and never knew exactly when, consciously understands and appreciates that reading is a delight. Little Miss Frances knew, but she was "a story-maniac."

"Have you any books you could lend me?" she always ended by asking a new acquaintance.

"That child has a book again!" she used to hear annoyed voices exclaim, when being sent up or down stairs, on some errand, she found something to read on the way, and fell through the tempter. It was so positively unavoidable and inevitable that one should forget, and sink down on the stairs somewhere to tear the contents out of the heart of a few pages, and it was so horrible, and made one's heart leap and thump so guiltily, when one heard the voices, and realized how bad, and idle, and thoughtless, and disobedient one was.[3]

Naturally the ideal situation is that of having eagerness to read welling up in the minds and spirits of all the young and of also having available to them a generous variety of literary concoctions which may lead them forever deeper into the realm of literature. But this is never so, and perhaps is not for mourning, for all beings are individuals with strange quirks and differences, and if everything written attained the same level of good and stimulating writing, how would readers learn to judge and distinguish among styles and talents? A hodgepodge is ever more interesting, both as to inhabitants and as to what some of them write.

That brings any reader to the subject of what he wants to read. It has often been presumed that adults should prescribe materials for young readers, and probably it has also usually been that children prefer to choose their own books once they depart the infantile stage. In the beginning, when the world of Mother Goose comes into view, the infant engrosses himself with the exciting new pastime of turning pages and finding images of kits, cats, hungry dogs and pigs in wigs, and with rhythmic sound of verses harmonious with the pictures. Later, if read-aloud stories prove uninteresting, the listener gives a verbal thumbs-down or simply focuses attention on something else. When he finds a story to his liking, he wants to hear it over and over and over again. Even by that time he is making choices.

Yet adults who are in power in the schools may present unseasoned pap that introduces words shockingly limited as to number, and dull words at that. Some of the old-timers who put together textbooks were more perceptive. While they did not overlook moral lessons they also included stories, light verse and examples from the works of established poets. The impression is evident that compilers of such readers did not consider that they were selecting material for dull-witted children at all but for intellects ever on the verge of expansion. Even the *New England Primer*, adding to the preliminary text the "Assembly of Divines, and Mr. Cotton's Catechism, Etc.," gave listings, within the first few small pages of "easy" syllables, and words of one, two, three, four, five and six syllables!

When Bruno Bettelheim, child psychologist and psychoanalyst, wrote an essay entitled "A Primer for Literacy" as part of a child development research presentation by *Harper's* magazine a few years ago, he voiced indignation over the ludicrous simplicity and repetition of pre-primers and primers used in American schools.

As he enters school, the child is both proud of his past achievement and apprehensive about his ability to learn. He resents nothing more than feeling belittled. By this time, there are probably at least 6,000 words that he knows well and comprehends accurately;...Yet he may very well be presented with basic readers that will treat him as though he possesses no vocabulary at all....[4]

With the view of reading only as a tool necessary to success in school, method can cancel interest, Bettelheim believes. "But that's the way we still teach reading: as a skill, rather than as a meaningful pursuit." As he pronounces elsewhere in the essay, "Reading permits the child to procure man's accumulated knowledge for himself, without having to rely on the verbal communication of others." Bettelheim expressed the conviction that children desire esteem and that textbooks should reveal respect for children as well as for education and school itself. And intent should extend far beyond the schoolroom.

If the stories we use in teaching our children to read do not reflect purpose..., if they do not give the child immediate pleasure, and add meaning to his life by opening up new perspectives—if, in short, these stories fail to provide the child with deep satisfactions—then they also unintentionally belittle reading itself.[5]

That education is in need of correction is a view shared by some institutions and by the public at large. "One of the aims" of a California county's project, as stated in a news account, is that of turning children from television to "a good book." (One can only surmise as to the identity of the others.) With federal aid the county has been testing a program administered through public libraries and linked with child care centers. This has involved everyday visiting of such centers for purposes of storytelling and of checking out books, with services expanded to evening and weekend hours for the benefit of parents as well. Workshops were set up to train individuals providing day care in the employment of storytelling and of library and other community resources. Libraries themselves held sessions for children, using puppets, musical instruments and props suitable for skits. The Story Tailors, a professional group, performed in child-care centers, while the county reading council scheduled a speaker whose purpose was to promote reading aloud to children.

There is nothing new about recommendations for improvement in education, even though results have not always been forthcoming. Several years ago *McGuffey's Readers*, introduced into American schools in the 1830's, when Jacob Abbott began writing Rollo stories, came into some favor again. Not only people with fondness for the old days unknown to them but also some schools have been the buyers. Teachers have selected portions that appealed to them to use in the classroom as supplementary material, and children have accepted them, with some curiosity, one may suppose, which means that they are not averse to small lessons in the virtues of punctuality, patriotism, kindness and honesty, fairness and industry.

When author and editor Horace Scudder devised the idea of Riverside Literature Series for Young People, he was thinking in terms of using entire works instead of the fragments sometimes chosen for school readers. His aim coincided with that of Bettelheim.

> ...he wanted reading to be a joy and not a task. The right kind of reading should be chosen "to stimulate interest, rouse the imagination and fix the attention, reading at the same time healthy and sound and which shall lead to better things in the future."[6]

In Scudder's era, which was less complex except for early expectations in schooling, the child respected books and sought and discovered adventure in them. They were numbered, and thus precious, and meant to be read and re-read. School readers themselves were small semi-literary collections with romance, true and imagined, with myth and fairy tale, brief essays and poetry. "Look, here is the world," these readers sometimes offered silently. There was the unspoken practice of reading to oneself, and half recognition of means that others used in expressing themselves; thus with the invitation or instruction to compose thoughts upon paper, there existed a guide of sorts. Reading teamed itself with an apprenticeship at constructing phrases

Relatively few among the procession of series survived, but all had at some time found places in readers' hearts.

and stating one's thoughts, and at use of the imagination and the wits. Old diaries and letters and autograph albums testify to this practice as do accounts of "literary societies" functioning at high school level. Naturally, well-worded recounting was superior to trite terms and ill-phrased composition. Just as a being needs to make the acquaintance of all manner of people in order to understand human nature, he needs to experience all kinds of writing in order to understand communication and self-expression and to make some kind of judgment.

Of course that old world was more of a reading world. School meant required reading from day to day although the bookworm read all the choicest material in a new reader the very first day. But printed matter opened to unsuspected and unending horizons, and reading was, as it is now, the implement that society demanded of an individual lest he be a blockhead, and blockhead he was if he did not learn to read.

The means was provided in one way or another. Sometimes a child had the stimulation of charts illustrating sounds, letters and words, of cardboard squares printed with one letter each which, placed together in a row with proper spacing, magically spelled out a thought or fact. Thus all along the way the fortunate child's mind developed through listening and through the practice of reading silently. It learned to feed itself and matured with self-education almost as much as with study in the schoolroom, and all this without benefit of television feeding. There was no mincing of mental nourishment, no pre-digesting, and scheduled activity outside of school limited itself to such things as music lessons or practice for plays or other programs meant for school or church presentation. The challenge faced the child directly, to improvise, create, instigate his own play and entertainment, often guided indirectly by nuclei from what he read. The inner eye, self-stimulated, came to flame under its own power. This could embrace the various kinds of romance which made older classics so readable.

Once the printed or written word drew respect. Of an evening family members took turns at reading aloud to the group. Individuals read to each other, older children and adults to the young and to the infirm. Books cost money, and money was not always at hand in sufficient quantity to warrant spending for something possibly available in a library. However, books continued to come from varying publishers in reprints of low price and cheap, fast-yellowing paper. Still, the stories were the same. Likely there were at least supplementary readers at school, and, in the libraries, outdated *St. Nicholas* magazines bound in heavy boards. Sunday Schools provided weekly papers and, as occasional prizes, books themselves. Eager readers found no dearth of material. They read whatever books their parents owned, and those that older family members brought from the library. They paged through any and all publications that came through the mail, and read borrowed books, advertising flyers, old magazines collected by brothers for disposal at a small price to the junkman, religious publications and western magazines or whatever else was in sight during early evening baby-sitting hours in neighbors' homes. Simply—they read. And prominent among books available were volumes from series, cherished if self-owned, re-read whether or not, sometimes dramatized in part, books peopled with characters referred to as familiar acquaintances.

Certainly there is now no lack of material, old and new, from which to choose one's reading, for there is scarcely time enough to read it all even if one adopted Theodore Roosevelt's alleged custom of going through two books daily. Possibly there is so much printed that it seems, to some, too common to be of consequence simply too voluminous or, to some of today's children, "boring."

That children in general are neglecting adult-recommended reading worries educators. Yet the pastime requires a certain solitude or concentration not always accessible under common conditions of the present whirlwind world, for the young live under regimentation, and this not alone during school hours. Cause is in part that often both parents—if there are two— are working and must make provision for the child's free time. Consequently the small person's day is scheduled closely with paid-for enrollment in sports groups (in summertime, "sports camps" as well), in classes of all description and/or in day-care centers. However the days are spent, they are in company of others so that an individual acts as part of a group and largely under adult direction. And at a cost, even if subsidized. At-home entertainment may be the passive one within view of TV programming. Rare is the simple old neighborhood play, the freedom to follow instinct, to allow imagination independent play and to make discovery. Ironically, people refer frequently to the "freedom" of this era.

While society's current codes differ, problems, but for the use of drugs, are essentially the same as during the past century and a half. Social and racial inequalities and poverty certainly existed; homes were impaired by death rather than divorce; there were parents inclined toward alcoholism as well as toward child desertion or neglect. Crime against the young was not unknown, although not necessarily of today's kind. War, or the threat of war, if not the nuclear menace, hung like a Damoclesian sword. And life, while more isolated, was precarious because of few remedies for overcoming disease and early death. Those long-gone children were well acquainted with death and disorder; they watched infant siblings die and witnessed firsthand the deterioration of the several generations of close association. They learned to accept responsibility for themselves and for other family members, and they learned to work. In one way they were more fortunate than today's children, for they grew up with religious faith, and in the extended family of their day usually could single out adults as role models. The nihilism glimpsed in the present time was generally outside their ken. And they believed in the old saying of "Hitch your wagon to a star." That was romantic, and romance aids in enduring the travail of the universe.

Despite some likenesses, differences exist in moral outlooks and the treatment of subjects. Current philosophy is that of revealing all to the child as well as to the mature. Sexual knowledge, once veiled, comes in for casual and frank discussion along with human misconduct and vulgarities which a portion of the adult population greedily absorbs in paperbacks and watches on common television showings. Naught is presented subtly and this extends to everything from advertisements printed, pictured or spoken, to inhuman physical conduct by man against man as if human beings were brutes. Realism goes its length and beyond bounds into a savage no-man's land.

Reflection of barbarous behavior and its tolerance is visible in matter of speech and vocabulary. In the old series, mentors frowned upon slang as a careless habit leading to careless comportment, and use of correct phrases both in speech and writing came in for emphasis. Current "freedom" has brought to the tips of tongues not only heedless grammar but offensive, trite and glib phraseology used so repetitiously that it is almost without meaning, and adopted as readily by adults as by children, as though fashion and the pretense of intelligence dictate the use.

Realists, devoid of fancy's flight, carp or sneer, declaring that a writer "should tell it like it is." Yet straight realism in fiction is as misleading as straight romance, and total baseness as deluding as total idealization. While clarity and direct style are always effective in themselves so long as free of obscenities, the magic of fiction lies with the ingredient of romance.

Associations of individuals may supply it; an event may startle the mind; setting or invisible atmosphere may dilate the imagination, or illusion enhance an impression. Comic charm, if reasonably natural, is one of the most magnetic qualities, particularly if it be allied with a child. How many fictional children remain in the memory for their inborn grace and gracelessness residing side by side and coming to expression! And the mind's dreaming as it wanders into dark and bright regions finds harmony with almost any intellect. Introduction of romance in a controlled manner does not indicate that corruption does not exist, and fiction-reading above all other ought to produce temporary release from unrefined reality.

Young Henry Davidson of Boston, in *Zigzag Journeys Around the World*, knew of the need. He told his father as they spoke of "story-places" awaiting them that "A story is not a story unless it rises above common life."[7]

Paradoxically, despite the urge toward straightforward recounting, those now plunging into realms beyond the earth on explorative voyages find romance and creativity in outer space, while those bound to this planet build up science-fiction spheres. Yet new insights of the already-known universe can generate elation just as any of the various arts elevates the senses to a plane that individuals have tried to reach with drugs.

Glancing back superciliously, fretful observers of the literary scenes look down their noses at sentimentality, traces of piety, and lack of literary felicity in old series. Apparently they cannot see that series served the purpose, if nothing else, of leading children to follow fictional friends from one volume to the next, in other words, to continue reading. They do not understand that readers delighted in stepping into the roles of other boys and girls, participating in the pleasures and small rebellions, in the moments of crisis as well as of success. A child is not a literary critic. He builds up a discrimination in his reading but this is a gradual constructing of judgment. On the way a weed may seem a flower, and a flower no more than a weed. Instinctively he knows how to circumvent expression of morality; a "lesson" does not block his progress in the least. What other children did or are doing and how they conduct themselves is reason for investigation and leads to revelation.

Who can say, and believe entirely his own argument, that it is not better that a child read sentimental or formulistic stories than that he not read at all? Adults may not care for hot dogs and peanut-butter sandwiches but these often make up a child's choice during growing-up years. So be it with certain of the old series. Today's offerings, by no means always displaying improvement over yesterday's, could be rated even more barren since "here and now" is a wider world and children early acquire a veneer of sophistication which, however, can be surprisingly thin.

A subject brought frequently into prominence regards the "rights" of a child, that he may appear before an arbitrator to express his desire, that he may withhold information from those who support him, or that he may be granted something that a guardian does not wish him to have. Yet he has lost, too, with the slipping of anchorage from family and home into the province of child-care authorities. Still more instability may result with visits to or from blood-parent living apart. So long as his reading remains in the bounds of child-literature, he ought to have some right of choice. One can but hope that fast and ruthless TV shows of an adult nature have not already spoiled his taste for fiction involving his particular segment of the population.

Perhaps it is necessary to ponder the fact that mediocre books are really all that some youthful as well as mature persons will ever desire, and that all the efforts of institutions and individuals may not be able to persuade child X in higher direction. The important consideration is that he read, because there is no way of telling at what point he may take position on that magic carpet by opening a book of greater power and launch out into a fascinating realm of invention. There is always the old-fashioned dream of that happening in a world in which appear indications of the return of people caring about people, with public and private concern fastening upon the well-being of the young and the elderly, the unemployed and the unemployable, the right to live and the right to die—all of this despite a confused and confusing universe caught in rapid motion.

Children in an earlier era, too, had to combat disapproval of reading matter. In the beginning adults considered fiction less than wholesome. "Novels are the alcahol [sic] of the mind"[8] was the gloomy pronouncement in a children's periodical of 1852. Along with the stories once sanctioned, young readers were obliged to accept moral guidance contained therein. Yet the time came that everyone wanted a hand in the production of fiction. Evidences of the results stand on any well-furnished series of shelves open to children.

The truth is that a good many children's classics emerged from these old groups of books and that some of today's youths, like those preceding them in all the decades that have been rolling off and away since the heyday of series, are burrowing their noses in editions of Oz and Tarzan, Green Gables' Anne, Alcott stories, and a good many others, and dreaming their universal or inherited dreams by means of literature that ties together whole generations. And that is no mean accomplishment.

And a second truth is that every series, distinguished or undistinguished, served a purpose for someone. Every series somehow enlightened a young mind, nudged an imagination, functioned as outlet for restrained emotions and fancies and, above all, lured children on to reading more of something. Every series, almost, dove-tailed to help fill niches or wide gaping spaces in an environment.

The curator of Early Children's Books at the Morgan Library, Gerald Gottlieb, gave sagacious judgment which surely applies.

"Children's books have traditionally been treated with disdain by adults, because many of the early ones were written by hack writers and were sometimes printed somewhat sloppily. But it has been said that the best way to learn about another era is not from the great writers but from those that are second-rate. Great writers transcend their times, but second-rate writers are mired in theirs. So if you look carefully at these books you will catch fascinating glimpses of the joys and sorrows of growing up in a world that is very remote from the one we live in."[9]

Collectors who search for the old series and examine early editions and early reprints often tattered, dog-eared, fractured of spine, missing a clumsy illustration or two, find anthropological testament of much handling. Lots of someones buried their noses in Abbott and Alcott, Altsheler and Alger, Baum and Burroughs and Butterworth and Burgess, Castlemon and Kellogg, Finley, Garis and Johnston and Knox, May, Lofting, Montgomery and Optic, Phelps and Perkins and Porter, Rice and Richards, Sidney and Stratemeyer, Twain, Trowbridge and Tarkington, Wiggin and Wilder. And someone read all of the others, too, all along the years from Rollo—*Bessie at the Seaside* to *Jolly Good Times* to *Peck's Uncle Ike and the Red-Headed Boy* to *A West Point Yearling* and *Girls of the Morning Glory Camp Fire* and *Boy Scouts in an Airship* to *Princess Polly's Gay Winter, Jerry Todd and the Waltzing Hen* to *Billie Bradley and the School Mystery* and *The Hunniwell Boys in the Secret Service.*

From slightest story line to crowded plot, the series in one infinitesimal way or another helped fill out the jig-saw puzzle that a life becomes, and in addition took care of some need of that instant, like bread or meat at table, like a carrot pulled right out of the garden loam, or an apple plucked from the backyard tree, a roasted potato excavated from the ashes of an autumn-leaf fire or an unexpected lollipop when a taste of sweetening seemed vital.

Even clumsy writing can manage this; it can arouse the spirit in some mysterious way more than an instructor's efforts to teach literary standards. Likely a style is really not important to a young reader unless it be so excellent as to start a chill along the spine. He reads for the story and judges a book by that and by the feeling it invokes, and sometimes he writes a curt impression in the book or on a school-library card. "This is the dummest book I ever read." Or, "This is a very good book." Or he may in private re-enact the story, taking the most admired part himself, of course. Or he may even be inspired to write a like tale, boldly following the original.

When the aged lady nearing the century mark after a life spent in known and out-of-the-way places, in university and museum atmospheres, astride a camel on an Australian field trip over a desert, or afoot on a fashionable avenue in Paris, recalls the pleasure of the weekly Elsie books drawn from the Sunday-School library of a Southern town, her memory is an honest and just one. Someone else did truly long to be Honey Bunch, and another Dorothy Dainty, and there may be a wistful tinge to a man's voice recalling his Rover Boys books as he wonders what on earth happened to them. The bookseller, too, understands what this is all about when he pencils in prices on the fly-leaves of these rectangular pieces of the past. So do the hucksters when they cast about for drama to present in some other form to the passive audience of television.

And if a series is sentimental, what of it? At least it offered, as well as reading matter, an outlet when society did not favor too visible a reaction of individual sensibilities. One needs to accept the fact that women were and are more likely to write with sentiment than are men and that, being women, they know what the young female heart craves and sometimes they supply it. There is nothing shameful about controlled sentiment; it may even be that girls and women, secretly or not, still welcome a chance to spill over a bit, emotionally speaking, and thus retain better balance. After all, there has been little objection to the furious, the almost unbelievable action that boys like in their reading. That element in turn supplies something which the male heart and mind need, apparently. Appetites are not always the same, despite the current philosophies and determined attempts at equalization. Let all tastes have some means of satisfaction, and that includes the TV heroes who unashamedly weep.

It should be understood and accepted that while quality is always desirable, one can neither demand nor expect only that. Let the simple desire to read find stimulation somehow so that the mind opens out to soak up breathtaking adventures and homely accounts. With wits sharpened by much reading, with views extended by the same, the individual has reason to pursue subjects and can begin to evaluate. Thus the world becomes his. That is the way some children learn really to read: to happen upon a subject of such intense interest that they must find out more about it. If this be through books written in haphazard style, what matter? A child is uncovering for himself the enchantment of the wonderfully silent world of books in which all the action and the spoken words can re-dramatize themselves in the imagination, and what greater miracle can there be?

Judging by observations of today's child, one can conclude that these small people need a refuge from all that is thrust upon them, to help fill the place of that old family security and attain growth and vitality for facing all that is expected of them as members of a highly changeable and highly charged society with its caravans of fashionable crusades.

Notes

Chapter I

[1]Jacob Abbott, *Rollo at School*, p. 149, Boston: Phillips, Sampson, and Company 1838.

[2]Ibid, Prefatory Note.

[3]Jacob Abbott, *Lucy's Stories*, Revised, 1841 New York: Clark, Austin & Smith.

[4]Alice Morse Earle, *Child Life in Colonial Days*, p. 228, New York & London: The Macmillan Co. 1899.

[5]John A. Nietz, *Old Text Books*, p. 50, Pittsburgh, Penn.: University of Pittsburgh Press 1961.

[6]American Sunday School Union, *Hymns for Infant Minds*, pp. 29-30, Chiefly by the Author of Original Poems, Rhymes for the Nursery, etc. Revised by the Committee of Publication of the Amer. Sunday School Union, n.d. Philadelphia.

[7]Ibid, p. 54.

[8]*Historical Statistics of the U.S.*, Colonial Times to 1970, Part I, p. 56, U.S. Dep't of Commerce, 1975.

[9]*Lessons for the Little Ones* by a Teacher of Infants, p. 166, Philadelphia: Presbyterian Board of Publication n.d..

[10]Josef & Dorothy Berger, *Small Voices*, p. 25, New York: Paul S. Eriksson, Inc. 1966.

[11]Ibid, pp. 58, 60.

[12]Jacob Abbott, *Rollo at School*, pp. 16, 105, Boston: Phillips, Sampson, and Company 1838.

Chapter II

[1]Frank Luther Mott, *A History of American Magazines*, Vol. I, p. 492, New York & London: D. Appleton & Co. 1930.

[2]Ibid, p. 144.

[3]Cornelia Meigs, Anne T. Eaton, Elizabeth Nesbitt, Ruth H. Viguers, *A Critical History of Children's Literature*, New York: The Macmillan Co. Revised Ed. 1969 Part III, p. 384 (Elizabeth Nesbitt).

[4]*Encyclopaedia Americana*, Vol. 26, p. 22, Danbury, Conn.: Grolier Inc. 1983.

[5]Alice B. Cushman, "A Nineteenth Century Plan for Reading," Part II, *Horn Book*, April 1957, p. 159.

[6]Joanna H. Mathews, *Bessie in the City*, New York: Robert Carter & Brothers, 1874.

[7]Cornelia Meigs, Editor, *A Critical History of Children's Literature*, Part III, p. 385 (Elizabeth Nesbitt).

[8]Annie Fellows Johnston, *The Little Colonel's House Party*, pp.31- 33, Boston: L.C. Page 1900.

[9]*Historical Statistics of the U.S.*, Colonial Times to 1970, Part I, p. 15.

[10]Peter Parley, *The Tales of Peter Parley about America* Facsimile of the 1828 Edition. With a new introduction by Barrows Mussey, p. xvii, New York: Dover Publications, Inc. 1974.

[11]Frank Luther Mott, *A History of American Magazines*, Vol. I, p. 492.

[12]Ibid, Vol. III, p. 175, Cambridge. Mass.: Harvard University Press 1938.

[13]Ibid, Vol. II, pp. 100-101, Cambridge, Mass.: Harvard University Press 1938.

[14]W.H.G. Kingston, *Schoolboy Days: or, Ernest Bracebridge*, Boston: Lee & Shepard, 1869.

[15]Oliver Optic, *Poor and Proud; or, The Fortunes of Katy Redburn*, Boston: Lee & Shepard 1867.

[16]Oliver Optic, *The Starry Flag; or, The Young Fisherman of Cape Ann*, Preface, Boston: Lee & Shepard 1867.

[17]Frank Luther Mott, *A History of American Magazines* Vol. III, p. 175.

[18]Ednah D. Cheney, Ed., *Louisa May Alcott, Her Life, Letters and Journals*, p. 152, Boston: Little, Brown & Co., 1889, 1930.

[19]Frank Luther Mott, *A History of American Magazines* Vol. III, pp. 176-78.

[20]Ibid, Vol. II, pp. 268-71.

[21]Ibid, Vol. III, p. 176.

[22]Ibid, Vol. III, p. 501.

Chapter III

[1]Cornelia Meigs, Editor, *A Critical History of Children's Literature*, Part II, p. 221 (Anne Thaxter Eaton).

[2]Ibid, Part I, pp. 124-25 (Cornelia Meigs).

[3]Jacob Abbott, *Rollo at School*, Preface, Boston: Phillips, Sampson & Co., New York: James C. Derby 1888

[4]Margaret Sidney, *Ben Pepper*, Preface, Boston: Lee & Shepard 1905

[5]Arthur Winfield, *The Rover Boys on Treasure Isle*, Preface, New York: Grosset & Dunlap Copy. 1909.

[6]L.M. Montgomery, *Anne of the Island*, Boston: The Page Co. 1915.

[7]Horatio Alger, *Tattered Tom*, p. 282, Phil.: John C. Winston. 1st Copy. 1871.

[8]Horatio Alger, *Luck and Pluck*, p. 343, Phil.: Porter & Coates 1869.

[9]Sophie May, *Little Folks Astray*, p. 203, Boston: Lee & Shepard, N.Y.: Lee, Shepard and Dillingham 1872.

[10]Harry Castlemon, *Frank on the Prairie*, p. 245, Phil., Chicago, Toronto: The John C. Winston Co. 1st Copy. 1865.

[11]Elijah Kellogg, *The Young Deliverers of Pleasant Cove*, p. 304, Boston: Lee & Shepard, N.Y.: Lee, Shepard and Dillingham 1871.

[12]Howard R. Garis, *Uncle Wiggily in the Country*, p. 166, Copyright 1915, copyright renewed 1943 by Howard R. Garis. Reprinted by permission of Platt & Munk.

Chapter IV

[1]Jacob Abbott, *Lucy Among the Mountains*, Preface. N.Y.: Clark & Maynard 1870.

[2]Oliver Optic, *Freaks of Fortune; or, Half Round the World*, p. 303, Boston: Lee & Shepard. Copy. 1868.

[3]Horatio Alger, *Luck and Pluck*; or, John Oakley's Inheritance, p. 343, Phil.: Porter & Coates, 1869.

[4]Laura Lee Hope, *The Bobbsey Twins at Meadow Brook*, pp. 6-7, New York: Grosset & Dunlap, 1915.

[5]Hezekiah Butterworth, *Zigzag Journeys Around the World*, pp. 27-8, Boston: Dan Estes & Co. 1895.

[6]L. Frank Baum, *Wizard of Oz*, Introduction. Indianapolis and New York: The Bobbs-Merrill Co. 1900.

[7]Thornton Burgess, *Mother West Wind "Where" Stories*, p. 3, New York: Grosset & Dunlap, 1st Copy. 1918 (By arrangement with Little, Brown & Co.).

Chapter V

[1]Aunt Florida, *Phebe Travers*; or, One Year at a French Boarding School, Introduction. San Francisco and New York: A. Roman & Co. 1869.

[2]*Notable American Women 1607-1950*, A Biographical Dictionary, Edited by Edward T. James, Vol. III, p. 668, Cambridge, Mass.: The Belknap Press of Harvard University Press 1971.

[3]Roger Garis, "My Father Was Uncle Wiggily," *Saturday Evening Post*, Dec. 19, 1964, pp. 64-66. Reprinted from The Saturday Evening Post, c. 1964 The Curtis Publishing Co.

[4]Roger Garis, *My Father Was Uncle Wiggily*, p. 71, New York, Toronto, London, Sydney: McGraw-Hill Book Co. 1966.

[5]Ibid, p. 155.

Chapter VI

[1]Alice M. Jordan, *From Rollo to Tom Sawyer* and Other Papers, p. 78, Boston: The Horn Book Inc. 1948.

[2]Peter Parley, *The Tales of Peter Parley about America*, p. 9.

[3]Oliver Optic, *Little by Little*, "Biography and Bibliography," 1911 reprint from The New York Book Co.

[4]Oliver Optic, *Poor and Proud*: or The Fortunes of Katy Redburn, Preface, Boston: Lee & Shepard 1858.

[5]*American Authors 1600-1900*, A Biographical Dictionary of American Literature, Edited by Stanley J. Kunitz and Howard Haycraft, p. 758, New York: H.W. Wilson Co. 1938.

[6]Harry Castlemon, *Our Fellows*, back-page, Phil.: John C. Winston, 1st Copy, 1872.
[7]Ibid.

[8]Cornelia Meigs, Editor, *A Critical History of Children's Literature*, Part II, p. 222 (Anne Thaxter Eaton).

[9]Alice M. Jordan, *From Rollo to Tom Sawyer*, p. 110.

[10]Elijah Kellogg, *Boy Farmers of Elm Island*, p. 300, Boston: Lee & Shepard 1869.

[11]Frank Luther Mott, *Golden Multitudes*, The Story of Best Sellers in the U.S., p. 158, New York: The Macmillan Co. 1947.

[12]Horace E. Scudder, *The Doings of the Bodley Family*, back page. Boston: Houghton, Osgood & Co. 1875.

[13]*Dictionary of American Biography*, edited by Allen Johnson & Dumas Malone, New York: Charles Scribner's Sons, Vol. II (1958), p. 376.

14*National Cyclopaedia of American Biography*, New York: James T. White & Co, Vol. 23 (1933), p. 122.

15Cornelia Meigs, Editor, *A Critical History of Children's Literature*, Part II, p. 221 (Anne Thaxter Eaton).

16Harry Castlemon, *Our Fellows*, back page, Phil.: John C. Winston 1st Copy. 1872.

17James D. Hart, *The Popular Book*, A History of America's Literary Taste, p. 120, New York: Oxford University Press 1950.

18Elizabeth Stuart Phelps, *Gypsy Breynton*, Preface, New York: Dodd, Mead & Co. 1894. First entered 1866.

19Ibid.

20Katharine Anthony, *Louisa May Alcott*, p. 62, New York, London: Alfred A. Knopf 1937, 1938.

21Ibid, p. 80.

22Ednah D. Cheney, Ed., *Louisa May Alcott*, Her Life, Letters and Journals, p. 99.

23Katharine Anthony, *Louisa May Alcott*, pp. 94-5.

24Ednah D. Cheney,. Ed., *Louisa May Alcott*, p. 127.

25Ibid, p. 135.

26*Notable American Women 1607-1950*, A Biographical Dictionary, Vol. I, p. 344.

27Ibid, p. 32.

28Ibid, p. 619.

29 Martha Finley, *Elsie's Motherhood*, p. 33, New York: Dodd, Mead & Co. 1876.

30*Notable American Women 1607-1950*, A Biographical Dictionary, Vol. III, p. 669.

31Laura E. Richards, "When I Was Your Age," (serialized) *St. Nicholas*, Vol. XIX, Part II, May-Oct, 1892, p. 692, July issue.

32*Notable American Women 1607-1950*, A Biographical Dictionary, Vol. III, p. 148.

33Stanley J. Kunitz & Howard Haycraft, *The Junior Book of Authors*, p. 13, New York: The H. W. Wilson Co. 1940 1st Copy, 1934.

Chapter VII

1Frank Luther Mott, *Golden Multitudes*, The Story of Best Sellers in the U.S., Appendix A, p. 303.

2Anne Commire, *Something About the Author*, Vol. I, p. 2, Detroit: Gale Research Book Tower 1971.

3Ibid, p. 210.

4Irwin Porges, *Edgar Rice Burroughs*, The Man Who Created Tarzan, p. 2, Provo, Utah: Brigham Young University Press 1975.

5Frank Luther Mott, *Golden Multitudes*, p. 238.

6James D. Hart, *The Popular Book*, pp. 219-20.

7Alice Hegan Rice, *Mrs. Wiggs of the Cabbage Patch*, New York: The Century Co. 1901.

8Stanley J. Kunitz & Howard Haycraft, *The Junior Book of Authors*, p. 262.

9*The National Cyclopaedia of American Biography*, Vol. 42, 1958, p. 393.

10*Notable American Women 1607-1950*, A Biographical Dictionary, Vol. III, p. 559.

11Ibid, p. 559.

12Ibid, p. 560.

13Roger Garis, *My Father Was Uncle Wiggily*, p. 75 (McGraw-Hill Book).

14Stanley J. Kunitz & Howard Haycraft, *The Junior Book of Authors*, p. 199, Second

Edition Revised 1951.

[15]Anne Commire, *Something About the Author*, Vol. I, p. 210.

[16]Ibid, p. 210.

[17]Roger Garis, *My Father Was Uncle Wiggily*, p. 72 (McGraw-Hill Book).

[18]Anne Commire, *Something About the Author*, Vol. I, p. 2.

[19]*Oxford Dictionary of Quotations, Cahier, Quelques six mille proverbes, Tout passe, tout casse, tout lasse*. p. 12.

Chapter VIII

[1]George C. Needham, *Street Arabs and Gutter Snipes*, Preface, p. iv Boston: D.L. Guernsey 1st Copy. 1883.

[2]Ibid, p. 453.

[3]Alice Maude Fenn, *St. Nicholas*, Vol. XV, Part II, pp. 509-15, May-Oct. 1888 May issue.

Chapter IX

[1]John Stuart Mill, *The Subjection of Women*, p. 46, New York: D. Appleton & Co. 1869.

[2]Ibid, p. 47.

[3]Ibid, p. 43.

[4]Jacob Abbott, *Malleville*, Preface, New York: Harper & Bros. 1st Copy. 1850.

[5]Martha Finley, *Elsie Dinsmore*, p. 228, London: George Rutledge & Sons reprint, 1st Copy. 1867.

[6]Joanna H. Mathews, *Bessie in the City*, p. 31, New York: Robert Carter & Bros. 1st Copy. 1868.

[7]Ibid, pp. 31-32.

[8]Pansy (Isabella Alden), *Julia Ried*: Listening and Led, p. 342, Cincinnati: J.G. & F.C. Monfort 1st Copy. 1872.

[9]Sophie May, *Little Prudy's Cousin Grace*, pp. 9-10, Boston and New York: H.M. Caldwell Co. 1st Copy. 1864.

[10]Susan Coolidge, *What Katy Did*, p. 12, London & New York: Frederick Warne & Co. 1st Copy. 1873.

[11]Elizabeth Stuart Phelps, *Gypsy Breynton*, p. 15, New York: Dodd, Mead & Co. 1st Copy. 1866.

[12]Louisa May Alcott, *Little Women*, p. 9, Boston: Little, Brown & Co. 1st Copy. 1868.

[13]Margaret Sidney, *Five Little Peppers and How They Grew*, p. 37, Boston: Lothrop Publishing Co. 1st Copy. 1881.

[14]Lucy Fitch Perkins, *The Japanese Twins*, pp. 37-8, Boston and New York: Houghton Mifflin Co. 1st Copy. 1912.

[15]Laura Ingalls Wilder, *Little House on the Prairie*, pp. 46-7, New York, Evanston, San Francisco, London: Harper & Row 1st Copy. 1935.

[16]L.M. Montgomery, *Anne of Green Gables*, p. 33, Boston: The Page Co. 1st Copy. 1908.

[17]Ibid, p. 34.

[18]Kate Douglas Wiggin, *Rebecca of Sunnybrook Farm*, pp. 36-7, Boston and New

York: Houghton, Mifflin & Co. 1st Copy. 1903.

[19]Eleanor H. Porter, *Pollyanna*, p. 27, Boston: L.C. Page & Co. 1st Copy. 1913.

[20]Alice Ross Colver, *Babs at Birchwood*, pp. 56-7, Phil.: The Penn Pub. Co. 1st Copy. 1919.

[21]Carolyn Keene, *The Sign of the Twisted Candles*, p. 160, New York: Grosset & Dunlap 1st Copy. 1933.

[22]Oliver Optic, *The Starry Flag*, pp. 14-5, Boston: Lee & Shepard 1st Copy. 1867.

[23]Arthur M. Winfield, *The Rover Boys at School*, p. 162, New York: Chatterton-Peck Co. 1st Copy. 1899.

[24]*American Authors 1600-1900*, A Biographical Dictionary of American Literature, p. 13.

Chapter X

[1]Jacob Abbott, *Caroline*, pp. 149-50, New York: Harper & Bros. 1st Copy. 1853.

[2]Oliver Optic, *The Young Fisherman of Cape Ann*, pp. 17-8, Boston: Lee & Shepard 1st Copy. 1867.

[3]Ibid, pp. 284-85.

[4]Elijah Kellogg, *The Boy Farmers of Elm Island*, p. 167, Boston: Lee & Shepard 1st Copy. 1869.

[5]J.T. Trowbridge, *The Pocket-Rifle*, p. 229, Boston: Lothrop, Lee & Shepard 1st Copy. 1881.

[6]Ibid, p. 257.

[7]Joseph A. Altsheler, *The Riflemen of the Ohio*, p. 269, New York: Appleton-Century Crofts, Inc. 1st Copy. 1910.

[8]Edgar Rice Burroughs, *Tarzan of the Apes*, p. 97, New York: Ballantine Books A Division of Random House 1984; Copyright 1912 Frank A. Munsey Company.

[9]Harry Castlemon, *Frank on the Prairie*, p. 13, Phil.: John C. Winston 1st Copy. 1865.

[10]Arthur M. Winfield, *The Rover Boys at School*, pp. 9-10, New York: Chatterton-Peck Co. 1st Copy. 1899.

[11]Edward Ellis, *Lena-Wingo, the Mohawk*, pp. 68-9, Phil.: John C. Winston Co. 1st Copy. 1893.

[12]Louisa May Alcott, *Little Women*, p. 37, Boston: Little, Brown & Co. 1st Copy. 1868.

[13]L.M. Montgomery, *Anne of Green Gables*, p. 427, Boston: The Page Co. 1st Copy. 1908.

[14]Mary P. Wells Smith, *Two in a Bungalow*, p. 187, Boston: Little, Brown & Co. 1914.

[15]Alice Morse Earle, *Child Life in Colonial Days*, p. 225.

Chapter XI

[1]Jacob Abbott, *Lucy's Stories*, p. 54, New York: Clark & Maynard 1st Copy. 1841.

[2]Laura Ingalls Wilder, *On the Banks of Plum Creek*, p. 5, New York and Evanston: Harper & Row 1st Copy. 1937.

[3]Horace Scudder, *Doings of the Bodley Family*, pp. 71-2, Boston: Houghton, Osgood & Co. 1st Copy. 1875.

[4]Margaret Sidney, *Five Little Peppers and How They Grew*, pp. 247-48, Boston: Lothrop Pub. Co. 1st Copy. 1881.

[5]Annie Fellows Johnston, *The Little Colonel*, pp. 25-7, Boston: L.C. Page & Co. 1st Copy. 1895.

[6]Bruno Bettelheim, *The Uses of Enchantment*, p. 8, New York: Vintage Books, Division of Random House 1977, Orig. pub. by Alfred A. Knopf in 1976.

[7]L. Frank Baum, *The Wizard of Oz*, p. 135, Chicago: The Reilly & Lee Co. 1st Copy. 1900.

[8]Hugh Lofting, *The Story of Doctor Dolittle*, pp. 160-61, New York: Frederick A. Stokes 1920.

[9]Mark Twain, *Adventures of Tom Sawyer*, pp. 74-5, New York & London: Harper & Bros. 1st Copy. 1875.

[10]Horatio Alger, *Tom Thatcher*, p. 258, New York: A.L. Burt 1st Copy. 1888.

[11]Victor Appleton, *Tom Swift and his Giant Cannon*, p. 147, New York: Grosset & Dunlap 1st Copy. 1913.

[12]Ibid, pp. 170-71.

[13]Harry Castlemon, *Frank at Don Carlos' Rancho*, pp. 155-56, Chicago: M.A. Donohue & Co. 1st Copy. 1867.

[14]Arthur M. Winfield, *The Rover Boys in Alaska*, p. 283, New York: Grosset & Dunlap 1st Copy. 1914.

[15]Edward Ellis, *Lena-Wingo the Mohawk*, pp. 220-21, Phil.: John C. Winston 1st Copy. 1893.

[16]Edgar Rice Burroughs, *Tarzan of the Apes*, p. 140, New York: Ballantine Books A Division of Random House 1984; Copyright 1912 Frank A. Munsey Company.

[17]Ibid, p. 156.

[18]Elijah Kellogg, *The Boy Farmers of Elm Island*, pp. 261-62, Boston: Lee & Shepard 1st Copy. 1869.

[19]Thomas W. Knox *The Boy Travellers in Egypt and the Holy Land*, p. 57, New York: Harper & Bros. 1st Copy. 1882.

[20]Joseph A. Altsheler, *The Eyes of the Woods*, p. 262, New York: Appleton-Century 1917.

[21]Kate Douglas Wiggin, *Rebecca of Sunnybrook Farm*, p. 13, Boston & New York: Houghton, Mifflin & Co. 1st Copy. 1903.

[22]Elizabeth Stuart Phelps, *Gypsy Breynton*, pp. 45-6, New York: Dodd, Mead & Co. 1st Copy. 1866.

[23]Emma C. Dowd, *Polly of the Hospital Staff*, p. 62, Boston & New York: Houghton Mifflin & Co. 1st Copy. 1912.

[24]L.M. Montgomery, *Anne of Green Gables*, p. 17, Boston: The Page Co. 1st Copy. 1908.

[25]Kate Douglas Wiggin, *Rebecca of Sunnybrook* Farm, p. 10, Boston: Houghton, Mifflin & Co. 1st Copy. 1903.

[26]Louisa May Alcott, *Under the Lilacs*, p. 1, Boston: Little, Brown & Co. 1st Copy. 1878.

[27]Laura E. Richards, *Queen Hildegarde*, p. 250, New York: Grosset & Dunlap 1st Copy. 1889.

[28]Ibid, pp. 255-56.

[29]Annie Fellows Johnston, *The Little Colonel's Christmas Vacation*, p. 333, Boston: The Page Co. 1st Copy. 1905.

[30]Lucy Fitch Perkins, *The Scotch Twins*, pp. 150-51, Boston & New York: Houghton Mifflin Co. 1st Copy. 1919.

[31]Alice Hegan Rice, *Lovey Mary*, p. 47, New York: The Century Co. 1st Copy. 1902.

Chapter XII

[1]New England Primer, Twentieth Century Reprint, unpaged, Boston, New York, Chicago, London: Ginn & Co. n.d. Inscription dated June 1905 Foreword: "...a facsimile production from an original published, as nearly as can be determined, between the years 1785 and 1790..." Read "f" as "s" in proper places. (Final "s" of "parents" printed as is.).

[2]Mrs. Sarah Stickney Ellis, "The Education of the Heart, Woman's Best Work," p. 412, *The Young Lady's Guide*, New York: American Tract Society 1st Copy. 1870.

[3]Ibid, Hannah More, "Public Amusements," p. 309.

[4]Ibid, Rev. John Angell James, "The Influence of Christianity on the Condition of Woman," pp. 441-42.

[5]Anonymous, *The Five Talents of Women*, p. 16, New York: Charles Scribner's Sons 1888.

[6]Ibid, pp. 113, 123.

[7]*Good Manners*, Metropolitan Culture Series, Third Ed., New York: The Butterick Pub. Co. 1889.

[8]John H. Young, *Our Deportment*, pp. 280-84, Detroit and St. Louis: F.B. Dickerson & Co. 1879, 1881.

[9]Jacob Abbott, *Rollo in London*, pp. 165-66, Boston: Taggard & Thompson 1st Copy. 1854.

[10]Cousin Mary, *Christmas Holidays at Chestnut Hill*, p. 102, Boston: Lee & Shepard 1st Copy. 1853.

[11]Sophie May, *Little Prudy's Sister Susy*, p. 74, Boston: Lothrop, Lee & Shepard 1st Copy. 1864.

[12]Joanna H. Mathews, *Bessie in the City*, pp. 62-3, New York: Robert Carter & Bros. 1st Copy. 1868.

[13]Martha Finley, *Elsie Dinsmore*, p. 116, London: George Routledge & Sons 1st Copy 1867.

[14]Martha Finley, *Elsie's Womanhood*, p. 296, New York: Dodd, Mead & Co. 1st Copy. 1875.

[15]Pansy, *Julia Ried*, pp. 246-47, Cincinnati: J.C. and F.C. Monfort 1st Copy. 1872.

[16]Oliver Optic, *Little By Little* or The Cruise of the Flyaway, p. 23. N.Y.: The New York Book Co. 1911. No Copy date.

[17]Horatio Alger, *Luck and Pluck*; or, John Oakley's Inheritance, Preface Phil.: Porter & Coates 1st Copy. 1869.

[18]J.T. Trowbridge, The *Pocket-Rifle*, p. 25, Boston: Lothrop, Lee & Shepard 1st Copy. 1881.

[19]Elijah Kellogg, *The Young Deliverers*, p. 102, Boston: Lee & Shepard 1st Copy. 1871.

[20]Charles Stephens, *A Great Year of Our Lives*, p. 174, Boston: The Youth's Companion 1912.

[21]Mary P. Wells Smith, *Jolly Good Times*, pp. 99-100, Boston: Little, Brown & Co. 1st Copy, 1875.

[22]James Otis, *Toby Tyler*, pp. 250-51, New York & London: Harper & Bros. 1st Copy. 1880.

[23]Elizabeth Stuart Phelps, *Gypsy Breynton*, pp. 290-91, New York: Dodd, Mead & Co. 1st Copy. 1866.

[24]Louisa May Alcott, *Little Women*, p. 16, Boston: Little, Brown, & Co. 1st Copy. 1868.

[25]Ibid, p. 17.

[26]Louisa May Alcott, *Eight Cousins*, pp. 197-98, Boston: Roberts Bros. 1st Copy. 1874.

[27]Ibid, p. 199.

[28]Margaret Sidney, *Five Little Peppers and How They Grew*, p. 15, Boston: Lothrop Pub. Co. 1st Copy. 1881.

[29]L. Frank Baum, *The Emerald City of Oz*, p. 268, Chicago: The Reilly & Lee Co. 1st Copy. 1910.

[30]L.M. Montgomery, *Anne of Green Gables*, p. 55, Boston: The Page Co. 1st Copy. 1908.

[31]Kate Douglas Wiggin, *Rebecca of Sunnybrook Farm*, p. 92, Boston & New York: Houghton, Mifflin & Co. 1st Copy. 1903.

[32]Eleanor H. Porter, *Pollyanna*, p. 60, Boston: L.C. Page & Co. Copy. 1913.

[33]Annie Fellows Johnston, *The Little Colonel: Maid of Honor*, p. 147, Boston: L.C. Page & Co. 1st Copy. 1906.

[34]Alice Hegan Rice, *Mrs. Wiggs of the Cabbage Patch*, pp. 16-9, New York: The Century Co. 1st Copy. 1901.

[35]Lucy Fitch Perkins, *The French Twins*, p. 8, Boston and New York: Houghton Mifflin Co. 1st Copy. 1918.

[36]Arthur M. Winfield, *The Rover Boys in Camp*, p. 258, New York: Grosset & Dunlap 1st Copy, 1904.

[37]Laura Lee Hope, *Six Little Bunkers at Mammy June's*, p. 70, New York: Grosset & Dunlap 1st Copy. 1922.

[38]Laura Ingalls Wilder, *Little House on the Prairie*, p. 146, New York, Evanston, San Francisco, London: Harper & Row 1st Copy. 1935.

Chapter XIII

[1]Oliver Optic, *The Boat Club*; or, The Bunkers of Rippleton, p. 85, New York: Hurst & Co. n.d..

[2]Horatio Alger, *Sam's Chance* and How He Improved It, p. 7, New York: Hurst & Co. n.d..

[3]Arthur M. Winfield, *The Rover Boys in Camp*, p. 34, New York: Grosset & Dunlap 1st Copy. 1904.

[4]Victor Appleton, *Tom Swift and His Photo Telephone*, pp. 115-16, New York: Grosset & Dunlap, 1st Copy. 1914.

[5]George W. Peck, *The Grocery Man and Peck's Bad Boy*, pp. 82-3, Chicago: W.B. Conkey 1st Copy. 1883.

[6]Thomas W. Knox, *The Boy Travellers in Northern Europe*, pp. 206-07, New York: Harper & Bros. 1st Copy. 1891.

[7]Charles A. Stephens, *The Knockabout Club in Spain*, p. 160, Boston: Estes & Lauriat 1st Copy. 1889.

[8]Mark Twain, *Adventures of Tom Sawyer*, p. 1, New York & London: Harper & Bros.

1st Copy. 1875.

[9]Ibid, pp. 54-5.

[10]Booth Tarkington, *Penrod*, p. 5, Garden City, N.Y.: Doubleday, Page & Co. 1st Copy. 1914.

[11]Ibid, pp. 312-13.

[12]Clarence B. Kelland, *Mark Tidd in Italy*, p. 2, New York: Grosset & Dunlap, by arrangement with Harper & Bros. 1925.

[13]L. Frank Baum, *The Patchwork Girl of Oz*, p. 188, Chicago: The Reilly & Lee Pub. Co. 1st Copy. 1913, by L. Frank Baum, copyright renewed 1940 by Maud Cage Baum.

[14]L. Frank Baum, *The Wizard of Oz*, p. 231, Chicago: The Reilly & Lee Pub. Co. 1st Copy. 1900.

[15]*Webster's New World Dictionary*, réd-o-wa (Czech, rejdovak) 1. either of two ballroom dances of the 19th century, one like a polka, the other like a waltz.

[16]Louisa May Alcott, *Little Women*, p. 41, Boston: Little, Brown & Co. 1st Copy, 1868.

[17]Ibid, p. 50.

[18]L.M. Montgomery, *Anne of Green Gables*, p. 301, Boston: The Page Co. 1st Copy. 1908.

[19]Elizabeth Stuart Phelps, *Gypsy Breynton*, p. 80, New York. Dodd, Meade & Co. 1st Copy. 1866.

[20]Laura E. Richards, *Queen Hildegarde*, p. 20, New York: Grosset & Dunlap 1st Copy. 1889.

[21]Alice Hegan Rice, *Lovey Mary*, p. 146, New York: The Century Co. 1st Copy. 1902.

[22]Ibid, p. 170.

[23]Howard R. Garis, *Uncle Wiggily in the Country*, pp. 23-4. Copyright 1915, copyright renewed 1943 by Howard R. Garis. Reprinted by permission of Platt & Munk.

[24]Frances Boyd Calhoun, *Miss Minerva and William Green Hill*, pp. 196-97, Chicago: The Reilly & Lee Co. 1st Copy. 1909.

[25]Mary P. Wells Smith, *Jolly Good Times: or, Child Life on a Farm*, pp. 13-4, Boston: Little, Brown, & Co. 1st Copy. 1875.

[26]Sophie May, *Little Prudy's Captain Horace*, p. 73, Boston & New York: H.M. Caldwell 1st Copy. 1864.

Chapter XIV

[1]Jacob Abbott, *Rollo at School*, pp. 38-9, Boston; Phillips, Sampson & Co., New York: James C. Derby 1st Copy. 1838.

[2]Elijah Kellogg, *The Boy Farmers of Elm Island*, pp. 140-41, Boston: Lee & Shepard 1st Copy. 1869.

[3]J.T. Trowbridge, *The Pocket-Rifle*, p. 86, Boston: Lothrop, Lee & Shepard, 1st Copy. 1881.

[4]Ibid, p. 237.

[5]Oliver Optic, *Little by Little*, p. 70, New York: The New York Book Co., 1911.

[6]Horatio Alger, *Luck and Pluck*; or, John Oakley's Inheritance, p. 149, Phil.: Porter & Coates 1st Copy. 1869.

[7]Edward Ellis, *The Wilderness Fugitives*, pp. 234-35, Phil.: Henry T. Coates & Co. 1st Copy, 1893.

[8]Everett T. Tomlinson, *Three Young Continentals*, p. 246, New York: Grosset & Dunlap

1st Copy. 1896.

[9]Edward Stratemeyer, *With Taylor on the Rio Grande*, p. 261, Boston: Lothrop, Lee & Shepard 1st Copy. 1901.

[10]Clarence Young,*The Motor Boys in the Clouds*, pp. 7-8, New York: Cupples & Leon, 1st Copy. 1910.

[11]Harry Castlemon, *Frank on the Prairie*, pp. 69-70, Phil.: John C. Winston.Co. 1st Copy. 1865.

[12]Charles A. Stephens, *A Great Year of Our Lives*, p. 222, Boston: The Youth's Companion, 1st Copy. 1912.

[13]Horace Scudder, *Doings of the Bodley Family in Town and Country*, p. 9, Boston: Houghton, Osgood & Co. First Copy. 1875.

[14]Joseph A. Altsheler, *The Lost Hunters*, p. 24, New York: Appleton-Century 1st Copy. 1918.

[15]Hezekiah Butterworth, *The Wampum Belt*, pp. 99-100, New York: D. Appleton Co. 1st Copy. 1896.

[16]Louisa May Alcott, *Little Women*, pp. 55-6, Boston: Little, Brown & Co. 1st Copy. 1868.

[17]Elizabeth Stuart Phelps, *Gypsy Breynton*, pp. 106-07, New York: Dodd, Meade & Co. 1st Copy. 1866.

[18]Margaret Sidney, *Five Little Peppers and How They Grew*, p. 213, Boston: Lothrop Pub. Co. 1st Copy. 1881.

[19]Rosa Abbott, *Upside Down; Or, Will and Work*, pp. 10-11, Boston: Lee & Shepard 1st Copy. 1868.

[20]Susan Coolidge, *What Katy Did*, pp. 37-8, London: Frederick Warne & Co. 1st Copy. 1873.

[21]L.M. Montgomery, *Anne of Green Gables*, p. 26, Boston: The Page Co. 1st Copy. 1908.

[22]Kate Douglas Wiggin, *New Chronicles of Rebecca*, pp. 4-5, Boston & New York: Houghton, Mifflin & Co. 1st Copy. 1907.

[23]Eleanor H. Porter, *Pollyanna Grows Up*, p. 307, Boston: The Page Co. Copy. 1915.

[24]Annie Fellows Johnston, *The Little Colonel: Maid of Honor*, pp. 130-31, Boston: L.C. Page & Co. 1st Copy. 1906.

[25]Martha Finley, *Mildred's Boys and Girls*, pp. 302-03, New York: A.L. Burt 1st Copy. 1886.

[26]Amy Brooks, *Dorothy Dainty's Vacation*, pp. 132-34, Boston: Lothrop, Lee & Shepard 1st Copy. 1913

[27]Edgar Rice Burroughs, *The Beasts of Tarzan*, p. 23, New York: Ballantine Books A Division of Random House 1980; Copyright 1914 Frank A. Munsey Company.

[28]Ibid, p. 23

[29]Mark Twain, *The Adventures of Huckleberry Finn*, pp. 270-71, New York: Macmillan Co. 1st Copy. 1884.

[30]Booth Tarkington, *Penrod and Sam*, p. 74, New York: Grosset & Dunlap 1st Copy. 1916 by Doubleday, Page & Co..

[31]George W. Peck, *Peck's Bad Boy and the Groceryman*, pp. 171-72, Chicago: W.B. Conkey 1st Copy. 1883.

[32]L. Frank Baum, *The Wizard of Oz*, p. 186, Chicago: The Reilly & Lee Co. 1st Copy. 1900.

[33]Thomas W. Knox, *The Boy Travellers in the Far East*, p. 110, New York: Harper & Bros. 1st Copy. 1882.

[34]Mary Hazelton Wade, *Our Little Eskimo Cousin*, p. 29, Boston: L.C. Page & Co. 1st Copy. 1902.

[35]Lucy Fitch Perkins, *The Japanese Twins*, pp. 78-9, Boston & New York: Houghton Mifflin Co. 1st Copy. 1912.

[36]Clara Ingram Judson, *Mary Jane in France*, p. 84, New York: Grosset & Dunlap 1st Copy. 1930 .

[37]Sophie May, *Dotty Dimple Out West*, pp. 11-12, Boston: Lee & Shepard 1st Copy. 1868.

[38]Laura Ingalls Wilder, *By the Shores of Silver Lake*, p. 52, New York, Evanston, San Francisco, London: Harper & Row 1st Copy. 1939.

Chapter XV

[1]Marshall Saunders, *Beautiful Joe*, Introd. Toronto: Standard Pub. Co. 1897, Fifth Canadian Edition. 1st Copy. 1894.

[2]Tucked in, here and there, among the readers surveyed are three excerpts from the Rollo stories, one concerning Sophie May's Prudy, and one from *What Katy Did*.

[3]Hugh Lofting, *The Story of Doctor Dolittle*, p. 9, New York: Frederick A. Stokes 1st Copy. 1920.

[4]Anne Parrish, *All Kneeling*, p. 265, New York & London: Harper & Bros. 1st Copy. 1928.

[5]Cornelia Meigs, Editor, *A Critical History of Children's Literature*, Part III, p. 340 (Elizabeth Nesbitt).

[6]D.L. Kirkpatrick, Editor, *Twentieth Century Children's Writers*, p. 140 (Lucien L. Agosta) New York: St. Martin's Press 1983.

[7]Stanley J. Kunitz and Howard Haycraft, *The Junior Book of Authors*, p. 71 (Thornton Burgess).

[8]D.L. Kirkpatrick, Editor, *Twentieth Century Children's Writers*, p. 140 (Lucien L. Agosta).

[9]Albert Bigelow Paine, *The Hollow Tree and Deep Woods Book*, p. 79, New York: Harper & Bros. 1st Copy. 1900.

[10]Thornton Burgess, *Mother West Wind "Why" Stories*, p. 165, Boston: Little, Brown, & Co. 1st Copy. 1915.

[11]Thornton Burgess, *Mother West Wind "Where" Stories*, pp. 136-37, New York: Grosset & Dunlap 1st Copy. 1918 (By arrangement with Little, Brown & Co.).

[12]Arthur Scott Bailey, *The Tale of Solomon Owl*, pp. 52-3. Copyright 1917 by Grosset & Dunlap, Inc., copyright renewed 1945 by Arthur Scott Bailey. Reprinted by permission of Grosset & Dunlap, Inc.

[13]Howard Garis, *Uncle Wiggily in the Country*, pp. 9-10. Copyright 1915, copyright renewed 1943 by Howard R. Garis. Reprinted by permission of Platt & Munk.

[14]Howard Garis, *Uncle Wiggily's Airship*, p. 179, New York: A.L. Burt 1931.

[15]Frances Trego Montgomery, *Billy Whiskers*, The Autobiography of a Goat, p. 114, New York: Dover Publications, Inc. 1st Copy. 1902.

[16]Hugh Lofting, *The Story of Doctor Dolittle*, p. 77, New York: Frederick A. Stokes 1st Copy. 1920.

[17]Ibid, p. 137.

[18]Cornelia Meigs, Editor, *A Critical History of Children's Literature*, Part IV, p. 468 (Ruth Hill Viguers).

[19]Hugh Lofting, *Doctor Dolittle and the Green Canary*, Introd., Phil., New York: J.B. Lippincott Co. Copy. 1924, 1925, 1950.

Chapter XVI

[1]*A St. Nicholas Anthology* The Early Years, Selected and edited by Burton C. Frye, Foreword by Dr. Richard L. Darling, New York: Meredith Press, 1969.

[2]James D. Hart, *The Popular Book*, pp. 119-120.

[3]Hezekiah Butterworth, *Zigzag Journeys Around the World*, Introd., p. 7, by Allan Eric, in the *Journalist*, Boston: Dana Estes & Co. 1st Copy. 1895.

Chapter XVII

[1]*New England Primer*, Twentieth Century Reprint, unpaged.

[2]Kate Douglas Wiggin, *My Garden of Memory*, pp. 31, 354, Boston: Houghton Mifflin Co. 1st Copy. 1923.

[3]Frances Hodgson Burnett, *The One I Knew the Best of All*, A Memory of the Mind of a Child, pp. 112-13, New York: Charles Scribner's Sons 1st Copy. 1893.

[4]Bruno Bettelheim, "A Primer for Literacy," Part V of special section entitled "The Child's Mind," *Harper's*, April 1978, p. 56.

[5]Ibid, p. 58.

[6]Alice M. Jordan, *From Rollo to Tom Sawyer* and Other Papers, pp. 117-18.

[7]Hezekiah Butterworth, *Zigzag Journeys Around the World*, p. 30, Boston: Dana Estes & Co. 1st Copy. 1895.

[8]*Merry's Museum* and Parley's Magazine, edited by S.G. Goodrich, New York: S.T. Allen & Co. 1852, Vol. XXIII, "Scraps," p. 153.

[9]Gerald Gottlieb, "Small Mischief," from The Talk of the Town, *New Yorker*, Dec. 24, 1984, pp. 26-28.

Bibliography

A *St. Nicholas Anthology* The Early Years, Selected and edited by Burton C. Frye, New York: Meredith Press 1969

Adams, Bess Porter, *About Books and Children*, New York: Henry Holt & Co. 1953

American Authors 1600-1900, A Biographical Dictionary of American Literature, Edited by Stanley J. Kunitz and Howard Haycraft, New York: H.W. Wilson Co. 1938

Anthony, Katherine, *Louisa May Alcott*, New York, London: Alfred A. Knopf 1937, 1938

Berger, Josef & Dorothy, *Small Voices*, New York: Paul S. Eriksson, Inc. 1966

Bettelheim, Bruno, *The Uses of Enchantment*, New York: Vintage Books, Division of Random House 1977. Originally published by Alfred A. Knopf 1976

Bettelheim, Bruno, "A Primer for Literacy," Part V of special section entitled "The Child's Mind," *Harper's* April 1978, pp. 56-58

Burnett, Frances Hodgson, *The One I Knew the Best of All*, A Memory of the Mind of a Child, New York: Charles Scribner's Sons 1893

Cheney, Ednah D., Editor, *Louisa May Alcott*, Her Life, Letters and Journals, Boston: Little, Brown & Co. 1889, 1930

Commire, Anne, *Something About the Author*, Facts and Pictures about Contemporary Authors and Illustrators of Books for Young People, Detroit, Michigan: Gale Research Book Tower, Vol. I 1971

Cushman, Alice B., "A Nineteenth Century Plan for Reading," Part II, *Horn Book* April 1957, pp. 159-166

Dictionary of American Biography, edited by Allen Johnson and Dumas Malone, New York: Charles Scribner's Sons, Vols. 1 (1957), 2 (1958), 5 (1933)

Earle, Alice Morse, *Child Life in Colonial Days*, New York & London: The Macmillan Co. 1899

Encyclopaedia Americana, Danbury, Conn.: Grolier Inc. 1983, Vol. 26

Fenn, Alice Maude, "Girard College," *St. Nicholas*, Vol. XV Part II, May-Oct. 1888, May issue, pp. 509-515

Garis, Roger, "My Father Was Uncle Wiggily," *Saturday Evening Post*, Dec. 19, 1964, pp. 64-66.

Garis, Roger, *My Father Was Uncle Wiggily*, New York, Toronto, London, Sydney: McGraw-Hill Book Co. 1966

Good Manners, Metropolitan Culture Series, Third Ed., New York: The Butterick Pub. Co. 1889

Gottlieb, Gerald, "Small Mischief," from The Talk of the Town, *New Yorker*, Dec. 24, 1984, pp. 26-28

Green, David L. and Martin, Dick, *The Oz Scrapbook*, New York: Random House 1977

Handbook of Pseudonyms and Personal Nicknames, compiled by Harold S. Sharp, Metuchen, N.Y.: The Scarecrow Press, Inc. 1972

Hart, James D., *The Popular Book*, A History of America's Literary Taste, New York: Oxford University Press 1950

Historical Statistics of the U.S., Colonial Times to 1970, Part I, Bicentennial Edition 1975, U.S. Department of Commerce

Hymns for Infant Minds, Chiefly by the author of Original Poems, Rhymes for the Nursery, etc. Revised by the Committee of Publication of the American S.S. Union, Philadelphia: American Sunday School Union n.d.

Hymns for Sunday Schools, Youth and Children, Cincinnati: Swormstedt & Poe, Sunday-School Union 1860 First entered New York 1854

Jordan, Alice M., *From Rollo to Tom Sawyer* and Other Papers, Boston: The Horn Book Inc. 1948

Lessons for the Little Ones, by a Teacher of Infants, Philadelphia: Presbyterian Board of Publication n.d.

Meigs, Cornelia, *Invincible Louisa*, Boston: Little, Brown, & Co. 1933

Meigs, Cornelia (Editor); Eaton, Anne T.; Nesbitt, Elizabeth; Viguers, Ruth H., *A Critical History of Children's Literature*, New York: The Macmillan Co. 1953, Revised Edition 1969

Mill, John Stuart, *The Subjection of Women*, New York: D. Appleton & Co. 1869

More Junior Authors, edited by Muriel Fuller, New York: The H.W. Wilson Co. 1963

Mott, Frank Luther, *A History of American Magazines*, New York & London: D. Appleton & Co., Vol. I, 1741-1850, 1930. Cambridge, Mass.: Harvard University Press, Vol. II 1850-1865 and Vol. III 1865-1885, 1938. Cambridge, Mass.: The Belknap Press of Harvard University Press, Vol. IV 1885-1905, 1957

Mott, Frank Luther, *Golden Multitudes*, The Story of Best Sellers in the U.S., New York: The Macmillan Co. 1947

Needham, George C., *Street Arabs and Gutter Snipes*, Boston: D.I. Guernsey 1884

Nietz, John, *Old Textbooks*, Pittsburgh, Penn.: University of Pittsburgh Press 1961

Notable American Women 1607-1950, A Biographical Dictionary, edited by Edward T. James, Cambridge, Mass.: The Belknap Press of Harvard University Press 1971 Vols. I & III

Peter Parley, *The Tales of Peter Parley about America*, Facsimile of the 1828 Edition. New York: Dover Publications, Inc. 1974

Porges, Irwin, *Edgar Rice Burroughs, The Man Who Created Tarzan*, Provo, Utah: Brigham Young University Press 1975

Laura E. Richards, *When I Was Your Age* (serialized), *St. Nicholas*, Vol. XIX, Part I, Nov. 1891-April 1892, March issue, pp. 371-374; Vol. XIX, Part II, May-Oct. 1892, July issue, pp. 692-696

Robert Merry's Museum, S.G. Goodrich, Editor, Vols. XXI-XXIV 1851-1852, New York: published by S.T. Allen & Co.

Sloane, William, *Children's Books in England and America in the Seventeenth Century*, New York: Columbia University 1955 King's Crown Press, A History and a Checklist, Together with The Young Christian's Library, the First Printed Catalogue of Books for Children

Smith, Dora, *Fifty Years of Children's Books 1910-1960*, Champaign, Ill.: The National Council of Teachers of English 1963

Targ, William, Editor, *Bibliophile in the Nursery*, Cleveland and New York: The World Publishing Co. 1957

The Five Talents of Women, author anonymous, New York: Charles Scribner's Sons 1888

The Junior Book of Authors, edited by Stanley J. Kunitz and Howard Haycraft, New York: The H.W. Wilson Co. 1934

The Junior Book of Authors, edited by Stanley J. Kunitz and Howard Haycraft, 2nd Edition, Revised, New York: The H.W. Wilson Co. 1951

The McGraw-Hill Encyclopedia of World Biography, New York, San Francisco and St. Louis: McGraw-Hill Book Co. Vol. I 1973

The National Cyclopaedia of American Biography, New York: James T. White & Co. Vols. 1-5, 7, 11 13, 18, 10, 23, 27, 32, 39, 42 1898-1958

The New England Primer, Twentieth Century Reprint (A facsimile reproduction "...from an original published, as nearly as can be determined, between the years 1785 and 1790...") Boston, New York, Chicago: Ginn & Co. n.d. Inscription of 1905

The Osborne Collection of Early Children's Books 1566-1910, A Catalogue Prepared at Boys and Girls House by Judith St. John With an Introduction by Edgar Osborne, Toronto Public Library, Toronto, Canada 1958

The Reader's Encyclopaedia, edited by William Rose Benet, New York: Thomas Y. Crowell Co. 1948

The St. Nicholas Anthology, edited by Henry Steele Commager, New York: Random House 1948

The Young Lady's Guide (various authors, no editor named), New York: American Tract Society 1870

Thornwell, Emily, *The Lady's Guide to Perfect Gentility*, Philadelphia: J.B. Lippincott & Co. 1865

Twentieth Century Authors, edited by Stanley J. Kunitz and Howard Haycraft, New York: The H.W. Wilson Co. 1942

Twentieth-Century Children's Writers, edited by D.L. Kirkpatrick, New York: St. Martin's Press 1983

Wiggin, Kate Douglas, *My Garden of Memory*, An Autobiography, Boston & New York: Houghton Mifflin Co. 1923

Young, John H., *Our Deportment*, Detroit & St. Louis: F.B. Dickerson & Co. 1881

And scores of series

Index

Fictional characters are listed according to given names or to titles as appearing in the series. Particular pen-names—Aunt Florida, Cousin Mary, Mark Twain, Oliver Optic, Peter Parley, Sophie May—appear in this same order.

Butterworth, Hezekiah, 16, 17, 24, 25,
    41-2, 89, 150-51, 164, 185-86, 195

Cabbage Patch, 58-9, 70, 114, 128, 139
Cady, Harrison, 64, 173, 182
Calhoun, Frances Boyd, 140
Calhoun, Mary, 178
Captain Horace, 21, 141
Carlson, Natalie Savage, 178
Castlemon, Harry, 15, 21, 24, 26,
    32, 42-3, 91-2, 104-05, 148-49,
    151, 182, 195
Champney, Elizabeth W., 25, 50
Charlie Bell, 89, 106-07, 123
Children, situation of, 7-9, 12, 13,
    14, 19; with Abbott, Jacob, 36;
    46, 70-1, 115-18, 120-22,
    125-26, 166-67, 189, 192-95
Clarke, Rebecca Sophia. See Sophie
    May.
Classics, 28, 177, 179, 180, 195
Cleary, Beverly, 178
Clemens, Samuel L. See Mark Twain.
Coatsworth, Elizabeth, 178
Condé, J. M., 168, 173
Coolidge, Susan, 15, 17, 31, 33,
    49, 77, 153, 179, 180
Coombs, Patricia, 178
Cousin Grace, 77
Cousin Mary, 10, 120
Critical opinions, 36, 37, 38, 39,
    41, 53, 58, 144, 169-70, 175,
    194-95

Denslow, W. W., 57, 182
Dixon, Franklin W., 32, 67
Doctor Dolittle, 6, 27, 65, 66,
    102, 165, 168, 174-75, 179,
    181, 195
Dodge, Mary Mapes, 16-7, 41, 176
Dorothy Dainty, 27, 156, 168, 182,
    196
Dotty Dimple, 15, 48, 54, 77,
    161, 181
Dovey Brome, 3, 75, 144
Dunn, Harvey, 185

Edwards, Esther and Jonathan, 9
Eight Cousins, 17, 24, 54,

125-26
Ellis, Edward S., 16, 17, 18, 32,
    43, 93, 105, 147
Elsie Dinsmore, 5, 13, 16, 22, 23,
    31, 49, 54, 75-6, 121-22, 182, 196
Enright, Elizabeth, 178
Estes, Eleanor, 178

Fairy tales, 7, 27, 101-02, 149,
    166, 174
Family, use of, 23, 41, 47, 49, 50,
    67, 69, 75, 78, 79, 86, 95,
    97, 98, 99-100, 109, 121, 122,
    125-26, 128, 129, 137, 139, 141,
    153, 155, 156, 158, 161
Farley, Walter, 178
Fiction, status of, 19, 55, 116, 195
Finley, Martha, 22, 31, 49, 54, 72,
    75, 122, 155-56, 195
Fosdick, Charles Austin. See Harry
    Castlemon.
Frank and Archie, 21, 91-2, 104-05
Frost, A.B., 173

Garis, Howard R., 21, 27, 33, 63, 64,
    93, 132, 134, 140, 148, 168-69,
    172, 195
Garis, Lilian, 33
Garis, Roger, 33, 63, 66-7, 168
Gilbert Blythe, 22, 94-5
Glad Game, 82, 109, 114, 127,
    154, 181
Golden Multitudes, 85. See Mott, Frank
    Luther.
Goodrich, Samuel G. See Peter Parley.
Great-aunt Sarah Crim, 137
Gypsy Breynton, 5, 45, 70, 77-8,
    109, 124-25, 139, 152

Hardy Boys, 28, 32, 177, 179, 180
Haywood, Carolyn, 178
Hegan, Alice Caldwell. See Rice,
    Alice Hegan.
Henry Davidson, 25, 193
Henry, Marguerite, 178
Henry Ware, 91, 107
Heroes, 10, 19, 23, 24, 26, 71-3,
    86-97, 103, 146, 151, 157
Heroines, 10, 19, 23, 26, 72-3,

DATE DUE	